Finding
the
ZONE

Finding
the
ZONE

A WHOLE NEW WAY TO
MAXIMIZE MENTAL
POTENTIAL

GORDON D. LAWRENCE

Prometheus Books

59 John Glenn Drive
Amherst, New York 14228–2119

Published 2010 by Prometheus Books

Inquiries should be addressed to
Prometheus Books
59 John Glenn Drive
Amherst, New York 14228–2119
VOICE: 716–691–0133
FAX: 716–691–0137
WWW.PROMETHEUSBOOKS.COM

14 13 12 11 10   5 4 3 2 1

Library of Congress Cataloging-in-Publication Data

Lawrence, Gordon, 1930–
    Finding the zone : a whole new way to maximize mental potential / by
Gordon D. Lawrence.
        p. cm.
    Includes an index.
    ISBN 978–1–61614–161–5 (pbk. : alk paper)
    1. Intellect. 2. Mental efficiency. 3. Thought and thinking. I. Title.

BF431 .L43199 2010
153.4—dc22

                                                        2009047808

Printed in the United States of America on acid-free paper

CONTENTS

1

IN THE ZONE

Being "in the zone" is an experience that comes to all of us from time to time. If it happens, it happens when we are totally absorbed in purposeful work or play. Our senses become more alert. Intuition brings keener insights. Skill, emotion, and reasoning blend in a flow that makes our work seem almost effortless. In the zone we feel energized, focused, and not distracted by worry. We are constructive, efficient, and effective in moving toward our goal because our best stuff is coming together. We want to be in the zone because it is so satisfying to feel we are at our best, and getting better.

THE ZONE EXPERIENCE

We can often recognize when someone is in the zone, and it is usually a pleasure to watch. It is a treat for me to see my brother Howard at the keyboard. Playing piano has been his hobby since childhood. Now he has an electronic keyboard that keeps him in the zone for long stretches of time—working with the endless combinations of back-up instruments, types of music, and chords and rhythms built into it. His pleasure is infectious, and the spread of this pleasure to others is part of his zone experience.

My grandson at age seven was a delightful child, but he had a short attention span. For Christmas he got his first Zoids kit, a box of many small parts that can be assembled into an unearthly creature. He carried it off to work on it. An hour or more later, we wondered where he was. We found him on the floor in a bedroom, totally absorbed in figuring out how to get the thing together. We were amazed that he could stay focused on one thing for so long. The challenge had triggered a zone experience for him. He now has a full collection of Zoids creatures he has constructed. His attention span doesn't come up as an issue anymore, and we believe this is somehow related to his experiences in working with these kits.

Athletes speak of being in the zone. The image that instantly comes to my mind is the basketball player at the top of his or her game—seeing the whole court, coolly reading the flow of play and anticipating the moves of the other players, then breaking with a hot hand toward the basket and sinking the ball in the hoop. Basketball players often report that the zone experience amazingly makes the basket seem to double in size.

Fortunately, the zone experience is available to all of us, not just the superstars. We can learn a lot about the zone from the superstars—how they get there, how they sustain it, what sometimes blocks them from being in the zone, and about the fire in the belly that gets them back to it after it has been blocked. Their insights can help us more ordinary folk find the zone. These superstars are not just athletes but people in all kinds of pursuits, with widely diverse talents, who can find the zone to an extraordinary extent.

Although the zone experience is available to all of us, some of us don't get there very often. While we can agree that the zone is a good place to be, many of us have no idea how to set the conditions for entering the zone. Having a passion for something and pursuing it diligently are essential to the zone but not enough to make it happen. We can't just go after it or make it happen by willpower; it has to come to us. It is elusive, but it does come when the conditions are right. Consider, for example, something as ordinary as preparing a meal for one's family. It can be a zone experience for some and mundane for others. What makes the difference?

All of us have our own zone stories and can reflect on the conditions that help put us in the zone. Whatever our talents—mechanical, social, cerebral, physical, musical, creative expression, nurturing, exploring, organizing, harmonizing—when in the zone we are working at the fresh edge of our gifts and skills, and we are getting better. We are focused and not distracted. And we are absorbed in the process, not in ourselves. We are challenged and energized as we proactively pursue our goal. These, in brief, are the conditions for the zone identified by researchers. What circumstances make these zone characteristics happen for you?

Of course, we can't stay in the zone all the time. Every day we have many mundane things to do that take us off the crest of the wave. And we need the pleasure of zoning out with things that are just enjoyable without challenging us. But the zone experience calls us back because of the emotional charge that comes with experiencing growth in our skills and capacities.

The zone I am writing about is not the zoning out that comes with entertainment, such as watching a good movie, reading a good book, listening to music, or playing slot machines. In those activities we are often carried along as a relatively passive participant. But some zoning-out activity *could* help spark a zone experience. Zoning out could turn into a zone experience if it prompts us to take charge, bring our skills to bear, and hone them to better functioning. For example, great books have the capacity to do that—to engage us deeply, challenge us, and provoke us to grow.

But whenever we are in the zone we are initiating action, moving toward a goal, creating—as we more likely would be if we were making the movie, writing the book, creating the music, or absorbed in playing the basketball game. Alternating between being in the zone and zoning out is common. For example, I see it in my brother as he plays his keyboard, alternating between stretching his skills and just having the comfort and fun of zoning out with something familiar. The distinction between being in the zone and zoning out is an important one, and it is examined seriously in this book.

As you might suppose, research supports what our experience

tells us: most people don't find the zone very often. Every day we see depressing reminders of wasted human potential—people who go through life without much joy, people who do not know how to move toward a satisfying discipline of themselves that can take them to a higher level of functioning, and people who settle for a mundane life punctuated by passive zoning out. And the problem is most frightening when we see such behavior in our young people.

PROMOTING THE ZONE EXPERIENCE

This book has three main themes. The first is that the zone experience is a phenomenon that can be examined to yield clues about how it works and how it can be made more available to more people. While it cannot be willed to happen, it can and should be planned for, as a catalyst for our growth and development, individually and collectively. If the zone is a place where we find powerful motivation to keep improving, we surely want to be promoting it for ourselves and those we influence through our leadership and example.

Promoting the zone for others—in parenting, coaching, teaching, and all the helping roles—has been my main focus in shaping this book. Because these roles differ so widely from each other, it is not realistic for one book and one author to deal with the zone experience in relation to all of them. Promoting the zone with two dozen or more people at once, as would the classroom teacher or work supervisor, is a very different responsibility from that of the parent or the mentor who works one-on-one. I have taken the latter as the book's emphasis, and the examples I use are mainly of individuals helping other individuals find the zone.

So the key questions are these:

- How can we make the zone experience more available to any of us, rather than just waiting for chance to bring it?
- If being in the zone is truly catalytic for our growth and development, why don't more of us get there more often?
- Everyone's experience with the zone is so subjective; how can we objectively understand it well enough to know what conditions can bring it about?

Before we can answer these questions, we have to break through two major roadblocks, two basic and essentially hidden assumptions about the nature of mind and motivation. These assumptions prevail in our culture, and our being caught up in them—mainly unconsciously—seriously limits our access to the zone. They are the second and third main themes of the book: the commonplace view of mind that has been shown by research on brain/mind functioning to be clearly wrong, and the prevailing view of motivation that limits our ability to see constructive, alternative ways of promoting mental development. These prevailing conceptions, and replacements for them, are the subjects of chapters 2 and 3 and are briefly discussed below.

In the practical business of daily life, why should we worry about or take the time needed to ponder misconceptions of something as esoteric as the nature of mind? Because the assumptions we hold about other peoples' mental processing profoundly affect the way we treat them. And how we treat them has a direct effect on their development and performance, and on our own as well. It is the Eliza Doolittle phenomenon—is she the flower girl or the lady? Professor Higgins came to realize that his view of Eliza—his assumptions about how her mind/psyche/soul worked—also affected his own development and his understanding of human nature, and perhaps his own capacity to be in the zone.

ASSUMPTIONS ABOUT MENTAL PROCESSES THAT NEED REEXAMINING

The second and third themes of the book are concerned with tackling what I see as two major prevailing assumptions about the mental equipment we are born with and carry with us all our lives. These assumptions harm us in virtually all important human interactions and institutions, and they keep most of us from the zone experience much of the time. This book is a proposal for making two fundamental shifts in our view of human mental processing, shifts that have the potential to release a lot of constructive energy for our growth and development, regardless of age.

The first assumption is that the mind we are born with is essentially unformed and unorganized, in need of life experiences—with good parents and good teachers especially—to activate and organize it to take in the knowledge, skills, and character traits needed for mature functioning in the world. The work of teaching—and coaching, nurturing, and training—most commonly begins with the assumption that the learner's mind is gradually moving from an unformed to an organized state through the planned stimulation provided by the teacher, parent, and other authorities (*author*ities, in effect, authors of what is written into the learner's forming mind). It is assumed that the mind is ready to absorb. It is "impressionable" and "receptive," but to become organized, it needs the initiatives of the teacher. It is a blank slate to be written upon. Cognitive scientist and popular science author Steven Pinker summarizes this view of mind as the assumption that our biology equips us with "five senses, a few drives like hunger and fear, and a general capacity to learn. Then our culture molds the clay of our biology."[1]

This view of mind is truly pervasive. It is everywhere—in the folk wisdom of child rearing, in the structure of our schools and colleges, in the manner of religious education and practices, in the typical approaches to training and motivation in our workplaces. This blank-slate assumption is so deeply embedded that it is virtually unseen and unacknowledged, accepted as a given feature of human nature, generally beyond question.

Some will argue that we long ago gave up the idea that the mind is a blank slate ready to be written upon or a vessel ready to be filled. Some have intellectually abandoned that concept of mind, but there is no doubt that it persists as an unspoken assumption in the structure of our institutions and the ways they treat the learning mind. The aforementioned Steven Pinker, one of the most accomplished contemporary students of human nature, has written a five-hundred-page book demonstrating the pervasiveness of the assumption. The book is titled *The Blank Slate: The Modern Denial of Human Nature*.[2]

The blank-slate assumption underlies virtually all versions of schooling. Young children and college students alike face a curriculum that was preplanned, before they ever entered the classroom, for a steady presentation of preorganized materials designed for the generic absorbing, unformed mind. Teachers and printed materials lead them through a sequence of encounters, along a progression the curriculum makers and textbook writers believe will take them from relatively unformed mental activity toward a well-ordered mind. What's missing in this formula is allowing for the possibility that students enter new learning opportunities with minds already exquisitely organized to make sense of their world—that they come in with their own existing mental organizations that are dynamic components of classroom transactions. What's missing is the realization that all substantial learning involves unlearning first, the reorganizing—however minutely—of mental systems already in place. The blank-slate assumption keeps this vital fact from being recognized. Some of us were fortunate enough to have had teachers who *connected* with us as unique individuals, who saw what made us tick, and saw how we processed information. In doing that they consciously or unconsciously rejected the blank-slate assumption and tapped into our own distinctive mental organization that we brought to the learning situation.

How we can root out the blank-slate assumption is addressed directly in chapters 2 and 6. The question for us here is what we put in its place.

THE BLANK SLATE DRAWS A BLANK

The blank-slate view of mind seems obviously supported by our own experiences with babies; we see them as starting out with unformed minds that rely just on instincts. They seem so helpless, unaware, and in need of our attentive efforts to give them a sense of the world into which they have been born. This is a misconception. In the last thirty years, the research of neuroscientists and developmental psychologists has demonstrated beyond any question that babies are born with minds already organized, preorganized one might say, to take the initiative in engaging their environments to support their own growth and development. This is exciting stuff. The research methods they used with babies are ingenious. Chapter 2 of this book covers the research and gives you a sampling of the studies and their outcomes.

Some of the evidence that babies are born with preorganized, inquiring minds has been available to all us parents, but it wasn't recognized as evidence. For example, just after birth babies can recognize the difference between voices and other sounds, and they show by their behavior that they much prefer the voices. They also recognize the difference between faces and other objects, and they prefer the faces, especially a mother's face. It seems clear they were born with a brain preorganized to make these discriminations. No one taught them.

Even when infants can focus their eyes no more than a distance of a foot or so, they can duplicate the facial expressions of people they are seeing for the first time. They can smile back. (No, it is not just a gas bubble.) Stick out your tongue and the baby is likely to do it too. As one set of researchers put it: "At first glance this ability to imitate might seem curious and cute but not deeply significant. But if you think about it a minute, it is actually amazing. There are no mirrors in the womb: newborns have never seen their own face. So how could they know whether their tongue is inside or outside their mouth? . . . In order to imitate, newborn babies must somehow understand the similarity between the internal feeling and the external face they see, a round shape with a long pink thing at the bottom moving back and forth."[3]

Young babies' minds are organized to have coordination among the senses. A researcher gave pacifiers to two groups of one-month-old infants. They held the pacifiers in their mouths but didn't see them. One group had regular pacifiers, while the other group had pacifiers with a bumpy surface. Then the researcher showed the babies smooth and bumpy objects. The babies saw but did not touch them. The videotapes showed that "The babies looked longer at the object that was the same shape as the one they had just been sucking on. Somehow, they could relate the feel of the pacifier in their mouths with its visual image."[4]

Babies *anticipate* that they can engage and influence their world, that they can find experiences and resources that will help them meet their needs. In no way are their minds blank slates. We will explore the research behind this assertion in chapter 2.

THE INVESTIGATIVE MIND
AND THE ZONE EXPERIENCE

In light of the research findings, what kind of image of mind should replace the blank slate and empty vessel? The image that makes sense to me is the mind as *investigator*—the mind as an organized system of *figuring out and making sense of experiences, forming plans and playing them out in action, and learning from the consequences.* The research shows babies are born investigators who seek and probe to find ways to make their world *responsive to them*, to their growth and development processes. Even newborns, who have not yet developed a sense of themselves as beings who are separate from their mothers, are already investigating. I am not just rehashing the nature versus nurture argument, coming down on the side of nature. I am not saying that the motivations for our behavior are provided by our genes *rather than* by environment. I am not endorsing the view that babies are born with an internal blueprint that will chart healthy development if we give it favorable conditions. Or that they are born with a self that will become actualized or stunted, depending on the environment they encounter. These explanations of human nature, all well elaborated in psychological theory, have been bypassed by the new research on babies. I am arguing the case of a more comprehensive theory of human nature: that the investigative mind is an intricate dance of inborn resources *and* environment, an intimate transaction of environment and individuals who have an inner nature evolved through natural selection to *anticipate* and search for outer resources to support their development.[5] The anticipatory organization is the key.

Such investigative transactions are the stuff of the zone experience. I offer the view that the zone experience is the rich and exhilarating by-product of investigative energy focused on one's interests. It generates the joy, the payoff, that carries us into disciplined growth and development. How we can help make this happen more often in teaching-learning situations is the subject of chapter 6.

CHILDREN'S MINDS

Do we *all* start out as investigators? Reflecting on our own experiences, we all know some children who are truly interested in finding out and making sense of things, and even some who continue this investigative mind-set into adulthood, becoming more and more resourceful and effective. What about the other children, the ones who don't show the investigative traits? If we assume that all babies do start out as investigators, as the research is suggesting, we would have to conclude that they may have stopped being investigators because their environments didn't support that kind of mental processing. In chapter 2 I argue that most institutions in our culture—intentionally or unintentionally—discourage the investigative mind-set to the point that some or perhaps most children become passive responders to the constraints and prompts of the adult world grounded in the tacit assumption that humans are born with blank-slate minds. As a consequence, some of us have our investigative skills atrophy—synapses die because they aren't used.

What is the connection to the zone experience? One thesis of this book is that an investigative mind-set is essential to the zone experience. I will argue that passive responding will never carry anyone into the zone. In contrast, a mind that maintains an investigative approach is naturally inclined to be actively seeking to find the conditions that support growth, including those necessary for the zone experience. For example, skill practice for the athlete and the rest of us, too, is an important prerequisite for the zone experience. But consider the contrast between practice planned by the coach or teacher with the unconscious assumption of dealing with blank slates versus dealing with investigative minds. Of course, there are teachers and coaches who treat students and players as having inquiring minds. Unfortunately, teachers have to work within a system that prescribes input-output teaching and learning targeted to good performance on standardized achievement tests. The teachers are obligated to teach prepackaged input that most closely resembles the form of the output contained in the questions on the achievement tests. This kind of instruction is grounded in the blank-slate assumption.

Generally, athletic coaches have more flexibility. They are working mostly with players who passionately want to perform well and are more likely to actively investigate ways to improve their game. We all know young people who, for various reasons, have far more enthusiasm for sports than for classroom work. One reason may be the ways their minds were treated in the classroom versus the playing field or court. Reflecting back on our own experiences in classrooms and sports, in light of the blank-slate/investigator contrast, we may see that our interest was directly related to the extent that we were being respected as investigators.

The reasoning behind the blank-slate treatment of young people has always been something like this: If I follow a tried-and-true agenda and teach you what I know you will need to learn—and check to make sure you get it—I can have confidence you are likely to turn out OK. If I let you mostly just be absorbed in things you want to investigate, how can I have any assurance you will turn out well-rounded? You can't get well-rounded just by following your interests.

As we were growing up, some adults in our lives, perhaps many, may have had no intention of nurturing our investigative nature. They worried about stimulating "too much curiosity" and opening the door to "radical ideas." After all, the investigative process has no mandate to follow a standard path. It can lead to outcomes adults cannot control. But I suspect most of these adults had no idea they were promoting a blank-slate agenda and discouraging investigative processes. The blank-slate assumption permeates our culture; one does not need to be aware of it to act on it.

Most of us came through a schooling process that was grounded in the blank-slate assumption. How did that assumption affect us? Did we start school with an investigative mind-set? My wife, a teacher and elementary school principal for many years, tells me that most children come to kindergarten excited about learning, and almost all carry the excitement into the first and second grades. When I have been an observer in these primary grade classrooms looking for evidence of kinds of mental processing, it was easy to see that the excitement was the energy generated by investigative strategies in action. I was seeing the children's natural delight in finding out about things of interest to them and making sense of life experiences. And I was often seeing children in the zone. In third grade classes I saw much less of this investigative energy. The exploration teachers encouraged in kindergarten was largely replaced in third grade by input-output, step-by-step lessons implicitly based on the blank-slate assumption. Approaches to dislodging the blank-slate assumption in schools and elsewhere are discussed in chapter 6.

NURTURING THE INVESTIGATIVE MIND-SET

Some of us came through school and into adulthood with our investigative mind-set intact. But there are many who did not. Can they get it back? I believe most of them can. If they are now our employees or people we coach or teach, can we help them move toward zone experiences and the investigative mind-set embedded in them? Can groups such as teams and families move toward collective, shared zone experiences? My answer again is yes. Individually we need access to the zone for our own renewal, our reenergizing. Those of us in leadership positions need to know how to set the conditions for the zone experience to come to others. Leaders know more about those conditions—people's natural motivation patterns—than most realize, and they possess the ability to tune in to those patterns, making them useful in helping others leverage and develop these skills.

Let's go back for a moment to the example of the game of basketball. The best coaches know how to read the motivation patterns of their players. Whether the knack came to them intuitively or with much intentional study, they know what to do. The best coaches know which players will respond well to an in-your-face passionate criticism and which will need a private, off-the-court critique and reassurance to help them reclaim the zone. The best coaches also know that the ability to set conditions for individual players to find the zone experience is only a component of a still more powerful skill for winning games: the ability to help the team find the zone collectively. People in leadership positions who have a natural intuitive knack for reading motivation patterns are, in my experience, extremely rare. The rest of us need to deliberately investigate and learn and practice the skills. Defining and refining that learning process has been my goal in writing this book.

THE SECOND ASSUMPTION
NEEDING REEXAMINATION

Another centuries-old concept of mind has been passed down through the generations, an assumption that I believe needs to be reconsidered in light of modern scholarship and recent research. Understanding the nature of mind is always difficult because mind cannot be observed directly and must be inferred from outward behavior. Recent observational research carries us in the direction of the possibility that there are several, perhaps numerous, kinds of mind, not just one. I am not referring to Howard Gardner's work on multiple intelligences that has so effectively called our attention to kinds of talents often not nurtured well by our schools. He has identified constellations of traits that give us important clues to people's differing motivations.[6] However, as I understand Gardner, the multiple intelligences are variations of a common mental framework we all share. I am suggesting that we take the hypothesis that there are qualitatively different kinds of mind, not just different sets of interests and intelligences.

The view that has been passed on to us is that "normal" humans all have the same basic mental equipment; we just differ in the amounts we possess of different traits: IQ, abstract reasoning, social sensitivity, artistic gifts, attention span, assertiveness, curiosity, optimism, and so on. The list is long. But the assumption is that these are variations within the one common mental framework we all share. This could be called a unitary model of mind. It is based on the assumption that everyone's mind has the same hardwiring but that we differ in our software. I believe there is a lot to be gained by testing an alternative hypothesis that there are different hardwiring configurations, different systems of mental processing that can be considered distinct kinds of mind, with each of us retaining our own kind as long as we live. The different hardwired kinds of mind are analogous to different computer operating systems, such as Windows and Apple. Programs can be written to allow these two computer systems to communicate with each other, but there is no direct, automatic communication. Similarly, we develop ways to communicate across our different human operating systems, but we all know that some people are a lot harder for us to understand than others. Programming that bridge is a lot harder, and we know some people who will always be hard for us to reach. In contrast, when we are with someone who shares our same operating system, the communication is almost effortless.

DIFFERING MENTAL SYSTEMS

Anyone born into a family of one or more siblings knows firsthand the reality that people have differing mind-sets. Not just different sets of traits, but different ways of processing life experiences. For example, the family has a heated discussion over supper. The next day, trying to reconstruct the supper conversation, family members tell distinctly different stories about what actually took place the evening before. Some heard one thing, others heard another. Features of the conversation that were weighty for someone were overlooked by others. They carried away from the suppertime discussion clearly different experiences of the event, different realities drawn from the dialogue they all had in common. Their mind-sets had different values, priorities, motivations, and prior experiences through which they filtered the events. Chances are, if someone had tape-recorded the supper conversation and played it the next day, each person would hear on the tape some things they hadn't the slightest memory of hearing.

Cultural anthropologist Clyde Kluckhohn gave us the expression "Each man is like all other men, like some other men, like no other man."[7] Drawing on his viewpoint, I am saying that each mind is like every other mind, like some other minds, and like no other minds. And my emphasis is on the middle distinction, "like some other minds," a feature of essential human nature that has been generally neglected, particularly in the field of psychology. The dominating assumption has been that we all have the same mental equipment with idiosyncratic variations. Evidence that the middle category is important is now coming from macroresearch at the level of behavior observations and microresearch at the level of brain functioning. It is possible and useful to consider that people have distinct *kinds* of mind, minds that vary in *systematic and categorical* ways. And it is possible to discover the features of those varied mental systems.

Among all the features of human nature, perhaps our grasp of human motivation stands to benefit the most from the study of this middle category—systematic variations. From examining systematic similarities and differences we can get very practical insights into motivation patterns that accompany each kind of mind, patterns that are clues to the gateway of the zone experience for each kind of mind. The example of the disagreeable supper conversation remembered very differently by the family members suggests that each brought to the table different value and motivation patterns. The well-functioning family recognizes the reality of the differences and tries to harness this diversity of opinion to benefit the family's collective interests.

By focusing on the middle category—different systems of mental processing—I am not denying the importance of inquiry into the commonalities of all minds or into what makes each person unique. They have been and continue to be studied with care; but they are not my focus. Undoubtedly human brains function alike in nearly all respects. But my intent is to show that the fraction of brain processes that show differences among people are not just idiosyncratic differences; some of that fraction consists of patterns of differences I am calling different kinds of mind.

That is the third theme of this book: to show that we can more effectively manage our roles as parents, coaches, teachers, or team leaders by tuning into the systematic variations in motivations—the *patterns* of motivation—in those we teach or supervise rather than by attending just to the varied idiosyncratic motivations each of them has. I want us to look at motivations in a way quite different from the conventional view, that of *intrinsic* or *extrinsic* forces prompting behavior. We will test the hypothesis that each of the types of mental processing carries within it predictable sets of motivations that are *integrations* of organic (intrinsic) and environmental (extrinsic) variables.

ARE THERE HARDWIRED MOTIVATION PATTERNS?

Motivation is a concept concerned with movement and behavior, and with explanations of factors that can account for action or intention. Beyond our automatic reflexes that do not involve cognitive processing, such as the eye blinking or sneezing, there is a wide field of behavior that the concept of motivation covers. While some of our motivations are conscious intentions, many are not; some are inborn, and many of them are culturally acquired. Motivation also encompasses emotions. We are essentially emotional creatures. Even our efforts at reasoning by way of cool logic are grounded in emotions. For example, many of us care passionately about being dispassionate in our reasoning.

The emotions we know anything about, of course, are the emotional reactions that register in our conscious minds, such as anger, fear, love, and resentment. But there is in us an emotional infrastructure outside our awareness that we can know about only indirectly, and in this book I explore the implications of this infrastructure for the zone experience.

No doubt we all have many motivating factors in common. But if we have different kinds of mental hardwiring, different kinds of mind, we are processing the common human impulses and cultural prompt-ings through differing mental systems. Each kind of mind has its own set of priorities and values, and each may come up with different behaviors and different explanations for our behaviors. Those expla-nations and behaviors will show up as similar in people who share the same hardwiring and be in contrast with the behavior of people with other kinds of mind.

Here's an example. A woman I know is the CEO of a nonprofit organization and she chairs its board of directors, which usually has seven members. The board takes an active role in shaping the organi-zation's policies. From many years of working with them in trying to find consensus on policies, the CEO has concluded that the members can be sorted into three kinds of mind. She can predict three sets of reactions from the members. As she prepares a new proposal to take to a board meeting, she constructs it to connect with their preferred kinds of mental processing. "Two members," she says, "are always preoccupied with the practicalities—budget details, resources. Their support of the proposal also depends on whether I can show them that the new ideas won't take us away from the tried and true. The other five members are big-picture people who are happy to leave the details to me and my staff to work out. But the priorities of those five board members sort them into two groups. Three of them are conceptualizers focused on innovative, ingenious initiatives. And the other two lead with their hearts. What brought these two to the board was their deep concern for broad, human-value issues that this nonprofit organization was formed to address. These two examine any new proposal according to personal, human consequences. When I touch all three bases, we come to consensus more often and more smoothly."

In the context of considering the zone phenomenon, the thesis here is that minds with different motivation patterns need to be approached differently as we try to promote the zone experience. The conditions that carry people to the zone, and sustain them there, differ according to their motivation systems. Some readers may not buy my thesis of hardwired differences. Acceptance of it is not needed to rec-ognize the reality of—and find value in—the motivation systems pre-sented here. And, of course, the zone phenomenon can be considered and investigated without attending to what I am calling the hard-wiring differences; but I believe understanding the zone experience and learning how to foster it are substantially advanced by taking the kinds of mind into account.

My starting point in considering that minds differ systematically and not just randomly is Carl Jung's work on psychological types. I first encountered Jung's explanation of psychological types over thirty years ago. As I began applying it in my own work, I became convinced that he had discovered some essential realities. But at that time I did not regard the psychological types he described as different kinds of mind. Now I do, and I explain why in chapter 3.

KINDS OF MIND

My interest in the psychological types grew from the startling clarity they brought to the puzzle of why the structure of schooling is such a poor match for the ways of learning that some children bring to the classroom. Their kinds of mental processing are not well served by the sit-down, soak-it-up, straight-ahead, and somewhat impersonal traditions of formal instruction. This mismatch is not a matter of the child's intelligence or mental discipline, but rather the varied patterns of children's mental processing. The distinction became clear to me as I studied Jung's descriptions of the types of mental processing. Not only does his construct of psychological type shed light on learning preferences, but it also presents distinct, broad patterns of motivation. The psychological types are not different sets of talents, but different systems for processing life experiences. As patterns of motivation—and kinds of mind—the types give the best window I have found to understanding what precipitates the zone experience for different people.

TYPE VERSUS TRAIT

Jung's approach to motivation is distinctly different from what is widely accepted. The view of motivation passed on through the generations—and systematized by psychologists—is a view that sees people's behavior as prompted by a collection of *traits*, such as fearfulness, optimism, assertiveness, sociability, practicality, compassion, and decisiveness. Over a thousand traits have been named, and psychologists have been interested in measuring the amount of these traits that people possess. In essence, a person's psychological makeup is regarded as a composite of the numerous traits he or she possesses in greater or lesser amounts.

Jung developed a different view. The psychological types, or kinds of mind, he identified are not traits. They are either/or, qualitatively different *categories* of mental processing, each with its own dynamic and each with its own motivation pattern and associated traits. It is important to remember, in the paragraphs that follow, that Jung's terms for identifying the types are names of discrete categories and not traits that are measured by degree. It is like the difference between *types* of fruit, such as apple and peach, contrasted with *traits* of the fruit, such as redness and sweetness. Take automobiles as another example. They all can be compared on the basis of *traits*, such as gas mileage, passenger capacity, cargo room, cabin comfort, exterior color, engine power, safety in crash tests, and so on. In addition, there is also a lot to be gained by considering vehicles by types as well as traits, which is what we usually do when shopping for a new one—types such as family sedan, minivan, pickup truck, SUV, sports car, and so on. Then after deciding on the type of vehicle we want, we consider the traits that are important to us. Both ways of classifying and judging vehicles, by types and by traits, have value. People who miss the distinction between type and trait in viewing mental makeup, who mistakenly treat Jung's type categories as just other traits, tend to miss his main idea.

An example of the confusion over type and trait can be seen in uses of the terms *extraversion* and *introversion* that Jung brought to the language of psychology to represent an aspect of the structure of his types. (Note that Jung spelled extraversion with an "a." The "extra" comes from a Latin term meaning "from the outside," the meaning he intended to capture.) His terms *extraversion* and *introversion* were picked up by other psychologists and have since entered common vocabulary, but Jung's meanings were eventually dropped, and they were treated as traits. When used as Jung intended in the context of *types* of mental processing, extraversion and introversion refer to turning outside or turning inward for sources of mental energy. They are two distinct categories—like family sedan and sports car—not traits. The common usage is to treat them as something one can possess more or less of, as in "She's more extraverted than I am."

It is like saying, "That vehicle is more SUV than mine is." Traits can be treated in more than/less than comparisons, while types cannot.

In terms of Jung's types, it is wrong to use the easy expression, "She's very extraverted, isn't she?" Consistent with Jung's categories would be an expression such as, "She's one of the more talkative (or outgoing or gregarious, and so on) extraverts I know." In Jung's framework, a person is an extravert *or* an introvert; that is, essentially an outward-turner or an inward-turner. There are no degrees of turning outward for mental energy; you just do or don't. One or the other is the default mode, the mode that automatically comes to the foreground in mental processing. Outward-turners *can* turn inward for mental stimulation, but they don't go there first.

My wife and her sister provide an example here. My wife is a gregarious extravert who gets energized when meeting new people and talking with people. These qualities served her well in her work as a school principal. Her sister, in contrast, is an introvert; she is energized by being alone with her thoughts. She turns outward easily and comfortably with family and close friends, but she is drained by having extraverted responsibilities. Are such differences in mental makeup related to where and how people find their zone experiences? Most certainly. Jung's construct of the types of mental processing gives us a fresh and powerful way of finding out what triggers the zone for different people.

We are all accustomed to looking at personality characteristics as traits that each of us possess in greater or lesser amounts or degrees. For example, assertiveness is a trait of which we have more or less. And we consider too much assertiveness "overbearing," or too little "wishy-washy," as less desirable than a "middle" amount. Some variation of this quantitative range applies to all traits. To understand and use Jung's concept of mental processing types, we have to have a clear distinction between type and trait in our own mental habits.

Try a brief two-minute exercise to examine the difference. Think of one person you know well—it could be yourself—and quickly list six or seven features of that person's personality. Pause here in your reading to make your list.

Now examine your list. Are the words on your list some features that people can possess more or less of? Mark them. Did you mark all the words? Can you see them as being on a continuum, as something psychologists might want to measure the degree of? With scales such as

- less . . . more
- poorly . . . well
- too little . . . balanced . . . too much

Are any of the terms on your list only categorical, either/or, in the way that pregnant or left-handed are examples of categorical? Some terms, such as stubborn or kind, seem to be categories without quantitative variations. But kind and stubborn can be converted to kindness and stubbornness, and we know there are degrees of these.

Essentially *all* the words we have in our vocabularies for features of psychological makeup are *trait* terms, representing qualities that can be measured. But Jung's types are discrete, either/or categories, psychological descriptors that are not measured. Back to our vehicle analogy: SUV is a discrete category, and there is no such thing as SUVness that vehicles have more or less of. Readers who are encountering this distinction between psychological types and traits for the first time may find it helpful to keep in mind the vehicle analogy when we turn to Jung's types of mental processing in chapter 3. I also explain there Jung's underlying rationale and the various motivation systems I draw from his work.

EMERGING ATTENTION TO TYPES OF MENTAL PROCESSING

People's awareness of the psychological types has come mostly through the work of trainers and consultants who specialize in management and organizational development, and counselors who focus on career and personal development and family relationships. They use paper-and-pencil (or computer-based) self-report instruments, mainly the Myers-Briggs Type Indicator* (MBTI) assessment, to introduce the type concepts. Their aim is to help people understand the natural differences in mental processing that can be an irritant if not understood and, more important, an asset for teams or families in harnessing members' different strengths. Whether the setting is work, family, or other relationships, understanding one's own psychological type and that of others improves communication and reduces misunderstandings.

The emergence of attention to the psychological types in organi-

---

*Myers-Briggs Type Indicator, Myers-Briggs, and MBTI are trademarks or registered trademarks of the MBTI Trust in the United States and other countries.

zational life is curious because this important psychological construct has been largely overlooked by mainstream American psychology. Jung's work on types is barely mentioned in most psychology textbooks, dramatically overshadowed by theories akin to those of Freud in past decades, and more recently by those that are grounded in a trait approach to psychology. American psychology is anchored in the assumption that personality is a composite of traits that combine in numerous ways to make an individual unique, and that the traits are undergirded by basic drives. The view that personalities come in types has been dismissed by many psychologists. But the type approach has gained credibility elsewhere. In effect, the concepts of the psychological types did an end-run around mainstream psychology and, through the vehicle of the MBTI assessment, got into practical use in organizations on a large scale. The publisher of the MBTI instrument reports that it is by far the most widely used psychological instrument that addresses normal mental functioning.

Unfortunately, many people who have been introduced to the psychological types got a superficial explanation. At least, that is what I observed over the years. While the quality of use of the MBTI concepts has been steadily improving, even the most basic concepts of the psychological types do not stay with most people unless they are coached and guided in specific applications of them in their lives—a hard lesson I learned by my own mistakes in introducing type concepts to client groups—without adequate follow-through coaching. The richer meanings that Jung uncovered are what I am emphasizing in this book, in chapters 3 and 5. The main theme I develop therein is that Jung's types have embedded in them a practical model of development that allows us to predict the kinds of circumstances that will open the door to the zone in those people we teach, coach, and nurture, and, equally important, avoid actions that will close their door to the zone.

A CONCEPT OF MIND BEYOND THE BLANK SLATE

The focus of this book, the zone experience, has a research history. My own approach to the zone phenomenon draws substantially from the work of a group of social psychologists, particularly Mihaly Csikszentmihalyi.[8] His seminal book, *Flow: The Psychology of Optimal*

Experience, synthesizes his extensive research and that of others, and he has since written numerous other books and research reports. "In the zone" and "flow" have been used interchangeably in most literature. I am characterizing the zone experience in a way that I believe extends and somewhat differs from Csikszentmihalyi's view of flow. In my approach, the zone experience is entered only through the actions of an initiating, investigative, inquiring mind. When we teach or coach or nurture from a blank-slate assumption—whether knowingly or, more likely, unwittingly—we are not promoting investigation and not promoting zone functioning. We may be helping with skill practice, practice that is needed for the zone experience. But when we teach from the blank-slate assumption, that assumption is blocking the door to the zone, not opening it. If those we teach get to the zone, it will be because they managed to get through the blockage and turn on their own investigative minds. Weeding out the blank-slate assumption—from ourselves, our dealings with others, and our institutional forms—is a huge undertaking, one that may take generations. Considering the scope of the task, we need to decide what deliberate, incremental steps we can take to give the process momentum. We can start by examining our basic assumptions about mental functioning.

Starting from the solid evidence that we are born with *organized* minds, we can move to the next step: the assumption that it is in the nature of mind to *remain* organized, to move continually toward equilibrium. Disequilibrium, the experience of disorganization, is distressing and immediately energizes us to find ways to restore a sense of order. Any disruption of our mental habits sets in motion a search for a new organizational scheme that can absorb or eliminate the disturbance. The new organization that emerges after the disequilibrium is, however minutely changed, a reconstruction of mind. The computer has rebuilt itself. But equilibrium doesn't last long because new challenges to it are always appearing. And so the cycle of equilibrium/disequilibrium is repeated, as long as a person lives.

If we accept the view that minds are naturally organized and seek organization, it is a short step to seeing that the backdrop provided by nature for *all* our experiences is exquisite natural order and interconnectedness, and not entropy or chaos as some scholars contend. *Dynamic disequilibrium/equilibrium* is a term scientists are using to reflect the order in nature. We do not need to *try* to stay organized to avoid chaos. That's because our systems automatically seek order beyond the disturbances. These disturbances have the *appearance* of impending chaos, but are, in this view, not chaos but rather the workings of ordered minds in a restoration process. In this view, even deep mental illness is reorganization, however flawed, in an attempt to find a new equilibrium, to accommodate painful events that disrupted the mental order. Order—and the automatic, urgent flow of energy to restore it when disruptions occur—is in the nature of things.

ZONING OUT: SMALL-SCOPE ZONE
AND LARGE-SCOPE ZONE

This brings us back to the zone and zoning out. Sometimes the term *zoning out* is used to mean tuning out, drifting, or daydreaming. I use the term to mean an active process that has focus and intention but does not stretch one's growth and development. In the context of the last two paragraphs, the zoning-out process is an effort to restore order with a minimum investment of psychic energy. The aim is to find comfortable order, or apparent order, and not to stretch our gifts into richer, more complex order. The step beyond zoning out is to achieve what I am calling small-scope zone functioning. In the small-scope zone, we have available all the conditions that make the zone experience possible. What makes it small scope is the size of its goal and the role it has in the larger picture of a person's experience. The range of scope extends from something as small as getting really good in a contest of who can spit watermelon seeds the farthest, all the way to addressing major issues of human concern. It is a long continuum.

I contend that the way to help ourselves and others find rich zone experiences with significant human goals at the heart of them is to find deep satisfaction in smaller-scope zone experiences first. The joy of the zone experience is something we want to repeat again and again, as is the pleasure of seeing the positive consequences of stretching one's gifts. The stretching process leads us to greater complexity of mental functioning, and in that greater complexity we need new and progressively more challenging experiences to carry us to the zone the next time and the next time.

My thesis is that we get to large-scope zone experiences progressively by finding satisfactions in small-scope zone experiences. This point of view has dramatic implications for our approach to teaching, nurturing, coaching, and supervising. Teaching *of* or *about* the knowledge and skills needed for growth and achievement has only a modest chance of promoting the zone experience, even in its small-scope form. Filling the empty vessel with instruction in the fine points of the game and in how to evaluate your own performance according to those standards may be setting up unintended roadblocks to the zone experience. The potentially bad consequences of teaching this kind of self-criticism were demonstrated convincingly years ago by W. Timothy Gallwey in *The Inner Game of Tennis*.[9] The only way to teach or coach to make the zone experience more available to students is by bringing them into a partnership of investigation, an engagement in looking for the natural order of things (an assumption of order is essential to the concept of minds as being investigative!) and in experiencing directly the dance of organism and environment, the serious play that is the doorway to the zone. This is lofty language, but I use it deliberately to point the direction for change. Some concrete steps for moving in that direction are in chapters 5 and 6.

FEATURES OF THE ZONE EXPERIENCE

Envisioning a continuum or progression from zoning out to small-scope zone to large-scope zone raises the question of where the dividing lines are between the three. What features distinguish them? One was mentioned a few paragraphs back: zoning out is an experience in which one aims for comfort or pleasure obtained with a minimum investment of psychic energy. For example, watching an entertaining movie.

To make the distinction sharper, let's review the elements that accompany any zone experience. I described them generally in the first part of the chapter. They have been identified quite clearly by Csikszentmihalyi.[10]

1. The first component is that attention is concentrated and focused on a clear goal. This is an absorbing involvement, a keen interest, so engaging as to block out distractions and worries. And it is relaxed concentration. When worries intrude,

such as, "Am I doing this right?" the flow of the zone experience is broken.

2. Second, the focus is on something other than the self. Self-consciousness, self-doubt, and self-criticism are bypassed because total attention is on the goal. The self is out of con-sciousness, as in the expression, "I lose myself in the game." It is invested and absorbed in the task. If self comes back into awareness, even for a little self-congratulation for a job well done, the zone is broken.

3. In the zone, self-criticism is replaced by a third condition—a feedback loop that provides immediate information to be used in making adjustments needed for moving closer to the goal. In effect, the cognitive work needed to make the adjustments is not routed through the self for self-aware critical analysis. This is not the same as autopilot, or "Let the force be with you," or just going on instinct. A dramatic example that comes to mind is flying a fighter jet at a speed that calls for instant decisions on data supplied by electronic instruments. Skill in processing data very quickly, using a feedback loop that bypasses the self, is essential.

4. Fourth, the tasks in pursuit of the goal are challenges that stretch one's skills, and typically for youth and adults they are well-practiced skills; they are "barely manageable difficulties," that, when managed, bring the joy that sustains the zone expe-rience. Andrew Cooper refers to the well-practiced skills as craftsmanship, "a broader term that includes skill but also sug-gests a certain attitude that elevates the skill beyond the level of self-concern."[11]

5. Finally, there is a sense of control over one's actions, a control that seems almost effortless.

I would supplement the five components with a sixth one. It was identified earlier: The zone experience comes when mind is working proactively, not passively. It is the investigative mind that participates in the zone experience. Of course, we often use active minding on daily work when we are not in the zone, but we do not arrive in the zone without it.

We do not help our children or clients or team members get to zone functioning with blank-slate coaching or instructions, pouring information into their brains. Rather, we need to entice them into being fellow investigators, together taking on a goal and together deciding what action to take, and taking it. I see an example of this each time I watch my wife, Carolyn, tutor children who are blocked on reading. Typically when they come to her they are profoundly discouraged about reading because they stumble on words they don't know, can't get the meaning of the text, and are embarrassed at their clumsiness. She does a brief assessment to find their actual reading level, to get a starting point, and then she says, "I think your teachers haven't taught you the *tricks* about unlocking the meanings of words. Would you like know the tricks? It's like learning a secret code." She then leads them sequentially through word lists, showing them the decoding process, one trick (decoding rule) at a time. It is a mutual investigation of the snags the children have encountered in the reading process, producing a continuous series of little victories over the former reading frustrations. As they learn the tricks, the investigation then shifts to seeing how quickly they can decode the word lists, faster and faster until they have the skills mastered to the point that the decoding is automatic. This phonics process is usually taught with uneven success in blank-slate fashion, but my wife has converted it into an investigative excursion. And the children's joy in it is easy to see on their faces when they begin to read with comprehension, ease, and confidence. Carolyn's secret is that she gets the children beyond self-doubt and self-criticism by engrossing them in the investigative process. She finds a match between the child's existing skill and the challenge she poses for them. Carolyn finds her own zone in these tutoring sessions, and her zone—being contagious—spreads to the children.

Zone contagion is a joy to be part of and a pleasure to watch. Carolyn and I watched it happen from the stands as the University of Florida basketball team found zone contagion again and again during the seasons that culminated in the 2006 and 2007 NCAA championships. The players and their coaches were attuned to each other in unusually synchronous and synergistic ways. We knew we were witnessing something very rare.

Now we can better identify the contrast between the zone phenomenon—small scope and large scope—and zoning out. As I see it, the components of the zone experience identified above as number

4—stretching one's skills—plus the sixth one I added, would *not* be present in zoning out to any substantial extent. A zoning-out activity, such as reading a suspense novel or watching an entertaining movie, can absorb us and we can lose ourselves in it, but it is not likely to prompt our growth and development or investigative inquiry. As for distinguishing the border between small-scope and large-scope zones, the assumption of ultimate order and connectedness I described earlier in the chapter seems essential for anyone to have as an admission ticket for entering the large-scope zone experience and is not necessary in the small-scope zone.

The movement from small scope to large scope is a progression in ethics. We need to remind ourselves that the zone experience does not happen just in the context of beneficial and benign activities. It can be found in all kinds of pursuits, including ones that are illegal, unethical, immoral, and destructive. In a heist movie, for example, we can see and identify with the emotional high the bank robbers experience as they carry out their carefully made plans. While we know the film is glamorizing an ugly side of life and may not be reporting reality, we overlook that because we can enjoy zoning out by witnessing someone else seeming to be in the zone, even when they are doing something illegal. Watching the film, chances are that we can even detect when the actors are actually in an actor's zone while portraying the characters.

Because the attraction of the zone experience is so strong, we have to be concerned about the ethics of each zone situation. When we pursue and promote the zone experience, we need to be aware of the social context and potential social consequences and choose activities that are constructive for society as well as for ourselves. Doing so carries us and those we influence from small-scope to large-scope zone experiences.

As I am writing these words, I am aware that working through the years with Carl Jung's psychological types has provided me with many large-scope zone experiences. Part of what attracted me to his work and has kept me fascinated with it is the symmetry, comprehensiveness, and order in his view of personality. It provided me with a better hypothesis as to why and how people get out of synch with each other and with the institutional forms they live in—and how they can find clues for moving toward optimal functioning. No doubt this is a large-scope matter. And besides the obvious ethical and moral implications of his work, there is an aesthetic aspect too: the symmetry.

In this book I have tried to bring together the strands of research and careful thought about the conditions that can precipitate and sustain the zone experience. No doubt the topic has a lot of facets I have not captured here. My intention has been to join the dialogue and deepen it, get some clarity around the key concepts and contribute some viewpoints that I believe add new dimensions to the seminal work done by others on this topic. The work has been done in various disciplines, from macrosocial psychology to microneuroscience. There is clear evidence pointing to the cultural importance and also the biological reality of the zone phenomenon. Researchers in brain chemistry, for example, have found that the neurotransmitter dopamine is released in the brain during zone and zoning-out experiences and is the neurological root of the experiences. While there is no clear agreement on just how dopamine release is triggered and how brain response to it works in relation to specific behaviors, there is no doubt this neurochemical research is a frontier that promises to yield vital understandings about motivations, enhancing performance, mental health, addictions, and so forth.[12] This pioneering work is beyond my field of expertise, so I have not tried to summarize it here. Judging by what I have read of it so far, I see no indications that the findings will be inconsistent with my efforts, which are on the macrolevel.

So how do we get to the zone? How do we get beyond self-conscious self-criticism to find life activities that bring us psychic energy? How do we make the most of our individual talents and interests so that our work and play reward us with the zone? And most of all, how do we help those we teach and coach find the doorway to the zone? The remaining chapters are devoted to answering these questions. There are no self-help, how-to lists here. I am convinced there is no one list that fits all. There is no standard, universal path to the higher functioning that is found in the zone. While researchers have fairly well identified the *general* conditions needed for creating the zone, I believe that we individually find our own set of conditions for moving into the zone experience. And we find our own ways of helping others move into the zone.

2

THE INVESTIGATIVE MIND

*M*ind is a slippery term. It shifts from one meaning to another depending on the context. Consider a few of the ways we use the term. *Mind your own business. A mind is a terrible thing to waste. Keep an open mind. Please keep in mind. . . . Don't mind me. Make up your mind. I wasn't in my right mind. I've half a mind to . . . ! I can't get this child to mind me.* You can see how the meaning shifts. These expressions, in order, use the term to mean *attend to . . . , intellect, be receptive to . . . , a place where memories are kept, be bothered by . . . , a decision process, being rational, intention,* and *to obey or respond.* Mind is also used to mean exercising judgment and a place where all these processes take place. And all of the phrases imply that mind is awareness.

My favorite illustration of the slipperiness of the term *mind* is, when you want someone to mind your dog for the day, you choose someone who doesn't mind dogs.

MIND IS . . .

In writing this book about mind and motivation in relation to the zone phenomenon, I could not work with a vague concept of mind. And I did not want to arbitrarily narrow down the choices of meaning to one—for example, treating mind as roughly synonymous with brain, as is frequently done. Some notable scholars, particularly in neuroscience, use *brain* and *mind* as interchangeable terms. I hold to the view that mind is a more comprehensive concept than brain. Brain is an object. It has a definite geography. There is no mind without brain, but brain is only part of mind. The whole being, not just what is in the skull, is involved in mind. Neurons throughout the entire nervous system carry the memories that are the basis of all mental processing.[1] Of course, any study of mind has to be done in concert with the brain sciences. It no longer makes sense to investigate mental processes independently of how the brain works.

Because I am treating mind in a technical way, I had a strong need to put a clear and distinct concept of mind in front of us. The best I have found comes from the work of the American philosopher John Dewey. His is a concept fully consistent with current research evidence, and it weaves the pieces of the puzzle together. Mind is not a thing or a place, an organ or entity that *causes* us to observe, reason, make decisions, and take action. Mind is not something that can be considered apart from behavior; it can only be observed *in* behavior. Mind is not an *it*. Mind is a *condition* of the whole being—the person in a state of mindfulness. Mind is minding.[2]

I use the term *minding* because it helps us remember that mind is a quality of functioning rather than a thing. Viewing minding as a continuum also helps us conceptualize what mind is. Consider a continuum stretching from mindless (unthinking, uncaring, oblivious) through intermediate minding to highly mindful. The investigative mind, the theme of this chapter, is at the high end of the continuum, the high end of minding.

To convey his meaning of mind, Dewey offered the image of a mother minding her new baby: she is alert to what is happening, attentive, engaged, responsive, and processing data carefully. Her whole being is focused and involved, that is, mindful. Her mind *is* the quality of her caring thoughts and overt actions. (It is easy to imagine this mother being in the zone with her baby!) Her mind is not a force behind the scenes causing her thoughts and actions, as an invisible spirit or mechanism with its hands on the levers of behavior. Mind (minding or mindfulness) is a quality of behavior the mother brings to the relationship with her child, and this definition applies to any person/person-to-person/environmental relationship.[3]

Dewey's example helps convey the scope of meaning I want for the term *investigative mind*. Any single term is inadequate in capturing the mindfulness of the caring mother with her baby. I had a potful of terms to choose from to convey the high end of the minding continuum: attentive, inquisitive, creative, wondering, analytical, inventive, curious, probing, problem solving, exploring, reflective, engaged, inquiring, and carefully processing. All of these apply to the mindful nurturing of the mother. I chose *investigative* over the other terms because it connotes more proactive and focused minding than the other terms. It suggests a mind-set concerned with finding out, making sense of one's experiences, and adjusting behavior for what is needed next. For me, *investigation* is the term that best captures what it is that babies do as they figure out how to make their environments responsive to themselves. And if babies come into the world already equipped with a capacity for mindfulness, that gives us some vital information about the essential nature of mind.

This view of mind as minding is unfamiliar and hard to hang on to. It is very easy to fall back to the unconscious assumption that mind is an *it*, a place. But if we are going to help people shake off the blank-slate/empty-vessel view of mind, we have to move away from the concept of mind as a thing and toward a concept of mind as the *quality of mental processing* invested by the whole person in thought and action. In subsequent paragraphs we will explore different qualities or levels of minding.

How does this concept of mind relate to the main theme of this book? The distinction between zoning out and being in the zone depends on understanding different qualities of mental engagement. Being in the zone doesn't happen except through investigative mindfulness, and without any doubt, developing the investigative mind we discuss in this chapter is a high-quality investment of mental energy.

Throughout the book I use the term *mind* as described above, and I use it to mean *conscious* mental processing. No doubt unconscious processing is going on all the time in the brain and nervous system, and on a scale that dwarfs the conscious. The unconscious processing consists of all the coordination of all the elements of our elaborate organic system, coordination that is happening out of our awareness. But the only mind that we can *know* is the part of the processing that enters our awareness.

MENTAL PROCESSING IN BABIES

What mental equipment are we born with? This sounds like a question about the organization of the mind as an organ, a thing. Of course, the brain is the organ, the *organ*ization, that is the basis of mind. A more accurately worded (but clumsier) question would be, "What is the mental organization we are born with—that can be inferred from examining the measurable evidence of the awareness of newborns?" The term *awareness* brings in the concept of mind, that is, the quality of mindfulness. Mostly I will be using the phrase "mental processing" to convey mind and mindfulness.

The question of what mental equipment we are born with has been asked in different forms for untold generations. Only recently have scientific answers begun to fill in some important blanks about the nature of mind. Research on brain functioning has moved ahead dramatically. Studies of infants by developmental psychologists, using new investigation methods, fill in other parts. But mind is still a difficult concept to pin down, and we have to go beyond the hard sciences and make some educated guesses about what the full picture looks like.

In the first chapter I referred to research evidence that babies are born with organized mental processes, organized to investigate their environment and to anticipate finding around them people and things that are responsive to them and their needs. The evidence is elaborated in this chapter.

WHAT BABY BEHAVIOR TELLS US ABOUT MENTAL ORGANIZATION

It seems obvious that anyone studying human nature, anyone wanting to know what kind of mental organization is a given in human nature, would study the behavior of babies and look for evidence of mental

processing. Detailed, systematic observation of children was pio-
neered in the early years of the twentieth century by Jean Piaget, Lev
Vygotsky, and, to a lesser but significant extent, Myrtle McGraw. But
the ingenuity of their observational work was largely neglected in psychology until the past thirty years.[4]

The coming of the videotape recorder and the computer turned
the tide in developmental psychology. The 1999 book *The Scientist in
the Crib: Minds, Brains, and How Children Learn,* by Alison Gopnik,
Andrew N. Meltzoff, and Patricia K. Kuhl, contains a fascinating presentation of what videotaping has made possible in the detailed study
of babies' nonverbal behavior—their overt behavior that is the
window into their mental processing. The authors report their own
work and synthesize that of many other scientists who study babies.

One strand of the research on babies follows a basic design.
Babies are given something to look at, listen to, hold in their mouths,
and so on, and their reactions are videotaped or captured by computer. The babies are then given something else look at, listen to, hold,
and so on, and the two sets of recorded reactions can be compared to
see if (a) the babies can tell the difference and (b) if they prefer one
thing over the other. For example, to see if newborns can discriminate
human faces and voices from other sights and sounds, the experiment
is set up to have the human voices and faces on one side of the baby
to determine whether their eyes turn in that direction or in the other
direction toward other sights and sounds. The sources of the sounds
and images are off camera, so the research assistant who watches the
tapes (with the sound turned off) and records the babies' eye and head
movements doesn't know *what* the babies are looking toward, only
the direction of the looking. This technique of analyzing baby
behavior, and inferring from the behavior the mental processing going
on, is being used in many ways, some of them described below.

Remarkably, just after birth, babies *can* tell the difference between
voices and other sounds, between faces and other objects, and they
look longer at the faces and voices. This simple study by itself makes
the age-old assumption of the blank slate seem false. Moments after
birth the babies could make basic discriminations and demonstrate
preferences. They seem clearly to be equipped before birth to attend
to elements of their environment that will support them in their development. There was no time after their birth for the environment to

write on their slates. The babies brought mental organization into the world with them.[5] In the next paragraphs we will consider what kind of organization and its complexity.

To make their experiments possible, the scientists first had to understand the vision of newborns. They found them to be very nearsighted by adult standards, focusing well at about one foot, just the distance to the face of someone holding them. "Babies seem to be designed to see the people who love them more clearly than anything else."[6]

AT BIRTH

What else did the researchers learn about the mental organization of newborns?

- Newborns not only can distinguish voices from other sounds, but they can pick out their mother's voice, and they much prefer it. Babies sucking on pacifiers linked to audio or videotapes of voices will work more to keep their mother's voice going.
- Newborns demonstrate a coordination among their senses. When they hear a sound to the side of them, they will turn their heads expecting to *see* something to go with the sound.
- "Within a few days after they're born, they recognize familiar faces, voices and even smells, and prefer them to unfamiliar ones."[7]
- Just after birth, as I mentioned in chapter 1, babies can imitate facial expressions when the faces are a foot away. Stick out your tongue and the baby's tongue is likely to come out too. This is cute and may not appear to be of scientific significance. Actually, the ability of newborns to imitate shows a crucial, innate understanding that they are like us, and that they can connect with other people in nonverbal exchanges. More about this later.
- Babies a few days old attend carefully to edges of things, apparently using them to divide up the visual field into meaningful order, distinguishing objects from other objects. This making of meaningful order is no simple matter; even sophisticated computer vision programs are challenged by this task.
- Newborns give evidence of knowing that they live in a three-

dimensional world that has predictability in it. Their eyes follow movement of objects to distinguish them from the background, using the movement to identify objects in time as well as space. They seem to surmise the nature of objects by predicting their future behavior. Show young babies a ball rolling on a table. When it rolls behind a screen, their eyes shift to the far edge of the screen, anticipating the ball coming out there.[8]

IMPLICATIONS

There is no blank slate. The brain at birth is not an unformed organ waiting to be programmed. These and other studies of newborns give evidence that we are born with organized brains, organizational systems for engaging the world outside of the womb. What does the organization consist of?

1. Newborns have the preprogrammed capacity to make discriminations among sensations.
2. They then classify and bring order to what is experienced. The babies make some kind of rudimentary judgments about the sensations they experience to sort things into what they prefer and don't prefer. The sorting of experiences suggests there is an intuitive system for making categories of things according to properties they have or don't have. This sorting and classifying is what cognitive theorists are now calling the making of prototypes, or mental modules.
3. Babies then have the impulse to seek out more of the experiences in the categories they do prefer.
4. They make predictions and attend to whether their predictions prove valid.
5. Very young babies demonstrate *recognition* memory. For example, memory of faces and voices, even though they are not yet capable of conscious recall. As with all memories these early memories are stored in the nervous system as patterns of synaptic change. Stored as mental modules, the memories form the content the babies use in later investigations.
6. The facial imitation studies show that newborns are equipped with the brain organization needed for basic social interac-

tions: recognizing who is like them and in what ways, and engaging in social exchange, or turn taking.

7. Psychologist and noted science writer Daniel Goleman, synthesizing research on social intelligence, tells us that "Virtually from birth, babies are . . . active. . . . The two-way emotional message system between the baby and her caretaker represent her lifeline, the route through which passes all the traffic to get her basic needs fulfilled. Babies need be tiny masters at managing their caregivers through an elaborate, built-in system of eyes contacted and avoided, smiles, and cries; lacking that social intercom, babies can remain miserable or even die from neglect."[9] From her extensive review of research on mother-infant relationships, independent scholar Ellen Dissanayake concludes that the baby's emotional life is central in mental development. Babies are programmed "to seek and engage in intimacy with others before . . . anything else."[10]

8. The imitation studies and other experiments also show that babies have an innate coordination among the senses. In sticking out their tongues, for example, they demonstrate that the *oral* sensation of their tongue movement is matched to the *visual* image of the other person extending the pink thing from the lower part of his or her head. They stick them out even though they have never seen their own tongues! The folk wisdom about babies, assumed to be true even by many psychologists, is that imitation is an important way of learning but it involves no reasoning or investigation. These studies alone show that view to be false.

9. All of these features convey the clear picture that babies are born with the impulse and equipment to actively find out about and make sense of what they experience—to make meaning. There is no necessity to "motivate" them. They instinctively investigate.

These careful observations of newborns revealed behaviors that had to be programmed before birth, and they are evidence of an exquisitely organized brain. They also show that immediately after birth babies begin to learn by reflecting on experiences, deciding which experiences they prefer, and seeking more of those. This is a strikingly different image of infancy from the common view that babies are born with survival drives that are just emotion with no judgment involved in them.

Babies' mental processing takes raw sensations supplied by sound waves and light waves and converts them into meanings by sorting them into mental modules, or abstract representations. This processing then manipulates the representations into still other meanings. The image emerging from the research suggests a flowing together of sensation, intuition, judgment, and emotion in a combination that provides the impetus for mental growth.

All of these research findings lead us easily to the hypothesis that babies are born with the zone experience immediately available to them. They are investigating the world at the leading edge of their skills and experiencing the satisfaction of figuring things out. And all of this happens without babies having any sense of self as an individual separate from one's mother, and it happens without language! More about this to come.

The evidence of mental organization at birth carries us to the next question. What are the learning processes that build on the initial organization? If humans are born equipped with very powerful mental computers for processing experiences, how are they used to learn new things? For some additional answers we turn to studies of slightly older babies.

STUDIES OF BABIES, ONE MONTH TO ONE YEAR

Recall the study in which one-month-old babies were given one of two pacifiers to suck on, either a regular pacifier or a bumpy one. The babies never saw the pacifiers, only held them in their mouths. Then the babies were shown bumpy and smooth objects, without feeling them. "The babies looked longer at the object that was the same shape as the one they had just been sucking on. Somehow, they could relate the feel of the pacifier in their mouths with its visual image."[11] The babies go beyond the data obtained from one sensory system and link them to data provided by another sensory system. Part of the learning process evident here is the connecting of one experience to another to meet a fundamental need to makes sense of one's world.

- By five months babies show a much more sophisticated coordination of senses. Researchers "showed babies a silent video of a face saying either *ahhh* or *eeee*, and then they played the babies audiotapes of each vowel sound. Five-month-olds could tell which face went with which sound. They looked at the face with a wide-open mouth when they heard the *ahhh* sound and at the face with pulled-back lips when they heard the *eeee* sound."[12] This ability is clearly cross-sensory learning at a more complex level.

- Even at three months babies show evidence of awareness that they have the power to cause things to happen. One experiment, for example, that can be done by parents as well as researchers, involves tying one end of a ribbon to a baby's ankle and the other end to a mobile just above the crib but out of reach. When the baby kicks, the mobile moves. The baby quickly learns that it is just one leg's kicking that causes the mobile to move, and she kicks that one much more than the other leg. If the mobile is removed for a week and then returned and retied to the same ankle, she will immediately start kicking that leg.[13] At this age the baby has the memory capability to recall how the mobile was made to move, a memory spanning a week in this case, a capability used as a natural learning tool.

- From birth, babies' brains are designed so that sensory activity and motor skills promote cognitive development. "For example, at first a baby can release its grip only by accident, but when the coordination to let go deliberately is finally achieved, dropping objects becomes as enjoyable as grasping them was earlier. Not only is there an immediate, observable effect on the world, but *planning* to drop something and *predicting* that someone will pick it up and hand it back have the ultimate result of developing these cognitive pathways in the brain."[14]

- By nine months, babies have learned about the expression of basic emotions. When they watch a film showing a happy face alongside a film showing a sad face, then are played sounds of happy or sad voices, they look longer at the image that matches the tone of voice being played. They also know the facial expression that goes with an angry voice.

- Babies reach another level of understanding about emotions at about one year, the awareness that they can get important data about people by reading expressions of emotion. In one experiment, a researcher looks into two boxes while the baby watches. "She looks into one box with an expression of joy and into the other with an expression of complete disgust. Then she pushes the boxes toward the baby, who has never seen inside the boxes. Nevertheless, the baby figures out something about what is inside just by looking at the [grown-up's] face: the baby happily reaches into the box that made [the researcher] happy but won't open the box that disgusted her. The baby doesn't just understand that the other person feels happy or disgusted, but also understands that she feels happy about some things and disgusted about others—and that those emotions are information the baby can use to make her own judgments."[15]

- Pointing and having the baby look at what is pointed to is such a familiar event that it seems not to reveal anything important about mental processing. But it is evidence of babies' understanding that investigation of one's world is a social process as well as an individual process. Researchers have systematically recorded the fact that by one year "babies will look, precisely, at just the place the grown-up pointed to."[16] At this age babies also know they can enlist a grown-up's help by pointing to something they want, such as a toy out of reach, and the adult will comply with the request.

- By as early as their first birthday, babies are quite systematically investigating how things relate to each other. Given a rake to use to reach and pull a toy toward themselves, babies "forget all about getting the toy after a trial or two. They often deliberately put the toy back far out of reach and experiment with using the rake to draw it toward them. The toy itself isn't nearly as interesting as the fact that the rake moves it closer."[17] *The investigative process is more engaging than the outcome of the investigation.*

- Babies as young as three months have been shown to have a rudimentary sense of how the physical world works. In experiments similar to the observing of babies' eye movements as the ball rolls behind the screen, researchers observed that babies considered objects that moved together consistently were actually parts of one object. Babies also expect things that apparently belong together to stay together. When a researcher picked up an object and it didn't all lift but separated into two parts, the babies gave reactions of surprise. From these and similar studies the researchers concluded that even very young babies expect that they are operating in an orderly, predictable world.[18]

IMPLICATIONS

Clearly, normal babies are born with minds that include the capacity for keen observation of people and things. The keen observation skills make possible what is referred to as the cognitive triangle: the babies' perception of objects and events, their awareness of the grown-ups' attitudes or actions toward the objects and events, and their awareness of their own mental processing of ways to act in relation to the people and the objects. As the triangle is played out again and again, the babies spontaneously revisit and reconstruct over and over the mental modules they have formed for making sense of things.

Undoubtedly, babies' investigation of the minds of grown-ups begins early. The studies of reading emotions were done with one-year-olds. By one and a half years, babies start to become aware of differences between people, and they are fascinated by these differences. Experiments with fourteen- to eighteen-month-old babies show that they've learned—through their own investigations—that people have desires, that their desires may be different, and that they may even conflict. Their sense of self as separate from others emerges during this time.[19] During the "terrible twos," the babies' investigations shift to exploring the differences between their desires and those of others. While one-year-olds "may seem irresistibly seduced by the charms of forbidden objects (the lamp cord made me do it), the two-year-olds are deliberately perverse. . . . A two-year-old doesn't even look at the lamp cord. Instead his hand goes out to touch it as he looks, steadily, gravely, and with great deliberation, at you," investigating how your mind works. "The grave look is directed at you because you and your reaction, rather than the lamp cord itself, are the really interesting thing. If the child is a budding psychologist, we parents are the laboratory rats."[20]

Babies actively seek to find patterns in their experiences. From the earliest months, a baby's mental processing system is working at an abstract level. It is extracting and abstracting from various raw sensory experiences its own intuitive representations—mental modules—of how the world works, and it can mentally manipulate the representations to make further meanings. The abstracting goes beyond the data the babies have already processed. Babies go beyond the physical facial expression and read emotion in it. And they go beyond the visual image of the rounded shape of someone's mouth to intuit that an *oooo* sound is the one that goes with that mouth position.

In regard to the physical world, babies anticipate order and consistency. Their brains are preformed to expect order, continuity, predictability, and symmetry. We can speculate that they expect the world to yield meanings and explanations as they investigate it.

Babies' mental modules get reworked and refined as new experiences come along that don't fit in any early prototypes. The processing system reprograms the modules again and again to more comprehensive, subtle, and complex versions. The impetus for the reprogramming seems to come from dissonance in the system. The babies won't take in experiences that don't make sense to them. The need for making sense is what drives the system. Contrast this image of mind once again with the blank-slate assumption. Nothing in the blank-slate model accounts for the initiation of meaning-making activities seen in the experiments described in this chapter.

LANGUAGE DEVELOPMENT IN BABIES

How do babies acquire language? Do the features of mental processing described above also explain language learning? The research on babies' preverbal behavior provides a clear answer of yes.

The beginnings of language, and all social skills, probably are in the rhythms of mutuality in mother-infant interactions: the mother's vocalizations, facial expressions, body movements, and gestures. The mother makes all these actions exaggerated, clear, and rhythmic. And the baby responds, in a sequence of turn taking. As Ellen Dissanayake puts it, "Babies in turn respond with corresponding sounds, expressions, and the movements of their own, and over the first months a mutual multimedia ritual performance emerges and develops. Exquisitely satisfying to both participants, it inundates both mother and the baby with a special pleasure that is all the more powerful because it is not just felt alone (like the interest, excitement, or joy filled while privately thinking about or watching one's baby) but is mirrored or shared," as when the baby spontaneously and deliberately smiles.[21]

One-month-old babies who were given a pacifier to suck that was attached to a computer demonstrated that they heard all the distinctions of sound categories in the English language. The research method was ingenious. When the baby gave the pacifier a suck, it triggered a sound from the computer's speaker, one sound for each hard suck. "Babies love the sounds almost as much as they love milk: they may suck up to eighty times a minute to keep the sounds turned on. Eventually, though, they slow down; they get bored hearing the same thing over and over again." However, when the researcher changes the sound, "infants immediately perk up and suck very fast again to hear the new sound. That change in their sucking shows that they can hear a difference between the new sound and the sound they heard before." Their ability to distinguish between the sounds they judge to be the same and the sounds they hear as different is clearly demonstrated.[22] This result was the opposite of what scientists previously believed, probably based on the blank-slate assumption, that babies only gradually come to distinguish sounds.

Clearly, the babies grouped the auditory sensations they got into prototypical sounds. New sensations that then came along were identified as matching one prototype or another, or none. The learning pattern seemed the same: as with other abstract representations, these sound prototypes are in place until new experiences that don't fit them prompt a reconstruction that forms new, more complex ones. Tests showed that by one year of age babies' speech categories have, through this process, matured to resembled those of adults. And at that age they begin to shift from sounds to words. The sequences of sounds are transformed into sequences of ideas. The code of language, "far more baffling that any spymaster's cryptogram," can be deciphered by babies. "No computer has been able to figure it out. . . . There is no computer that can do what every three-year-old can do: understand a conversation."[23] In contrast to the human computation system that reprograms itself and adapts to changing situations, man-made computers are what Steven Pinker calls the ultimate blank slate, dependent on outside programmers and incapable of common sense.[24]

Language learning requires mental discrimination and generalization, complex processes showing judgment at work. One author uses the example of the word "bottle." The child learns that the word applies to whatever the color or shape the bottle may be, and whatever its contents.

Later the child discriminates the separate attributes—color, contents, nipple—and soon learns that "bottle" applies to other objects as well.[25]

By three years of age babies demonstrate an intuitive grasp of grammar as they make two- or three-word sentences. "[These] very young children already . . . seem to recognize that only some word orders are possible in their language. They say 'Mommy gone' but not 'gone Mommy'; 'more cookie' but not 'cookie more.' Second, they already use different word orders to express different meanings. 'Kiss Teddy' means Mommy should kiss the teddy bear, while 'Teddy kiss' means the teddy bear is going to kiss Mommy (undoubtedly assisted by the speaker). These very simple two-word sentences already follow certain rules, even though a two-year-old would never have heard the sentences from anyone else. Just as babies invent meanings, they also invent grammatical rules."[26] They don't just *learn* language. They actively structure it and restructure it in the process of making sense of their world.

BABIES IN THE ZONE?

All the infant studies mentioned so far suggest *investigative* mental processes at work, which for these subjects anticipates the finding of both meaning and supportive connections in the world around them. The investigative mind-set is one of the conditions needed for the zone experience. Four of the other conditions, described in chapter 1, also seem to be present in young babies' mental processing: concentrated attention on a keen interest; focus on something other than the self; a feedback loop not routed through self-criticism; and working at the edge of one's skills. The evidence points to babies having access to zone experiences from the beginning. They appear to be born with the expectation that they can make sense of the world, that their investigations will pay off. Their pure joy in figuring out something new radiates in their faces. Could these be zone experiences? It is easy for us to take the next step and speculate that when their investigation gets meaningful data from their world, the feedback and resulting joy sustain the zone.

No doubt the zone comes and goes for them as it does for us. One way of looking at the pacifier/computer tone experiments is that the excitement of causing a sound with each suck on a pacifier was a zone experience that was sustained just as long as the investigation of the new sound stayed engaging. The babies dropped out of the zone when the sound was no longer fresh, but they returned to the zone when the computer changed the sound. Whether the hypothesis that babies experience the zone proves out—or can even be tested—remains to be seen. But anyone who has observed babies at all closely has seen the absorption and delight they show when stretching their skills in exploring some person or thing new to them.

IMPLICATIONS OF THE EVIDENCE FROM BABIES

While this book is about mental processing, not specifically about babies, the study of babies just after birth is the right place to start. The clear demonstration that babies are born with organized brains designed to remain organized by reconstructing themselves is, I believe, a pivotal event in the study of human nature. None of the theorists who long ago shaped the fields of philosophy, psychology, and sociology had access to the data from this research. They had to make assumptions about the nature of mind and motivation, specifically about the kind of mental equipment we have at birth, without the evidence we now have available. It seems likely that those fields of study would have been vastly different if the scholars and scientists had the evidence from the research on newborns.

Now we have the evidence, and those disciplines and other ones will change because of it. The nature versus nurture arguments will eventually be seen as wrongheaded, based on a false dichotomy. The title of Matt Ridley's recent book, *Nature via Nurture*, characterizes the changing viewpoint.[27] Genes and experience collaborate in the shaping of human functioning. The question of which plays the initiating role will become irrelevant. Daniel Goleman sums up the collaboration in these terms: "It is biologically impossible for a gene to operate independently of its environment: genes are *designed* to be regulated by signals from their intermediate surround, including hormones from the endocrine system and neurotransmitters in the brain—some of which, in turn, are profoundly influenced by our social interactions. Just as our diet regulates certain genes, our social experiences also determine a distinct batch of such genomic on-off switches."[28]

The arguments around intrinsic and extrinsic motivation will likewise be seen as based on a false dichotomy. Moving beyond this argument is a big step. As I said in chapter 1, a new concept of motivation is emerging based on the understanding that we are born with an organized inner nature designed to *anticipate* outer resources. The collaboration of "inner" and "outer" is so fully mutual as to make even this distinction a false dichotomy.[29]

JOHN DEWEY'S CONTRIBUTION TO THE DIALOGUE

The comprehensive theory of human nature most consistent with the evidence and implications described above is that of John Dewey. I spoke with a philosophy professor recently who said, "We don't do Dewey much anymore." I told him that it is time for a Dewey renaissance. While the research evidence on mind functioning is new, the concept that we are born investigators is not. The findings of today's researchers with infants were anticipated by more than fifty years in the writings of John Dewey. Dewey worked on the leading edge of the study of human nature. He first published his insights into the nature of mind over a century ago. Through the years his books presented *inquiry*—basically what I am referring to as our investigative nature—as essential to individual and collective progress. Improvements in the human condition don't happen except through inquiry, or perhaps occasionally by accident.

Dewey's ideas were championed by educators in the Progressive Education movement, who tried various applications of Dewey's work from the early 1900s until World War II. While some of the innovations came into wide usage, the main theme—active inquiry based on keen interests—never came close to replacing conventional instruction. However, the ideas have continued on a small scale. Many of the proponents of the inquiry approach identify their view of mind as constructivist or constructionist, meaning that the brain is organized to continually reconstruct itself. That is, learning is not additive but instead is a reorganization process. I include this brief mention here to highlight the fact that while the investigative view of mind is alive and well among some educators, it has not gained acceptance broadly. The blank-slate assumption predominates in virtually all corners of our society, including our schools.

In my research I have studied the works of many scholars writing currently about the nature of mind. Dewey's work is not referenced in any of them. The fields of neuroscience, developmental psychology, cognitive science, and evolutionary psychology have their roots outside of philosophy. And the leading writers in these fields do not acknowledge the kindred work of Dewey and the rich philosophic framework he provided for the issues they are working on. As an admirer of Dewey's work, I am delighted to see that many of today's scholars and researchers have come, independently, through empirical work, to the view of mind that Dewey formulated through reflective philosophy. Part of my motivation in writing this book is to bring Dewey's powerful contribution into the dialogue. In the paragraphs that follow, I summarize his key points on mental processing and extend his ideas in the direction of the zone experience.

LEARNING

When the brain is viewed as always being organized, learning is re-organization. Learning always involves the unlearning of a pattern of thought or preconception that existed before the new learning event. The experiments with infants all point to the brain having innate organization, now viewed as templates or mental modules for making sense of experience, and some built-in rules for managing the modules. These were provided by natural selection as survival skills thousands of generations ago when the structure of our brains was formed.

The organization of the brain is changed, however slightly, when something new is learned, or else learning didn't happen. There is often the appearance of learning when something "taught" is held in short-term memory; but if some reorganization has not occurred, the "learning" does not become part of long-term memory, the store-house of mental habits. Someone wanting to teach a child a new fact, concept, or behavior will be effective to the extent that she can first identify the child's preconception or mental habit that is to be unlearned or modified and then engage the child in activity that prompts reorganization.

Here's an example of unlearning needed for new learning to occur. I happened to be on campus at the elementary school where my wife, Carolyn, was principal. I had a video recorder with me and caught on camera an episode of my wife coaching a discouraged kindergartner who could say her numbers, one to ten, but stumbled when counting objects. As Carolyn handed Sara chips one at a time for her to count, she could correctly count one and two, but she identified the third chip as "four." After about seven minutes of coaching, Sara could count sets of various objects to three. When Carolyn took the lesson up one more number and pointed to a set of four objects, Sara counted, "one, two, three, umm, umm . . . a thousand of 'em." There were at least two main preconceptions here that needed unlearning. Knowing the number names one to ten was mistakenly identified by her teacher as evidence that Sara understood how to *count* to ten. When counting objects with Carolyn, she got to only two. Sara needed to see (and touch) the reality of sets of objects having particular names according to how many were in the set. "A thousand of 'em" was in her mind, apparently, a name to go with a category meaning "too many to count." I believe Sara came away from the lesson with the understanding that any set of objects, no matter the quantity in the set, had a specific number name to identify it. In the nine minutes of coaching I recorded, Carolyn had identified the faulty preconception and had helped Sara reorganized her sense of what numbers mean.

Dewey's view was that learning is the outcome of experiencing the consequences of decisions made and actions taken. Since the time of his analysis of experience and learning, solely on the macrolevel, neurological researchers have demonstrated, on the microlevel, the power of experience in shaping the brain. As summarized by neurobiologist Lise Eliot, "The brain itself is literally molded by experience: every sight, sound, and thought leaves an imprint on specific neural circuits modifying the way future sights, sounds, and thoughts will be registered. Brain hardware is not fixed but living, dynamic tissue that is constantly updating itself to meet the sensory, motor, emotional, and intellectual demands at hand."[30] The child's brain produces billions of synaptic connections each day and loses billions of the connections that are produced but go unused.

The brain is never inactive, or "on hold," even in the quiet phases of sleeping. Besides not being a blank slate on which experience is written, the brain is always actively attending to and engaging with something and is mediating events. There is no such thing as inactive daydreaming. What may appear to a parent, teacher, or other outsider as a child's vegetating or mind wandering is actually active mind engagement in something, albeit something other that what the adult wishes. Mental activity always has a focus and direction, a purpose however well or poorly understood in consciousness. To focus a child toward some intended learning, the adult has to trigger in the child an awareness that the new mental construct is more important—to the child—than the activity already going on. Just as all learning involves unlearning, all direction is redirection. Patterns of mental activity already in place need to be experienced as inadequate for dealing with new events, and then the focus of activity shifts. All of these principles of learning apply to adult learning as well.

VALUING IN THE LEARNING PROCESS

Another inherent feature of our brains is prioritizing, or valuing. We humans differ among ourselves in what experiences and events we find more valuable, but we all prioritize. Long before young children have any conscious priority systems, they have clear preferences as to what is important. It is thought to be part of the survival instinct. Every action has an emotional component, a valuing component, an assigned importance among one's life experiences. The emotional component is just as much present in mature adults who have value systems that are consciously developed and well reasoned. As I said earlier, even impersonal logical reasoning has an emotional engine.

All learning has an emotional engine. Learning is not just the stimulation of and hooking up of unused synapses or connecting them in new ways. Before learning can happen, the person has to be seeking something, aiming toward some outcome that seems to be valuable. Research with primates shows this to be true for their learning, as well as for humans. Even chance encounters with ideas and information unrelated to what we are doing at the time grab our attention and refocus our mental activity, however briefly, because they strike some note of value in relation to our mental storehouse. As anthropologist Donald Symons described the emotional engine, "the proximate goal of mental activities always is the attainment of emotional states."[31]

MENTAL HABITS AND LEARNING

Mental habits, what now are being called mental modules or proto-types, whether innate or learned, operate our daily activities automatically, out of consciousness, until they run into circumstances that show them to be inadequate. We all know the experience, such as driving along the expressway with our conscious attention on something totally remote from driving. In effect, our habits, out of consciousness, are driving the car. Then something intrudes on our thoughts, say, the sight of a car ahead having a tire blowout. Our driving habits tell us they are inadequate to deal automatically with the situation, and our full awareness is instantly back on our driving and primed to deal with the uncertainty that triggered the conscious mental processing. The emotional engine gets to work and the conscious mental processing begins. It prompts us to a range of mental activities: sorting through data on hand, looking at things differently, searching for new data, conceptualizing alternatives, visiting values and priorities, applying logic, and putting all of this together in a tentative plan of action, trying it out and checking on its adequacy. All of this can happen in a split second. It can happen in a shallow and incomplete way and result in a poor plan. It can happen in a deep and (relatively) profound way. It happens whether we are considering very small matters or major ones. But it happens, or learning—a reconstruction that enters long-term memory—has not occurred. Not all conscious mental processing follows this pattern, but good-quality processing does. More about this later.

When a teacher, parent, or coach initiates some new *investigative* learning, the tasks needed are:

- sleuthing out the preconceptions (mental modules) students have that make their world sensible;
- in a caring context, planting doubts about the adequacy of the preconceptions;
- helping the doubts to crank up the emotional engine that fosters students' inquiry;
- providing "just in time" resources to help the inquiry;
- giving students space and time to try out their reconceptualized way of making sense of things; and
- recycling through the process as needed.

All of this can happen in a brief moment, as in helping a child figure out a printed word that is unfamiliar; or it may be a long-term quest built of many intermediate inquiries. Illustrations of such longer-term inquiries and shifts in mental modules are given in some detail in chapter 6.

When a student is stuck, sees that the preconception doesn't fit a situation, and seeks the teacher's help, the learning process is the same as identified above except the student's awareness of the inadequacy of the preconception is what initiates the sequence, not the teacher's action.

DEWEY'S FOUR LEVELS OF REASONING

When disequilibrium prompts conscious mental processing to deal with it, the quality of reasoning that happens can vary widely. Dewey identified four quality levels of reasoning that can come into play.[32] He described but did not name the first two levels of quality. The first level could be called *panic reasoning* or *barely reasoning*. At this level, the uncertainty or disequilibrium that triggers conscious processing and starts data gathering and reasoning also triggers fear, making the person so uncomfortable that he or she grabs the first solution that comes to mind—to push the difficulty away as quickly as possible. Obviously, this process has a very small chance of concluding with a good solution, especially in today's complex world. But if the person's conscious processing is clouded by fear, he or she may pay little attention to the consequences of the solution and draw from the process very little, if any, growth. And whatever equilibrium is attained comes with a strong message to always stay in familiar territory, to take no conscious risks, and to let unconscious habits and impulses run as much of one's life as possible. Put in the context of teaching and learning, instruction that evokes strong fear blocks sound reasoning.

The second level could be called *pat-answer reasoning*. When fear plays a smaller but still significant role and the person feels confident enough to pause to consider more than one way of dealing with a difficulty, the reasoning is likely to be of the pat-answer kind. Prior experiences (mental modules) and rules come to mind that may fit the difficulty. But the ideas that do come are treated as fixed and not open to inspection. Reasoning stays outside the substance of the idea. In other words, the ideas that come to mind are pat answers. "What was it my mother (or coach or teacher or boss) said to do in cases like this?" How well the rule or idea fits the difficulty is not examined; the fit is assumed *on authority*. I choose the pat answer that has the stamp of approval on it. If the consequences of the action I take turn out to be appropriate to the situation, the credibility of the authority is confirmed in my mind. Pat-answer reasoning is what's sponsored by the blank-slate approach to teaching. That is, someone else's reasoning and stamp of approval are written onto the student's blank slate.

Dewey called the third quality level *reflective thinking*, and in his later writings he called it *inquiry*. I am calling it investigative reasoning. In writing about this kind of reasoning, I have avoided the terms *reflective* and *thinking* because they are used by Carl Jung in a special way (see chapter 3), and I want to avoid confusion. This third type of reasoning is fundamentally different from the first two. The inquiry goes *inside* the rules and the facts that come to mind and inspects their adequacy and value in the new situation. Put in contemporary terms, the content of mental modules and the rules for manipulating them are inspected. Solutions that come out of investigative reasoning may or may not be sanctioned by authorities or custom. Authority and custom are not the test of new ideas. They may be considered as *data* in the pool of things being considered. But the investigative test is whether the new idea fits the requirements of the situation that triggered the reasoning. This inquiry tries out ideas, both in imagination and in action, by examining the consequences of the chosen action. Careful attention to consequences and learning from those consequences are the hallmarks of investigative reasoning.

The fourth level of quality reasoning has all the features of the third, plus two more: it is an intentional process and it is disciplined. Dewey called this reasoning *systematic inquiry*. While investigative reasoning can happen without any planning, as it happens to all of us from time to time, systematic inquiry is an intentional, practiced discipline. I believe this disciplined quality of reasoning emerges as we find satisfaction in investigative reasoning. There is an emotional lift that comes with finding that the consequences of our investigative actions are productive, and we want to keep the lift going.

The distinction between the levels of reasoning is not just theoretical but very practical as well. For example, the Jacob Wetterling Foundation, concerned with educating parents about how to help prevent child abductions, urges parents not to teach their children to fear strangers. The foundation reports that more than 80 percent of child abductions are not done by strangers, but by someone familiar to the child, usually neighbors or family. "The Stranger/Danger mantra is far overrated." In Dewey's terms, I read this as meaning that panic reasoning, with its heavy component of fear, is not workable in situations such as this. The foundation encourages parents to play out "what if" scenarios with their young children. Such as, what if we suddenly get separated while in the mall? In the subway? What would you do? As partners in an investigation, the parent and the child consider ways the child can find trustworthy adults—strangers, most likely—who can help, such as a sales clerk in a mall store or any mother with children of her own. In this vein, we are teaching the child to be cautious about situations, not people.

A comment here about the zone experience. My thesis is that the zone is available only through investigative reasoning, Dewey's inquiry. As everyone is capable of investigative reasoning, everyone has potential access to the zone. However, I believe we can often be in investigative reasoning without being in the zone. Many circumstances call on us to reason with care, but many of them don't engage the first condition of the zone experience: concentrated, absorbing focus on a goal related to something of keen interest. Or the circumstances that promote the investigation may not stretch our skills. We have many daily tasks to do that call for good-quality reasoning but do not grab our high-priority interests or stretch our skills.

INQUIRY AND THE ZONE

BABY ZONE AND ADULT ZONE

One could assume that Dewey's four qualities of reasoning suggest a progression from immature to mature, perhaps linked to age. Because I believe the evidence shows that investigative reasoning is available to newborn babies, I reject the assumption that the progression is highly correlated with age. However, systematic inquiry, being a disciplined version of investigative reasoning, is mature reasoning, and it is not, I believe, what newborns exhibit. It has to be learned. It is a habit of mind that is developed over time, as the brain matures. But just as we know children who show investigative reasoning, we all know adults who seldom show it. So age seems not to predict maturity of reasoning.

Reading through the description of Dewey's concept of inquiry, his third category, one gets the distinct impression that inquiry is a *conscious* manipulation of experiences. I believe Dewey saw it that way. But the evidence from research with infants shows them engaged in the process of investigative reasoning before they have any awareness of self as beings separate from their mothers. They have no awareness of the reasoning process as it happens or afterward. While babies can be investigators, their brains have not matured to the place where their consciousness extends to a sense of self. If babies do exhibit investigative reasoning, that means an awareness of self is not a condition needed for it to happen.

Looking at this from another angle, babies seem to slip into the zone naturally and easily, more easily than adults do. The mental conditions that make possible the zone experience seem to be the same for babies and adults: having a goal grounded in a keen interest; undistracted focus on something other than the self; a feedback loop that bypasses self-criticism; stretching one's skills; and an investigative, active mind-set. My own conclusion is that the zone is more accessible to babies precisely because the self is not a factor in their mental processes. Two of the zone prerequisites—focus on something *beyond oneself* and bypassing *self-criticism*—are conditions for the zone for adults but not for babies whose brain maturation does not extend to an awareness of self. I don't know if this hypothesis is one that could ever be tested. But there is ample evidence that babies appear to be in the zone often, much more than some adults.

The evidence from the study of babies tells us that humans are born with exquisitely organized brains, organized to instinctively try to make sense of the world, to make meaning, and to find supportive connections that will serve daily needs. The impulse to make sense of things is what drives the system. The impulse to investigate is built-in. A kind of investigative reasoning is built-in, even in infants. And the capacity for entering the zone experience is built-in. The evidence points to the conclusion that zone experiences put children on a fast track of mental growth and development. They want the exhilaration of the zone to come again and again. From birth on, somehow the memory of zone emotions prompts us to be zone seekers. I see zone seeking as a fundamental feature of human nature. When we seek the zone but can't find it, we settle for zoning out. And some of us have a very hard time finding the zone after early childhood.

LOSING THE MOTIVATION TO INVESTIGATE

If baby zone happens easily, why is the zone elusive for so many adults? If normal babies are born ready to use investigative reasoning, why do we see so many children and adults not using it? I believe the general answer is they encounter environmental conditions that support pat-answer reasoning but not investigative reasoning. In the beginning, the cocoon of support from parents and others that makes up the baby's mental environment is likely to encourage investigation more than discourage it. We adults delight in seeing our babies explore their new world, and we allow them to be investigators much of the time, keeping the door to the zone open, except of course when they start doing something that could jeopardize their safety. But at some point, sooner or later, the adult feels required to direct the baby's behavior, "for the child's own good," to steer her toward some actions or away from other actions. To "shape" the child to "fit life's realities." That is a shift to treating the child as a blank slate. This shift takes the baby out of investigative inquiry into pat-answer or panic reasoning. Of course, adult admonitions such as "This is the way we do things" and "NO! Don't ever touch that!" are essential in some situations. But they do block investigations and close the zone door.

I believe that many adults see the processes of investigative reasoning as being inefficient as a means for teaching their children. They believe that directing the child to prescribed conclusions is the quickest route to learning. All of us, reflecting back on our own school experiences, could sort our teachers into two categories: those who treated us as blank slates and those who encouraged us to investigate. All but the most lucky of us would have far more teachers in the first category. Why the blank-slate attitude persists and what might be done to counteract it are among the topics of chapter 6.

No doubt pat-answer teaching works, at least on one level. And it has an efficiency to it. It brings about a behavior quite directly that, on the surface, shows "learning" that the adult wants to have happen. But, if the process of accepting a pat-answer solution does not allow the child to figure out and make sense of the prescribed actions, the outcome is minimal minding, not zone-opening minding. The message the child gets is that the adult does not support inquiry in this situation. Sometimes the child's investigation continues anyway but it shifts away from a focus on what the adult wants the child to learn, switching over to trying to read the mind of the adult and stay in good graces. Some older children get very good at it. Once they have the adult figured out, they know how to give the outward appearance of compliance with what the adult has in mind while quietly giving their attention to whatever is of more interest. This dividing of effort between complying with others' wishes and satisfying one's investigative needs is not healthy. If the zone is an experience that integrates our resources, this dividing is disintegrative.

Readers of this book most likely grew up with pat-answer schooling and learned to manage in it fairly well. We came to not expect zone experiences in schoolwork and looked for them elsewhere in our lives—sports, other games, hobbies, nonschool reading, exploring nature, friendships, and so on. In effect we specialized in some activities that were of keen interest to us and the interest sometimes took us to the zone.

If we had teachers and parents who took a pat-answer approach with us, and we went along with it, there most likely was an unintended side effect of promoting some passivity in us. That is, we get the hidden message that most life situations that come along have solutions that have already been worked out; the situations that happen to us are not new, they have ready-made solutions, and our job is not to investigate but to remember which solution goes with which situation. We don't need to inquire into the quality of the fit of a solution to a situation, just match them up according to some learned formula.

Most of my own school experiences that I can remember were of this sort. Occasionally I had a project to do that got me into the zone. But mostly there wasn't much zest in my schoolwork. I found that spark in extracurricular activities—such as the school newspaper and stage crew—or totally away from school. Looking back on science and history lessons that didn't get my investigative juices going, I feel a lot of regret about the wasted opportunities. And I also feel that I fell into a certain passivity toward that kind of schoolwork. Luckily, beyond schoolwork I had many positive and energizing things going on in my young life, so the passivity didn't generalize into other aspects of my relationship to the world.

But we have all seen people in whom the passivity did become pervasive. They expect other people and resources in their environment to give them pat answers, to entertain them, to enliven their routines with zoning-out activities. Those of us who supervise, teach, or coach them recognize them as people in whom the passivity has generalized. And when we are responsible for their performance—as in the case of our employees, for example—we feel the heavy drag when they do not initiate ideas, take proactive roles, try to figure out what is happening, what is needed, and move toward making things work. The natural tendency of the supervisor or parent is to respond to such passivity by being more direct, more explicit about the behaviors that are expected. But responding in this way is falling into the trap of the blank-slate assumption: supplying a more explicit pat answer, with a carrot or a stick being displayed or implied. This response to passivity only extends it, promotes it. The trap looms anytime the focus is on the person's *performance* rather than on growth and development. But where is the luxury of time to attend to growth and development? Obviously a shift of focus to an employee's or a child's development has to be planned, with time given over to it; the shift won't happen spontaneously.

This subject is part of chapter 6.

HOW DO EMOTIONS FIT INTO THE ZONE EXPERIENCE?

THE EMOTIONAL MIND

Since John Dewey's time, scientists have discovered a lot about the emotional systems of the brain and how they work. The picture emerging from the research is strikingly consistent with Dewey's view of mental processing. Joseph LeDoux, who is highly regarded for his research on emotional processing in the brain, tells us that emotions have a mind of their own. They function in a brain structure quite independent of our rational brain, the neocortex. The amygdala, an organ at the base of the brain that is well formed by the time of birth, is the seat of our emotional mind and the source of neural pathways for emotional responses. The pathways of emotional minding can bypass the rational mind and directly affect the organs of the body.

While they are separate, the rational and emotional aspects of mind communicate with each other in intricate ways. In their communication the two systems provide input to each other: emotions alert the neocortex to engage reasoning when needed, and the neocortex sends messages to the emotional systems to modulate emotional responses based on outcomes of reasoning. But communication between the two is not balanced. The amygdala has greater influence, and that is evident when our emotions swamp our rational side. While our emotions have a circuitry that is capable of bypassing the neocortex and triggering action directly, the reverse is never true: our neocortex never operates without emotions playing a part. Arousal of the neocortex by emotions has to be the basis of our motivations.

In the evolution of humans, emotions were the primary survival mechanism long before the neocortex developed. Emotions were action impulses that provided split-second survival decisions. They still operate that way in modern humans. Because humans were emotional creatures for thousands of generations before the development of reasoning, our rational processing is grounded in the emotional infrastructure on which the neocortex was built over time.

We identify our emotions because they enter our consciousness from time to time. But having evolved long before consciousness did, their functioning certainly doesn't depend on our being aware of them.

The emotion systems operate largely out of awareness. The emotions just happen to us; we don't choose them. We do have some indirect control over them by choosing events and situations likely to evoke specific emotions. For example, on a particular evening we may choose to watch a video of, say, a light comedy rather than a tense drama partly because of the emotions we are likely to have while watching it.

LeDoux speaks for brain scientists generally, and for John Dewey as well, when he says, "I view emotions as biological functions of the nervous system. . . . This approach contrasts sharply with a more typical one in which emotions are studied as psychological states, independent of the underlying brain mechanisms. Psychological research has been extremely valuable, but an approach where emotions are studied as brain functions is far more powerful."[33]

MOTHER-INFANT INTIMACY AS THE BASIS OF EMOTIONAL AND SOCIAL DEVELOPMENT

Ellen Dissanayake's analysis of research on the interactions of mothers and their babies led her to the conclusion that babies are born seeking intimacy and that their mothers are biochemically designed to provide them intimate support. The birthing process and breastfeeding release the hormone oxytocin, which is thought to promote maternal feelings. Her nurturing behaviors match her baby's needs for emotional and social development. Mother and baby initiate social exchanges immediately after the baby's birth. The mother's natural rhythmic movements, facial expressions, and vocalizations draw her infant into communication sequences—reciprocal responses, exchanges that are often turn taking and often synchronized. Dissanayake refers to this as mother-infant *mutuality*. "These exchanges not only communicate emotional information but also allow for emotional state–sharing, or *attunement*. For both mother and baby (who are unaware of the complex intricacies of their duet), they are pleasurable—joyous, captivating, and fun."[34] This attunement appears to be a special kind of zone experience, a kind that is shared rather than happening to one person individually.

Dissanayake continues, "What are produced, matched, and exchanged in early mother-infant engagements are positive emotional and motivational states of interest, pleasure, amusement, desire to establish relationship, intention to please, and intention to communicate with the other."[35] All these are skills that eventually make possible the comprehending and predicting of the behavior of people outside the parental bond, helping the child identify with social groups and find confidence and meaning in the wider circle.

On this view, a culture that neglects to acknowledge the central importance of mother-infant mutuality and attunement is a culture in trouble. The American pattern of two-income families appears to be a permanent one. But the policy of expecting new mothers to return to work shortly after giving birth seems destined to reduce the time and the opportunities they will have for the vital cultural role they play, the role of giving their babies the intimate nurturing so essential to their development. This massive (uncontrolled) experiment we are engaged in needs careful monitoring.

THE NEUROLOGY OF MOTIVATION

In his book *The Synaptic Self: How Our Brains Become Who We Are*, Joseph LeDoux gives his definition of motivation as "neural activity that guides us toward goals, outcomes that we desire and for which we will exert effort, or ones that we dread and will exert effort to prevent, escape from, or avoid."[36] Emotions are involved in all our goals. All of our reasoned goals have an emotional component. That means there is no distinct line between rational and emotional experience.

It is emotions that alert the conscious mind when our mental habits—the autopilot—seem inadequate to deal with something in the environment. Emotions must arouse the neocortex and keep it optimally activated. In LeDoux's words: "Arousal is important in all mental functions. It contributes significantly to attention, perception, memory, emotion, and problem solving. Without arousal, we fail to notice what is going on—we don't attend to the details. But too much arousal is not good either. If you are overaroused you become tense and anxious and unproductive. You need to have just the right level of activation to perform optimally."[37] This view of arousal seems consistent with Dewey's four qualities of reasoning, with overarousal prompting panic reasoning and pat-answer reasoning, and with optimal arousal being associated with investigative reasoning and systematic inquiry.

The zone experience involves a flowing together of emotions, reason, and well-honed skills. The emotions that participate in the zone experience are well modulated by reason. And the reasoning that happens in the zone experience depends on emotional arousal. They are mutually supportive. And, of course, the zone is sustained by the emotions that bring satisfaction and joy to the activity.

In this book I am proposing that it is *investigative reasoning* that participates in the zone phenomenon. The zone is not available with pat-answer reasoning. But we have to acknowledge our ambivalence. On the one hand, we are attracted to the apparent efficiency of a pat-answer approach to teaching and coaching. On the other hand, we wish for our children and those we coach the energizing experience of being in the zone. And the only way we can precipitate the zone for them is to consciously, deliberately bypass our impulse to provide them with pat answers. The responsibilities of parenting don't easily allow the bypassing in many aspects of life. But we can't have both at the same time: the ease and familiarity of the pat-answer approach and the energizing, integrating learning that the zone brings. The latter certainly takes more work, especially more planning. The payoff for the extra work, of course, is the joy of helping others find the zone. In chapter 6 I propose some incremental ways to shift schooling and the workplace toward investigative minding and zone experiencing.

In the next chapter we examine aspects of Carl Jung's view of mind. His work is also grounded in a rejection of the blank-slate assumption, and it gives us a framework for exploring zone motivations.

3

FRAMEWORKS OF MENTAL PROCESSING

When people answer the question, "What puts you in the zone?" they report different qualities of experience that carry them to the zone and hold them there. An illustration of such differences came to light in a fascinating conversation I had with three alumni at a university homecoming gathering. They had been roommates in medical school and were enjoying catching up with each other's news since they had last been together. They had gone into three different specialties and all were very happy about their career choices. I asked about their specialties, whether they found the zone experience in their work, and what aspects of their work seemed to put them in the zone.

The three men seemed almost as interested in each other's answers to the questions as I was.

The first answer came from the former roommate who had gone into emergency medicine. He especially enjoyed working in emergency services because of the variety of challenges, the sense of urgency, and the high-stakes decision making that pervaded his daily work. The more complex and urgent cases seemed to be zone producing, when time stood still and all the elements of the work seemed to flow together seamlessly, with everyone synchronized in their roles. "When my skills are really being tested is when the zone comes."

The second to answer had gone into family practice in a small town. What appealed to him about the work was the personal rapport he developed with patients. He enjoyed being a respected, contributing member of the community—getting to know families well, helping them through illnesses, being the source of personal advice, and knowing them outside of the doctor's office. He did not believe any intense zone experiences happened very often in his office, but he felt a sense of shared zone with patients, friends, and neighbors in a variety of community contexts.

The emergency room doctor was intrigued by the contrast between the two of them. He said, "It certainly is not the rapport with patients that brings the zone for me. Many of them are unconscious most of the time, and I seldom see them after they leave emergency care. It is the solving of the problems they present that grabs me."

The third man, who had specialized in biomedical research, was nodding during these last comments. He said, "Part of the reason I chose medical research was a preference for doing medicine without having to deal with patients. The lab is where I find the zone, on the trail of elusive solutions and new knowledge in a quiet setting with no distractions. Actually solving a problem is not so much of a zone event as is the figuring out how to frame the problem so as to make a plan of action possible."

DIFFERENT REALITIES

In this chapter we consider how differences such as these can be the product of different frameworks of mental processing and not just idiosyncratic variations. We'll turn to the three doctors again as we examine the frameworks.

No doubt there are different mental realities. But are there *patterns* of differences we should attend to as we consider how to promote the zone experience for those we coach, teach, or nurture?

All of us know of instances when several people participating in the same situation, apparently observing the same phenomenon, afterward give distinctly different reports of what happened. If each were given a lie-detector test, all of them would pass. None of them would perceive what he or she says as a lie or a bending of the exact events as they happened. How can all of the versions be true? Here's an example that comes to mind. I was standing on the street corner near my office waiting for the stoplight to turn so I could cross. Two cars collided in the intersection. A police officer arrived very quickly. Two of us on our corner had witnessed the accident and so had another man across the street.

The officer asked to speak to each of us three witnesses separately. He took our statements of what we saw and heard, then he gathered the three of us together and read the statements as he had written them, asking each of us if there was anything we wanted to add or change in what we said. We all showed surprise at what he read. Our statements seemed to be describing three different accidents. None of us knew the occupants of the cars, and all said our statements were unbiased and accurate. The officer said he interviewed us separately because he frequently got conflicting statements that he needed to sort out to get a true picture of what happened.

Of course, our individual experiences color our perceptions and tell us what is real and not real, true and not true. In some respects, each person's experience is unique. Other aspects of experience are not unique but shared. Looking for predictable commonalities in human behavior, Carl Jung conducted research that led him to the conclusion that all life experiences are filtered through one's *type* of mental processing. He called these distinctive mental frameworks *psychological types*. People automatically apply the built-in filters of the framework of their type. They participate in the "same" event, attend to different aspects of it, experience it somewhat differently, and, at the time they are asked to recall what happened, they reconstruct the event in memory according their own kind of mental processing. Sometimes the perceptions are radically different. Their filters can provide wholly different mental landscapes because their brains registered different data. While people's accumulated life experiences are infinitely varied, a strong case is being made that the filters they use come in distinct types.[1]

As Jung viewed the frameworks, one has no experiences outside one's own type of mental framework. I cannot suspend my type of processing and stand outside of it, even temporarily. There is no "objective" viewpoint or framework. The hardwiring analogy works fairly well here. While translation is possible between the operating systems of Windows and Apple, there is no direct transmission between them. Each psychological type has a distinct operating system. Professionals who work with Jung's construct of psychological type see evidence continually that the sixteen different frameworks identified by Jung's work are realities we should not ignore.

How does this relate to the zone phenomenon? The doorway to the zone is different for each of the types of mental processing identified in Jung's typology. As with the three physicians described at the beginning of the chapter, each type has its own set of basic zone-precipitating motivations and values, and they are described in this chapter. Self-aware, mature people can describe—at least to some extent—the motivating conditions that carry them toward the zone. In this chapter I am concentrating not so much on *self*-awareness as I am on our efforts to find the zone-motivating conditions of those we teach or coach or nurture. Jung's contribution is especially helpful in providing us insights into the motivations of others—those we work with and intend to influence. In chapter 1, I drew on Clyde Kluckhohn's observation to say that each mind is like all other minds, like some other minds, and like no other mind. Jung's construct of the psychological types is a means to understand the patterns of motivation and behavior that represent the category, "like some other minds." Through the years I have become more and more amazed at the practicality and usefulness of Jung's insights, and their application to the zone experience is another extension of his concepts.

PART 1: THE BASIC ESSENTIALS

I have divided this chapter into two parts. In this first section are these elements:

- descriptions of the sixteen types of mental processing as identified in Carl Jung's work;
- a brief explanation of the rationale behind them;

- a discussion of the motivation patterns in the types as they bear on the zone experience; and
- the thesis that investigative minding is equally available to all the types, with each type requiring its own set of supportive conditions for inquiry.

Part 2 is a fuller presentation of Jung's rationale underlying the sixteen types. I have used this sequence in organizing the chapter because I know some readers do not share my fascination with theoretica. For *my* type of mental processing, and some kindred types, Jung's underlying research and the theory he devised to explain the research outcomes are essential here. But for those readers who would rather skip part 2, the rest of the book should hang together quite well without it.

PREFERENCES THAT MAKE UP THE SIXTEEN TYPES OF MENTAL PROCESSING

The types are sets of mental preferences among four dimensions. The dimensions are composed of pairs of opposite ways of processing one's experiences, designated by the letter pairs: EI, SN, TF, and JP.

E **Extraversion:** Interest in the people and things *outside* oneself

I **Introversion:** Interest in the ideas *inside* one's mind that explain experiences

S **Sensing:** Interest in what is real and can be seen, heard, touched

N **Intuition:** Interest in what can be imagined, seen with "the mind's eye"

T **Thinking:** Interest in what is logical and works by cause and effect

F **Feeling:** Interest in what is important and valuable, harmonious with one's values

J **Judging:** Interest in acting by deciding, organizing, planning

P **Perceiving:** Interest in acting by watching, trying out, adapting

The preferences combine in sixteen ways, representing the sixteen types of mental processing. Everyone has interests in all the categories and uses all of them, but each of us prefers one from each pair of opposites, much like being right-handed or left-handed; one hand takes the lead but we use both hands. The contrasts between the preference pairs can be seen in the box below. Each preference combination, such as ESFP or ISTJ, has a distinct way of processing experiences. The descriptions of the sixteen types of mental processing follow the box.

WORDS FOR UNDERSTANDING TYPE CONCEPTS

E: EXTRAVERSION
When extraverting, I am . . .
Oriented to the outer world
Focusing on people and things
Active
Using trial and error with
confidence
Scanning the environment for
stimulation

I: INTROVERSION
When introverting, I am . . .
Oriented to the inner world
Focusing on ideas, inner
impressions
Reflective
Considering deeply before acting
Finding stimulation inwardly

S: SENSING PERCEPTION
When using my sensing I am . . .
Perceiving with the five senses
Attending to practical and factual
details
In touch with the physical realities
Attending to the present moment
Confining attention to what is said
and done
Seeing "little things" in everyday
life
Attending to literal, concrete
experiences
Letting "the eyes tell the mind"

N: INTUITIVE PERCEPTION
When using my intuition I am . . .
Perceiving with memory and
associations
Seeing patterns and meanings
Seeing possibilities
Projecting possibilities for the
future
Imagining; "reading between the
lines"
Looking for the big picture
Having hunches, "ideas out of
nowhere"
Letting "the mind tell the eyes"

T: THINKING JUDGMENT
When reasoning with thinking, I am . . .

Using logical analysis to critique things

Using objective and impersonal criteria

Drawing cause-and-effect relationships

Being firm-minded

Prizing logical order

Being skeptical

F: FEELING JUDGMENT
When reasoning with feeling, I am . . .

Applying personal priorities

Weighing human values and motives, my own and others'

Appreciating

Valuing warmth in relationships

Prizing harmony; trusting

J: JUDGMENT
When I take a judging attitude, I am . . .

Using thinking or feeling judgment in my *outer* life, where people see it in action

Deciding and planning

Organizing and scheduling

Controlling and regulating

Goal oriented

Wanting closure, even when data are incomplete

P: PERCEPTION
When I take a perceiving attitude, I am . . .

Using sensing or intuitive perception in my *outer* life, where people see it in action

Taking in information

Adapting and changing

Curious and interested

Open-minded

Resisting closure to obtain more data

From *People Types and Tiger Stripes*, 4th ed.
Copyright © 2009 by Gordon D. Lawrence

DESCRIPTIONS OF THE SIXTEEN TYPES

The sixteen type descriptions were developed initially over fifty years ago by Isabel Myers, the primary author of the Myers-Briggs Type Indicator instrument, and Katharine Briggs. The indicator is a paper-and-pencil, self-report inventory. There is also a Web-based version, containing the same items. The MBTI is the most common way people are introduced to the types of mental processing. The responses are sorted and the individual is placed into one of the sixteen type categories. The MBTI report provides a starting point to consider which of the types is the best fit. The MBTI instrument was developed with great care and is accurate for most people. It is suggested to respondents that they read all of the sixteen descriptions of mental processing types, shown below, as they decide. Just as there are no right or wrong answers to the MBTI items, there are no good or bad types. Each type has its gifts and blind spots, and all types are valuable.

Readers interested in taking the MBTI can access it through the Web site www.cpp.com. There is also a children's type indicator, for children in grades 2 through 12, that can be taken online at www.capt.org. Both CPP and CAPT distribute and publish extensive support materials related to applications of the concepts underlying the two instruments.

The type descriptions written by Myers and Briggs and others are considerably longer than those below. I wrote these compacted descriptions so that people can fairly quickly read all of them in the process of deciding which description is the best fit for them, and they can hypothesize about the fit of other descriptions to people they know.

The sixteen type descriptions I have written are grouped in three ways.[2] The types preferring Extraversion are on the left side, and those having the opposite preference, Introversion, are on the right. The descriptions are also arranged with opposite types across from each other; for example, ENTJ is across from ISFP, the type that is opposite in all four dimensions. As you read the phrases listed for each type, you should *not* assume that a positive value listed for one type implies a negative trait for the opposite type. For example, when we read that ENTJs value efficiency, we must not infer that

ISFPs are inefficient. Similarly, because ISFPs value compassion does not mean that ENTJs are coldhearted. Opposite types are across from each other to help people decide their best-fit type. The contrasts shown by the opposites help to clarify what is given higher priority in our mental processing. What has high priority for ISFP is not given high priority by ENTJ, and vice versa. The descriptions emphasize the *values* and mental *priorities* of the types more than they tell what *behaviors* are associated with each of the types. The values are emphasized because they are the motivation energy behind the behaviors.

There is a third feature of the groupings to help in the recognition of similarities and differences of the types. Note that in each four-letter type designation one of the four letters is larger than the others, as in ENTJ and ISFP, and ESTJ and INFP. The larger letter identifies what Carl Jung called the dominant function, the mental process that is the centerpost of the type. In the sixteen types there are four with T dominant, four with F dominant, four with S dominant, and four with N dominant. The descriptions are arranged in these foursomes, with T and F dominant types on the first four pages and S and N dominant types on the second four pages. The role of the dominant process in the dynamics of each type is evident in the descriptions.

In the descriptions and throughout the rest of the book, I have capitalized the terms used to identify the eight categories of mental processing that make up the types, such as Intuition and Thinking. I have done it to distinguish them from the ordinary use of the terms. For example, thinking is a term used in a lot of ways, but Thinking means specifically Jung's category of mental processing, using his definition.

T AND F DOMINANT TYPES

ENTJ

Intuitive, innovative ORGA-
NIZERS; analytical, systematic,
confident; push to get action on
new ideas and challenges. Having
extraverted THINKING as their
strongest mental process, ENTJs are
at their best when they can take
charge and set things in logical
order. They value:

- Analyzing abstract problems,
  complex situations
- Foresight; pursuing a vision
- Changing, organizing things to
  fit their vision
- Putting theory into practice,
  ideas into action
- Working to a scheduled plan
- Initiating, then delegating
- Efficiency; removing obstacles
  and confusion
- Probing new possibilities
- Holding self and others to high
  standards
- Having things settled and
  closed
- Tough-mindedness, directness,
  task focus
- Objective principles; fairness,
  justice
- Assertive, direct action
- Intellectual resourcefulness
- Driving toward broad goals
  along a logical path
- Designing structures and
  strategies
- Seeking out logical flaws to
  improve things

ISFP

Observant, loyal HELPERS; reflective, realistic, empathic, patient with
details. Shunning disagreements,
they are gentle, reserved, and
modest. Having introverted
FEELING as their strongest mental
process, they are at their best when
responding to the needs of others.
They value:

- Personal loyalty; a close, loyal
  friend
- Finding delight in the moment
- Seeing what needs doing to
  improve the moment
- Freedom from organizational
  constraints
- Working individually
- Peacemaking behind the scenes
- Attentiveness to feelings
- Harmonious, cooperative work
  settings
- Spontaneous, hands-on
  exploration
- Gentle, respectful interactions
- Deeply held personal beliefs
- Reserved, reflective behavior
- Practical, useful skills and
  know-how
- Having their work life be fully
  consistent with deeply held
  values
- Showing and receiving
  appreciation

T AND F DOMINANT TYPES

ESTJ

Fact-minded practical ORGA-NIZERS; assertive, analytical, systematic; push to get things done and working smoothly and efficiently. Having extraverted THINKING as their strongest mental process, they are at their best when they can take charge and set things in logical order. They value:

- Results; doing, acting
- Planned, organized work and play
- Commonsense practicality
- Consistency; standard procedures
- Concrete, present-day usefulness
- Deciding quickly and logically
- Having things settled and closed
- Rules, objective standards, fairness by the rules
- Task-focused behavior
- Directness, tough-mindedness
- Orderliness; no loose ends
- Systematic structure; efficiency
- Categorizing aspects of their life
- Scheduling and monitoring
- Protecting what works

INFP

Imaginative, independent HELPERS; reflective, inquisitive, empathic, loyal to ideals: more tuned to possibilities than practicalities. Having introverted FEELING as the strongest mental process, they are at their best when their inner ideals find expression in their helping of people. They value:

- Harmony in the inner life of ideas
- Harmonious work settings; working individually
- Seeing the big-picture possibilities
- Creativity; curiosity, exploring
- Helping people find their potential
- Giving ample time to reflect on decisions
- Adaptability and openness
- Compassion and caring; attention to emotional needs
- Work that lets them express their idealism
- Gentle, respectful interactions
- An inner compass; being unique
- Showing appreciation and being appreciated
- Ideas, language, and writing
- A close, loyal friend
- Perfecting what is important

T AND F DOMINANT TYPES

esFj

Practical HARMONIZERS, workers-with-people; sociable, orderly, opinioned; conscientious, realistic and well-tuned to the here and now. Having extraverted FEELING as their strongest mental process, they are at their best when responsible for winning peoples' cooperation through personal caring and practical help. They value:

- An active, sociable life, with many relationships
- A present-day view of life
- Making daily routines into gracious living
- Staying closely tuned to people they care about so as to keep relationships positive
- Talking through problems cooperatively, caringly
- Approaching problems in tried-and-true, familiar ways
- Caring, compassion, and tactfulness
- Helping organizations serve their members well
- Responsiveness to others and to traditions
- Being prepared, reliable in tangible, daily work
- Loyalty and faithfulness
- Practical skillfulness grounded in experience
- Structured learning in a humane setting
- Appreciation as the natural means of encouraging improvements

inTp

Inquisitive ANALYZERS; reflective, independent, curious; more interested in organizing ideas than situations or people. Having introverted THINKING as their strongest mental process, they are at their best when following their intellectual curiosity, analyzing complexities to find the underlying logical principles. They value:

- A reserved outer life; an inner life of inquiry
- Pursuing interests in depth, with concentration
- Work and play that is intriguing, not routine
- Being free of emotional issues while working
- Working on problems that respond to detached intuitive analysis and theorizing
- Approaching problems by reframing the obvious
- Complex intellectual mysteries
- Being absorbed in abstract, mental work
- Freedom from organizational constraints
- Independence, nonconformance
- Intellectual quickness, ingenuity, invention
- Competence in the world of ideas
- Spontaneous learning by following curiosity and inspirations
- Using critical analysis to improve things

T AND F DOMINANT TYPES

ENFJ

Imaginative HARMONIZERS, workers with people; expressive, orderly, opinioned, conscientious; curious about new ideas and possibilities. Having extraverted FEELING as their strongest mental process, they are at their best when responsible for winning peoples' cooperation with caring insight into their needs. They value:

- Having a wide circle of relationships
- Having a positive, enthusiastic view of life
- Seeing subtleties in people and interactions
- Understanding others' needs and concerns
- An active, energizing social life
- Seeing possibilities in people
- Thorough follow-through on important projects
- Working several projects at once
- Caring and imaginative problem solving
- Maintaining relationships to avoid trouble
- Shaping organizations to better serve members
- Sociability and responsiveness
- Structured learning in a humane setting
- Caring, compassion, and tactfulness
- Appreciation as the natural means of encouraging improvements

ISTP

Practical ANALYZERS; value exactness; more interested in organizing data than situations or people; reflective, cool, and curious observers of life. Having introverted THINKING as their strongest mental process, they are at their best when analyzing experience to find the logical order and underlying properties of things. They value:

- A reserved outer life; a cool, logical inner life
- Having a concrete, present-day view of life
- Clear, exact facts—a large storehouse of them
- Looking for efficient, least effort solutions based on experience
- Knowing how mechanical things work
- Pursuing interests in depth, such as hobbies
- Collecting things of interest
- Working on problems that respond to detached, sequential analysis and adaptability
- Freedom from organizational constraints
- Independence and self-management
- Spontaneous hands-on learning experience
- Having useful technical expertise
- Critical analysis as a means to improving things

S AND N DOMINANT TYPES

eStp

REALISTIC ADAPTERS in the world of material things; good-natured, easy-going; oriented to practical, firsthand experience; highly observant of details of things. Having extraverted SENSING as their strongest mental process, they are at their best when free to act on impulses or responding to concrete problems that need solving. They value:

- A life of outward, playful action, in the moment
- Being a troubleshooter
- Finding ways to use the existing system
- Clear, concrete, exact facts
- Knowing the way mechanical things work
- Being direct, to the point
- Learning through spontaneous, hands-on action
- Practical action, more than words
- Immediately useful skills
- Plunging into new adventures
- Responding to practical needs as they arise
- Seeing the expedient thing and acting on it
- Finding fun in their work and sparking others to have fun
- Looking for efficient, least effort solutions
- Being caught up in enthusiasms

iNfj

People-oriented INNOVATORS of ideas; serious; quietly forceful and persevering; concerned with work that will help the world and inspire others. Having introverted INTU-ITION as their strongest mental process, they are at their best when caught up in inspiration, envision-ing and creating ways to empower self and others to lead more mean-ingful lives. They value:

- A reserved outer life; sponta-neous inner life
- Planning ways to help people improve
- Seeing complexities, hidden meanings
- Imaginative ways of saying things
- Understanding other people's needs and concerns
- Planful, independent academic learning
- Reading, writing, and imag-ining; academic theory
- Being restrained in outward actions; planful
- Aligning their work with their ideals
- Pursuing and clarifying their ideals
- Taking the long view
- Encouraging others through appreciation
- Finding harmonious solutions to problems
- Being inspired and inspiring others

S AND N DOMINANT TYPES

eSfp

REALISTIC ADAPTERS in human relationships; friendly and easy with people, highly observant of their interests and needs; oriented to practical, firsthand experience. Having extraverted SENSING as their strongest mental process, they are at their best when free to act on impulses, or responding to the needs of the here and now. They value:

- An energetic, sociable life, full of friends and fun
- Performing, entertaining, sharing
- Immediately useful skills; practical know-how
- Learning through spontaneous, hands-on action
- Trust and generosity; openness
- Patterning themselves after those they admire
- Concrete, practical knowledge; resourcefulness
- Caring, kindness, support, appreciation
- Freedom from irrelevant rules
- Handling immediate, practical problems and crises
- Seeing tangible realities; least effort solutions
- Showing and receiving appreciation
- Making the most of the moment; adaptability
- Being caught up in enthusiasms
- Looking for least effort solutions
- Easing and brightening work and play

iNtj

Logical, critical, decisive INNOVATORS of ideas; serious, intent, very independent, concerned with organization; determined, often stubborn. Having introverted INTUITION as their strongest mental process, they are at their best when inspiration turns insights into ideas and plans for improving human knowledge and systems. They value:

- A restrained, organized outer life; spontaneous, intuitive inner life
- Conceptual skills, theorizing
- Planful, independent, academic learning
- Skepticism; critical analysis; objective principles
- Originality, independence of mind
- Intellectual quickness, ingenuity
- Nonemotional tough-mindedness
- Freedom from interference in projects
- Working to a plan and schedule
- Seeing complexities, hidden meanings
- Improving things by finding flaws
- Probing new possibilities; taking the long view
- Pursuing a vision; foresight; conceptualizing
- Getting insights to reframe problems

S AND N DOMINANT TYPES

eNTP

Inventive, analytical PLANNERS OF CHANGE; enthusiastic and independent; pursue inspiration with impulsive energy; seek to understand and inspire. Extraverted INTUITION being their strongest mental process, they are at their best when caught up in the enthusiasm of pursuing a new project and promoting its benefits. They value:

- Conceiving of new things and initiating change
- The surge of inspirations; the pull of emerging possibilities
- Analyzing complexities
- Following their insights, wherever they lead
- Finding meanings behind the facts
- Autonomy, elbow room, openness
- Ingenuity, originality, a fresh perspective
- Mental models and concepts that explain life
- Fair treatment
- Flexibility, adaptability
- Learning through action, variety, and discovery
- Exploring theories and meanings behind events
- Improvising, looking for novel ways
- Work made light by inspiration

iSFJ

Sympathetic MANAGERS OF FACTS AND DETAILS, concerned with people's welfare; stable, conservative, dependable, painstaking, systematic. Having introverted SENSING as their strongest mental process, they are at their best when using their sensible intelligence and practical skills to help others in tangible ways. They value:

- Preserving, enjoying the things of proven value
- Steady, sequential work yielding reliable results
- A controlled, orderly outer life
- Patient attention to basic needs
- Following a sensible path, based on experience
- A rich memory for concrete facts
- Loyalty; strong relationships
- Consistency, familiarity, the tried and true
- Firsthand experience of what is important
- Compassion, kindness, caring
- Working to a plan and schedule
- Learning from planned, sequential teaching
- Set routines, commonsense options
- Rules, authority, set procedures
- Hard work, perseverance

S AND N DOMINANT TYPES

ENFP

Warmly enthusiastic PLANNERS OF CHANGE; imaginative, individualistic; pursue inspiration with impulsive energy; seek to understand and inspire others. Having extraverted INTUITION as the strongest mental process, they are at their best when caught up in the enthusiasm of a project. They value:

- The surge of inspirations; the pull of emerging possibilities
- A life of variety, people, and warm relationships
- An exciting outer life
- Following their insights wherever they lead
- Finding meanings behind the facts
- Creativity, originality, a fresh perspective
- An optimistic, positive, enthusiastic view of life
- Flexibility and openness
- Exploring, devising, and trying out new things
- Open-ended opportunities and options
- Freedom from the requirement of being practical
- Learning through action, variety, and discovery
- A belief that any obstacles can be overcome
- A focus on people's potentials
- Brainstorming to solve problems
- Work made light and playful by inspiration

ISTJ

Analytical MANAGER OF FACTS AND DETAILS; dependable, conservative, painstaking, systematic, decisive, stable. Having introverted SENSING as the strongest mental process, they are at their best when charged with organizing and maintaining data and material important to others and themselves. They value:

- Steady, systematic work yielding reliable results
- Practical systems and organization
- A controlled outer life grounded in the present
- Following a sensible path, based on experience
- Concrete, exact, immediately useful facts, skills
- Consistency, familiarity, the tried and true
- A present-day view of life
- Working to a plan and schedule
- Preserving and enjoying things of proven value
- Proven paths, commonsense options
- Freedom from emotionality in deciding things
- Learning through planned, sequential teaching
- Skepticism; wanting to read the fine print first
- A focus on hard work and perseverance
- Logical, detached problem solving
- Serious, focused work and play

Nearly everyone who reads the descriptions can find one that is a good fit for himself or herself. People recognize the pattern of their own mental processing, their motivations, their values, and their priorities. Of course, every person is unique, and most of us don't like to "be categorized." But those who read the descriptions generally have no difficulty in picking out one that fits best, some that are similar but not a best fit, and the descriptions that are distinctly in contrast. Moreover, as they read the descriptions, they recognize that the patterns describe other people they know well. And they usually start matching people's names to the type descriptions. My personal experience of seeing thousands of people go through this recognition process—validating one type as a best fit, validating the patterns as life realities, seeing other people in the descriptions, and so on—is part of what convinces me that Jung's types are distinct kinds of mind, different hardwiring, and not just variations on a unitary model of mind.

A reader can rather quickly see the contrasting motivation patterns. What is organically a high priority for the type on one side of the page is a low priority for the type on the other side, and vice versa. It is important to note that having a particular value as a priority does not imply *competence* in exercising or expressing that value. There is no guarantee that those traits will form well; that's a matter of maturity. For example, a person who identifies with the ENTJ type description is likely to agree with the statement that ENTJs value "holding self and others to high standards," listed in that description. But the statement indicates what is sought after and connotes nothing about whether the particular person pursues that value with skill or is not mature and pursues it clumsily. The terms in the descriptions must not be seen as skills. They are permanent dispositions—values, priorities, motivations—that make up the fabric of a filtering screen through which life events pass and become experiences. Each psychological type is a distinct filter.

Moreover, when a value is associated with a certain type, it means that type is naturally, structurally energized to pursue that value. If we accept the types as hardwired kinds of mind, "naturally" means *organically programmed with that value as a key component.* Take, for example, loyalty, a value associated with ISFP and INFP, among others. Loyalty is a priority this type automatically pursues. Does that mean the opposite types, ENTJ and ESTJ, don't care about loyalty? Not at all. Let's stay with the ENTJ type for an extended illustration.

An ENTJ boss, for example, may care a lot about having loyal employees. But knowing how to engender loyalty in others or how to be loyal to others is not organically part of her type. Her psychic energy doesn't flow into that channel. If employees bring loyalty into their relationships with this boss, it is not because the boss's type of mental processing naturally engages loyalty. So how does this boss learn and promote loyalty? If loyalty is not organically a priority of the ENTJ makeup, how can the energy of the ENTJ system be altered to incorporate attitudes and skills not organically in it? It is best accomplished in childhood, in the context of a sound and emotionally healthy family. If an adult ENTJ needs to work on loyalty, the basic answer is in enlisting the help of someone whose type has the loyalty value built in, most particularly an ISFP or INFP. The ENTJ has to *want* to learn the skills and attitudes of loyalty, to be prepared to take advice and coaching, and to find the discipline to channel energy toward that goal. Here is the key: she has to find, *among the ENTJ organic priorities*, values that will be well served by the skills of loyalty. The energy the ENTJ will need for developing loyalty skills must come from those organic priorities.

Two values that make up the ENTJ dynamic—and appear in the type description—seem good candidates for embracing the loyalty value: "foresight, pursuing a vision" and "designing structures and strategies." I can easily imagine the ENTJ boss having a vision of a smooth-running, cohesive organization in which people loyally support each other. And I can easily see this boss energized to design the strategies needed to make that happen. Here is the general rule: use a strength to strengthen a weakness. One's psychological type is a mental framework for processing life experiences, and all sorts of skills not organically part of the framework can be hung on the frame, provided that the dynamic of the type is respected and engaged. Having one's opposite type placed across the page in the type descriptions gives clues to what one's type is likely to neglect, what each person of that type is likely to develop only by conscious attention and discipline. And each description identifies values within that type that can be tapped for the energy to embrace and nurture the typically neglected values.

THE LANGUAGE OF THE TYPE DESCRIPTIONS

People have asked me how the wording of the compacted type descriptions came to be. That is, for example, why the phrases "personal loyalty" and "finding delight in the moment" are used to characterize facets of the motivation pattern of the ISFP type, and how the terms were chosen to distinguish this type from the others. While all the type descriptions I am aware of that others have written are constructed mainly of descriptions of *behaviors* associated with each type, they also include statements about values and priorities. I drew the latter from them, staying close to the language used by Isabel Myers, who undoubtedly, over a lifetime of study of the psychological types, understood the nuances of the types better than anyone else. She also collected more hard data than anyone else. With these value and priority statements in hand, I drafted type descriptions and had three-hundred-plus people critique them—people very familiar with the type concepts. After some editing based on their feedback, I expanded that group to more than a thousand to critique the second draft and offer suggestions. Then *Descriptions of the Sixteen Types* was published. At the time of the second and third printings of the booklet I made a few more adjustments.

For over thirty years I have administered the MBTI instrument to thousands of people, and I have worked for an extended time with many of them to help them understand and apply the concepts in their work and their life outside of work. Nearly all of them find a match of one of the type descriptions to themselves, and they recognize coworkers, family, and friends in the motivation patterns presented by the descriptions.

TYPES OF MENTAL PROCESSING AND THE ZONE

It is not hard to see in the descriptions important clues to the conditions that will be supportive or unsupportive for each of the types. This is the link between the mental processing types and the zone experience. The type descriptions give us a platform for finding conditions that are most likely to help lead people into the zone and sustain them there. For example, refer back to page 85 to the last pair of type descriptions, ENFP and ISTJ. Reread the bulleted portions and compare them line by line. Each bulleted item characterizes a path to personal satisfaction and fulfillment, and to zone experiences. Can there be any doubt that ENFPs and ISTJs will find the zone in distinctly different ways, under dramatically different psychological circumstances? If an ENFP and an ISTJ were partners at work or in a marriage, and they found the zone together in some activity, can there be any doubt that they had hold of different aspects of the project? You can make this kind of analysis more personal by comparing the bulleted items in your own type description with those of anyone else in your life whose type you know or can surmise.

Finding common ground with the other person for mutually satisfying activities is often a matter of trying to see how his or her values and perspective contrast with and complement your own. The type descriptions help the process. Isabel Myers put it very well:

> Whenever people differ, a knowledge of type helps to cut out irrelevant friction. More than that, it points up the advantages of the differences. No one man has to be good at everything. He only has to be good at his own stuff and decently appreciative of the other fellow's. Together, thanks to their differences, they can do a better job than if they were just alike.[3]

This is perhaps a good place to consider again the three physicians who were introduced at the beginning of the chapter. Their choices of medical specialty and their descriptions of work experiences that triggered the zone for them seem quite related to their type of mental processing. Although I did not tell them before our conversation, I was aware as I talked with them that their medical school routinely introduced incoming students to the psychological types through the MBTI instrument. I was, on occasion, the person who administered the MBTI to the students and gave them an explanation of their results, particularly as they related to learning preferences and study styles. I asked the three doctors if they remembered responding to the MBTI and getting an explanation. All three did remember, and two recalled the type they decided was the best fit for them. With some prompting from the rest of us, the third reconstructed what he thought was a good fit for himself. The emergency medicine physician identified himself as an ESTP, the family practice doctor as an ESFJ, and the medical researcher as an INTP. As you glance back over the descriptions of those three types, does that make sense to you?

JUNG'S FUNCTIONS AS QUALITIES OF MIND

I began chapter 2 with the thesis that mind is not an "it," a place that houses the forces that cause behaviors to happen. Rather, mind is minding, a quality of the whole being in action, a characterization of behavior that ranges from mindless to highly mindful. I believe it is important to view Jung's mental functions in that way. They should not be taken as entities, drives, or components of mind that make us behave in certain ways. They should be seen as action patterns, forms of activity of the whole person, expressions of preferred ways of addressing the world that are built into our mental makeup. For example, when I apply the label ENTP—or extraverted Intuitive—to myself, I mean to convey a dynamic action pattern of my mental processing, not to give a name to a set of forces or entities that drive my personality. I am referring to an ENTP kind of minding, not to E, N, T, and P as forces that make me tick. If we treat Jung's functions as observable action orientations of the whole person, we are reminded to keep observing, carefully observing the whole person to deepen our understanding of how mind (minding) works. We are reminded to stay away from regarding ENTP as a mechanism programmed in a certain way and also reminded to keep the concept of psychological types as a working hypothesis that we continue to test in various aspects of life, such as the zone experience.

KINDS OF MIND*

When descriptions of opposite types are read side by side, the contrasts are clear. Taken as a whole, the differences in mental processing among all the sixteen types are subtle and do not stand out in such bold distinctions as found in the pairs of opposites. So while I see the sixteen psychological types as sixteen kinds of mind, it is helpful in

---

*Adapted by permission from Gordon Lawrence, *People Types and Tiger Stripes*, 4th ed. (Gainesville, FL: Center for Applications of Psychological Type, 2009).

showing the distinctions between them to combine the sixteen kinds of mind to four sets—ST, NF, NT, and SF—the four function combinations. Stated in another way, the four ST types—ESTJ, ISTJ, ESTP, and ISTP—have in common the preference for concrete practicality (S) and logical, analytical decision making (T). This can be viewed as a distinctive kind of mind, and so on with the other three groups.

FOCUSING ON JUNG'S FOUR FUNCTION COMBINATIONS

When we say that four types have a common mind-set, for example, the four ST types, we know we are bundling together a lot of differences. But it is clear that we can expect a lot of commonality among people of the four ST types. The characterizations that follow are adapted from the work of Humphry Osmond, Miriam Siegler, and Richard Smoke, reported in their 1977 article, "Typology Revisited: A New Perspective," in the journal *Psychological Perspectives*.[4] They based their analysis on a careful study of Jung's writings about the types. I have adapted, with gratitude, their quite colorful descriptions of the ST, NF, NT, and SF combinations. They called the ST combination Structural, the NF Oceanic, the NT Ethereal, and the SF Expereal. As explained below, they invented the term *expereal* to contrast with ethereal. They developed their insights without knowing of the work of Isabel Myers and the extensive research done with the MBTI instrument. My presentation here differs somewhat from theirs because mine is based on Myers's work.

ST: THE STRUCTURAL MIND

Four types have the ST combination: ISTJ, ISTP, ESTJ, and ESTP. Similarly, four types have NF in common, four have NT, and four have SF. What the ST types have in common is their S way of experiencing life and their T way of organizing their experiences. They value what their senses experience that can then be turned by their Thinking directly into what they regard as objective reality. The best analogy for the structural mind is the computer as an elaborate filing system. STs want clean data that will file exactly where they want them, so the data can be easily retrieved in the same form that they filed them. The ST process works best with unambiguous facts and specifics that can be clearly and correctly sorted into mental files. Of course, life doesn't present just unambiguous experiences that can be neatly classified. The ST solution to that problem is to simplify experience by reducing it to what will fit the filing categories. Mature STs recognize that this solution may oversimplify things, but they believe the reality they hold on to is the part most needed for future use; they will have the essential things ready for use when they are needed.

NF: THE OCEANIC MIND

NFs process experience in an entirely different way. To NFs, the unique, subtle, personal, and "ambiguous" features of experiences are what make them most valuable and interesting. In their view, everything is ultimately connected to everything else; life is a seamless whole. To sort experiences and file them objectively is to lose the subtle features that make possible the rich connections and relationships between things and people. NFs see the ST way of reducing experiences to distinct, objective categories as destroying the essentials rather than saving them.

Rather than being a filing system, the NF mind is like an ocean. Swimming in the ocean, just over the rim of consciousness, are all the bits of distinctive experiences that the NFs want to save for quick reference. When the conscious mind is through with the bits, they are allowed to swim away, over the rim, to find their own place. When a new circumstance or problem is faced that requires recalling those bits of experience, they somehow become available—not from a systematic file, but from a process of letting associated memories come into consciousness, one pulling in another and another. Some that come are the exact ones sought, some are different. The NFs have faith that this process will preserve the best of experiences for future use; if the exact ones sought aren't found, others perhaps more interesting and just as useful will be retrieved and provide a creative and often surprising and refreshing solution to the new problem at hand.

NT: THE ETHEREAL MIND

NTs have in common with NFs the global approach provided by Intuition. In common with STs they have the concern for impersonal analysis that the Thinking function gives them. Ideas in the form of mental models are the central feature of the NT mind. Before they launch themselves into the hurly-burly of life events, the NTs want to have mental blueprints or maps to guide them, to provide an advance system of meanings by which they can stay oriented in daily life. Some NTs are bothered by the term *ethereal* as implying something insubstantial. One NT suggested to me the term *conceptual mind.* Osmond and his colleagues chose the term *ethereal* for the NTs to suggest their reliance on abstract constructs and principles, the etherlike material that is primary in their mental functioning. They also see NTs as tending to process experiences with "everything being grist for the mental mill." Directly experiencing life, without first conceptualizing it in a mental map, takes effort and seems awkward. NTs are keenly interested in objective data, not just facts as facts, but facts as evidence to support one of their mental models. (As you read this material, you are witnessing my NT mind doing what is most natural to me—presenting a mental model.)

SF: THE EXPEREAL MIND

The SFs have in common with STs the concreteness and matter-of-fact qualities that the Sensing function provides. With the NFs they share the personal, subjective approach of the Feeling function. *Expereal* is a term coined by Osmond and his colleagues to contrast with ethereal and to convey the central feature of SF mind: everything is validated in personal, practical, daily experience. Like the NTs, SFs believe in conducting their lives according to principles. But while the NTs seek out abstract principles first and then test them in life experiences, the SFs reverse the process. They take life events matter-of-factly; then, when their experiences show them what works and what doesn't work, rules-of-thumb emerge—personal, practical guidelines that are credible as guiding principles because their *own experience* in daily life produced them. SFs are immediately in touch with the tangible qualities of events, and they know directly the literal, personal meanings of what happens—and these experiences provide them with their rule-of-thumb principles. In contrast, STs turn events into objects before they react to them personally. In even sharper contrast, the NFs and NTs get their data not from the literal concreteness of Sensing but mainly from Intuition, which automatically probes behind literal experience before it settles on the meaning and value of it.

The contrasts in the paragraphs above highlight the mental filtering and processing differences that are the heart of the theory of motivation implicit in Jung's work. Turning back to the analogy of computer operating systems, it is quite easy to see that the ST, NF, NT, and SF operating systems compute experience in ways sharply different from each other. The practical implications become obvious. When, for example, an ST teacher and an NF student are trying to connect, or an NF parent and an ST child, a lot of energy goes into the necessary bridge-building software needed for communication. And the bridges are not just literal translations of input and output, but a connection of each other's emotional infrastructures to find an appreciation of the values of each other's kind of mind. That we can manage so large a task, day in and day out, is a tribute to the adaptability of the human brain.

INVESTIGATIVE MIND: GETTING PAST THE STEREOTYPES

All of the types, of course, are capable of investigative minding. But we all are saddled with a stereotype that leads us to the thought that some types would be better at it than others. A brief reading of the type descriptions does not break the stereotype. So we have to address it directly.

I chose the term *investigative* to characterize the quality of minding that is at work when we are in the zone, as I explained in chapters1 and 2. I mean the term to convey the idea of proactive inquiry that stretches our resources and talents. It is available to all of us, no matter which of the sixteen is our type of mental processing. But *investigative* needs to be freed from the stereotypical baggage that makes it seen more available to some types of minding than others. For example, consider which preference, Extraversion or Introversion, seems more connected to investigation. Because Introversion means, among other things, reflective engagement with ideas and considering things deeply, it has the connotation of being investigative. Consider Sensing and Intuition. Sensing perception is attention to

INTP

Inquisitive ANALYZERS; reflective, independent, curious; more interested in organizing ideas than situations or people. Having introverted THINKING as their strongest mental process, they are at their best when following their intellectual curiosity, analyzing complexities to find the underlying logical principles. They value:

- A reserved outer life; an inner life of inquiry
- Pursuing interests in depth, with concentration
- Work and play that is intriguing, not routine
- Being free of emotional issues while working
- Working on problems that respond to detached intuitive analysis and theorizing
- Approaching problems by reframing the obvious
- Complex intellectual mysteries
- Being absorbed in abstract, mental work
- Freedom from organizational constraints
- Independence and nonconformance
- Intellectual quickness, ingenuity, invention
- Competence in the world of ideas
- Spontaneous learning by following curiosity and inspirations
- Using critical analysis to improve things

ESFJ

Practical HARMONIZERS, workers with people; sociable, orderly, opinioned; conscientious, realistic, and well-tuned to the here and now. Having extraverted FEELING as their strongest mental process, they are at their best when responsible for winning peoples' cooperation through personal caring and practical help. They value:

- An active, sociable life, with many relationships
- A concrete, present-day view of life
- Making daily routines into gracious living
- Staying closely tuned to people they care about so as to keep relationships positive
- Talking through problems cooperatively, caringly
- Approaching problems through tried-and-true, familiar procedures
- Caring, compassion, and tactfulness
- Helping organizations serve their members well
- Responsiveness to others, and to traditions
- Being prepared, reliable in tangible, daily work
- Loyalty and faithfulness
- Practical skillfulness grounded in experience
- Structured learning in a humane setting
- Giving appreciation to prompt improvements

solid facts presented to the senses; perception by Intuition is the pursuit of intriguing possibilities beyond the givens. Intuition gets the nod for seeming more investigative. The stereotype favors Thinking over Feeling. And Judging, with its aim toward closure and predictability, seems distinctly less investigative than Perceiving, which aims for open exploration of curiosities. So I, N, T, and P seem to have an inside track to investigative minding. That's the stereotype, and it needs to be challenged so that we can see investigative minding as being equally available to all of the sixteen Jungian types.

To probe the stereotype problem, let's consider the two opposite types presented on the previous page, INTP and ESFJ. Does the INTP description seem to convey the conventional view of an investigative mind-set?

No doubt the INTP description presents the conventional image of investigative qualities. But if the concept of investigative minding being pursued in this book is worth anything, it has to be comprehensive enough to apply equally to ESFJ, and, of course, to all the types.

Starting with the basic idea that investigative inquiry is mindful behavior, we can fairly easily find plausible descriptors of this quality of mindfulness:

- alert, careful attention (full of care) to events, people, data
- focused, absorbing interest
- wholehearted engagement, aware and probing
- using sound reasoning to shape ideas for action
- testing the ideas in action, including mental action
- assessing consequences of the action
- using the feedback to improve the action

These features suggest the label *problem solving*, but *investigative mindfulness* is a better term, connoting something richer. It contains emotional loading, passion, a whole-person quality. And, defined in this way, investigative mindfulness is a construct that applies equally to all of Jung's types of mental processing.

Let's test the last statement. With INTP being the stereotypical investigative type, let's consider what investigative minding would look like for ESFJ, the type that differs in all aspects of mental processing from INTP. We can find clues in the ESFJ description. First of all, ESFJs play out their lives in a wholly different mental landscape from INTPs. So their mindfulness is grounded in other ways of experiencing life, other sorts of data, and other judgment processes.

ESFJs find their absorbing interest and wholehearted engagement in the circle of people who are part of their lives. It is the quality of the relationships with people that is their main agenda. "How are things with us?" is a question they always have in mind. Their extraverted Feeling, the dominant organizing feature of their mental processing, acts something like a set of antennae. The antennae are tuned instinctively to the significant people of their daily lives, especially to the emotional overtones of those people's behavior. Consider the contrast with INTP, whose mental processing is independent, impersonal, abstract, and analytical. What's the opposite of these INTP qualities? The ESFJ kind of minding is an immersion in the tangible, moment-by-moment interchanges of people, with the overriding purpose of harmonizing the relationships. When they have an impersonal kind of problem to solve, they often use their skills of personalizing things to find the solution. For example, enlisting other people's know-how. Many times I have seen them find just the right words and the touch of empathy that turns a stranger into a friend and ally, or at least a momentary friend and ally. The new friend then helps them break through some impersonal barrier to get a job done.

An example of ESFJ investigative strategy is vivid in my mind. I was a guest teacher for a college instructor who wanted his students to learn about Jung's psychological types in relation to their own learning styles. After the students had decided on a best-fit type for themselves, I turned the group to a discussion of their learning strategies and how they saw these habits as reflective of their type. I asked for volunteers to say their type and tell about how they study. After several had spoken, someone said, "Ask Katie here about her study style. She's the most serious note taker I ever saw." Katie volunteered, "I'm pretty sure I am an ESFJ. When we're having a lecture, I try to write down word-for-word what the teacher says. Then that night I go over my notes and highlight what I think the most important points are. During the first week or two of the course, I take my notes to the teacher—at least once, but maybe several times—and ask him or her if I got the key points highlighted. Sometimes I do that again later in the course, too. I don't want to be putting wrong stuff in my memory."

While Katie was talking, a student in the row behind her got wide-eyed and her jaw dropped. I asked her about her reaction and she said, "I'm an ESFJ too, and I do *exactly* the same thing. I can't believe it. I thought I was the only one in the *world* who studied this way." No doubt some ESFJs would study differently. But it is easy to see how this strategy fits the ESFJ mental priorities. Because their extraverted Feeling takes the lead, they quickly see the benefit of bringing the teacher personally into their study process. It makes perfect sense to them to have a learning style that includes their social skills—one that is interpersonal as well as intrapersonal. Katie wanted to be sure the teacher knew her as a person, not just a face in the classroom. The copious note taking reflects her trust in Sensing more than Intuition to catch all the important things to be remembered. She wanted the specific words the teacher spoke, not her own paraphrases.

Classrooms, as we generally see them, are not structured to draw on the strengths of ESFJs, or some of the other types as well. If classroom life were designed for Extraverts as well as for Introverts, there would be more time given to learning through outward action, movement, and dialogue. Sensing types are often put at a disadvantage as well. They thrive on having all their senses engaged, but most classrooms call mainly for just two: sight and hearing. Moreover, words and symbols, the mainstay of classroom instruction, primarily draw on Intuition for processing. The contents of textbooks and lectures are abstractions that are processed by Intuition, not concrete experiences that address the Sensing process. Notice that Katie treated the instructor's words as literal, concrete things she should transcribe and check for accuracy with the instructor. In effect, she needed to be certain that her Intuition, which she didn't trust as much as her Sensing, didn't seep into her thoughts and cloud the teacher's meaning. Katie's opportunities to use *investigative* minding were pretty much limited to checking for accuracy and figuring out how to please the teacher. The lecture format by itself is likely to prompt her into mental work that rests on the blank-slate assumption, is routine and mundane, and not near the upper end of the mindfulness continuum.

Glance back at the ESFJ description and consider what kinds of learning environments would engage Katie's investigative side. First of all, they would be *social* situations, ones that valued the taking of responsibility in group work. They would involve interactions far more varied than the typical lecture and recitation interchanges Katie likely encountered in her college classes. They would open up opportunities for ESFJs to manage essential details, particularly the social details. They would give ESFJs the job of winning people's cooperation on mutual goals. These kinds of challenges grab the natural investigative minding of ESFJs. They are the grounding of their growth and development, and the doorway to the zone for ESFJs.

ESFJs usually consider life beyond the classroom as the arena for their best learning. The quality of learning one does beyond school is distinctly affected by, among other things, the career path one chooses. There is extensive evidence that people tend to seek out and stay in occupations that are a good fit for their types of mental processing, fertile ground for their growth and development.[5] One example concerning ESFJs comes to mind from data on real estate salespeople. While ESFJ was not the most common type among real estate professionals, it was by far the most common type among those who were identified as real estate sales superstars. When some of them were asked how they accounted for their exceptionally high sales, they answered—almost uniformly—"It's all about relationships": staying in touch, networking with colleagues, building friendships, listening very closely to clients to figure out the specifics of their needs, getting them data, doing legwork and nice things for them, winning their trust, collecting feedback, doing the details, and bringing all these things together in closing a sale. This strikes me as investigative minding of a particular kind, in a particular arena.

I have used the example of the ESFJ superstar salespeople to test my proposed definition for investigative mindfulness. I believe the definition works for all sixteen types. The qualities of investigative minding specific to each type are implicit in the type descriptions. The qualities of high-level mindfulness described earlier in the chapter can be recast as questions to put to each type description. For each type,

- What values are likely to get their *alert, careful attention?*
- In what sorts of actions are they likely to focus their *absorbing interest,* their *wholehearted engagement?*
- What kind of reasoning—Thinking or Feeling, impersonal or person focused—will best draw on their resources and take them to sound conclusions?

- In what kinds of action—for example, Extraverted or Introverted, Sensing or Intuitive—are they likely to test their reasoned ideas?
- To what kinds of feedback are they likely to be most alert and responsive?

I believe the answers to these questions give a sound general picture of the kind of mindfulness one can expect in each type. And, because the zone isn't entered except through investigative mindfulness, answers to the questions point to the zone pathway for each type.

PART 2: JUNG'S KEY CONCEPTS

MENTAL CATEGORIES

Jung saw that we are born with certain categories of mind that are "antecedent to all experience and appear with the first act of thought, of which they are preformed determinants. The newborn brain is an immensely old instrument fitted out for quite specific purposes [that] actively arranges the experiences of its own accord." The categories make up "a kind of preexisting ground plan . . . inherent functional possibilities . . . like invisible stage managers behind the scenes."[6]

Today, cognitive scientists and developmental psychologists—particularly those who work with young children—independently seem to be moving toward a consensus that the brain, unlike manmade computers, makes computations by forming categories, that is, chunking experiences into data sets. The scientists identify these data sets with names such as mental modules or prototypes or schema or innate intuitive patterns that the individual person uses to identify and sort experiences to make sense of them.[7] When an event or thing then comes along that appears to be new to the person, he or she compares it to the prototype, categorizes it, and in doing so, gives it meaning and a place in an action scheme.

We all see this development of categories in young children just learning to name things. For example, when "doggie" is formed as a category, the child enjoys calling out "doggie" for any creature that seems to match the prototype. A horse or cat or any other four-legged animal will be called "doggie" until the child begins to differentiate large animals from small and sets up new categories for them. Emotions become components of these mental modules as they are formed. Fear, curiosity, joy, and caution can be associated with "doggie." And the time will quickly come when "good doggie" is distinguished from "bad doggie."

Mental categories reflecting temperament characteristics show up early too. A child's "I do it myself" category contrasts with a "Mommy help" category. Other such contrasts are: reflection versus action, practical versus imaginative, people oriented versus thing oriented, and planful versus open-ended.

The cognitive researchers also interpret their evidence as showing that individuals have *inborn* preferences among the prototype categories, giving higher value to some and using them more often—and more automatically—in doing their mental business.[8] This view of mental preferences, coming out of current empirical cognitive science, seems fully consistent with what Jung hypothesized nearly a century earlier. That is, his psychological types represent different *sets* of preferences among the prototype categories used in mental processing.[9]

To what extent might these mental filtering systems account for important variations in personality? Researchers say that about 50 percent of the variation in personality has genetic causes, as demonstrated by extensive studies of identical twins and fraternal twins, reared together and reared apart. Remarkably, they found that only an additional 5 percent of measured personality differences can be accounted for by the conditions of rearing, such as parenting styles, stability of the home environment, siblings, and so on. There is no consensus among psychologists about where the other 45 percent of the variation comes from.[10] Jung's mental frameworks may turn out to account for a good chunk of it. His typology is fully consistent with the widely held view that mental processing is accomplished by innate mental prototypes for categorizing experiences that carry emotional weights and priorities that differ for different people.[11] The reality of different priority paths for processing experience is exactly what Jung's typology is built on. And each typological prototype has its own logic and learning process.

DEVELOPMENT AND VALIDATION

First a few comments about Carl Jung and how he came to discover the types. He was a physician as well as a psychologist, and his work, which became the grounding of his writing, was in treating patients in psychotherapy. He left Switzerland to join Freud and Adler in Vienna in pursuing a clinical approach to psychology, and he expected a close collaboration with them. To better understand unconscious mental processes, Freud and Jung became psychoanalysts for each other. Despite their common mission, the clash of minds between Jung and Freud made collaborative work impossible. Jung's disappointment compelled him to find out why they clashed. This was a psychological puzzle he had to solve, a complexity that his young science had to be able to explain. This set him on the path that eventually led to his hypotheses about the types of mental functioning.[12]

After his discovery of the types, Jung refined and validated his construct through systematic observations during his many years of clinical practice.[13] In the decades since his work, his construct of the types has been validated by hundreds of studies. The studies were made possible by the development of a psychological instrument, the work of two American researchers, Isabel Myers and Katharine Briggs. Their instrument extended Jung's work beyond the psychiatrist's clinic by making it possible for people to identify in themselves an affinity for one of the types by responding to the instrument's questions. The Myers-Briggs Type Indicator instrument, first published in 1962 and based squarely on Jung's construct, opened the door for scores of researchers to devise studies that provide empirical evidence of validity, not just the validity of the instrument but of Jung's typology itself: different *types* of mind actually do exist, different kinds of hardwiring.

FOUR CONSCIOUS MENTAL FUNCTIONS

While Jung gave a large amount of his attention to the study of the unconscious mind, his psychological types are a characterization of *conscious* mental processing. At the center of his hypothesis was the recognition that all conscious mental functioning can be sorted into two categories: *perception* and *judgment*, that is, taking in information and making decisions about it. Perceptions are the mental experiences we engage in that do not involve judgment. They are sense impressions and insights that just happen, that involve no reasoning as they come into awareness; and they become the raw material of reasoning. Reasoning leads to judgments, the mental actions we take based on perception data, the closure needed before putting thoughts into action.

Further, all *perceptions* can be sorted into two mutually exclusive categories, *sensations* and *intuitions*—a perspective that is fully consistent with the work of researchers and theorists identified in chapter 2. Jung also observed that all *judgments* can be sorted into two mutually exclusive categories: reasoning by way of *Thinking* criteria and reasoning by way of *Feeling* criteria. Jung saw these four categories—Sensation, Intuition, Thinking, and Feeling—as accounting for all conscious mental functioning, and he called them the functions. The "Words for Understanding Type Concepts" lists that appear near the beginning of this chapter include some brief characterizations of the four functions.

CATEGORICAL OPPOSITES

I need to explain here Jung's concept of contrasting opposite functions. Sensing perception and Intuitive perception are categorically opposite, mutually exclusive ways of perceiving. Sensing perception is concerned with the tangible, immediate processes of sense organs bringing sensations into awareness. Sensing directs mental attention to what is seen, touched, heard, and so on. Intuitive perception is the process that brings abstract images, patterns, and intangible meanings into awareness. Intuition directs mental attention to meanings that have been extracted from prior experiences and stored in the memory bank as abstractions that we often call hunches, or "gut feelings." We may shift back and forth between Sensing and Intuition as we attend to our experiences—often shifting very rapidly—but we cannot be in both perception modes (Sensing and Intuition) at the same time. For example, as I sit at my word processor writing these words about abstractions, I am in my Intuition function. When something I have typed doesn't look right, I shift into my Sensing function to *see* what sort of typo or grammatical goof I have made. I can't have my attention on the big picture *and* the detail in the same instant. I shift back and forth. I use both, alternately, but prefer one over the other. One is my home base. In my case, the Intuition function is home. I stay easily in the abstractions. In this instant, as I am writing, I am reminded to say that Intuition is not in the here and now. Our dog, very much in the here and now, has just nudged my leg to ask for attention, and I am pulled back from the world of abstractions.

Now we turn to the two categorically opposite *judgment* functions: reasoning by Thinking criteria and reasoning by Feeling criteria. Once something has come into awareness by Sensing perception and/or Intuitive perception, we need to do something with the perception, that is, make a judgment about it: classify it, weigh it, evaluate it, analyze it, ignore it, and so forth. In our reasoning we may apply both Thinking criteria and Feeling criteria, but we favor one of them. The one we favor is our default mode, and we must *deliberately* choose to shift to the other mode if a situation calls for it.

WHAT THINKING AND FEELING ARE AND ARE NOT

Jung's distinctive and generally unfamiliar use of the familiar terms *Thinking* and *Feeling* needs clarification. Let's start with Feeling. *Feeling* is a term used just as loosely as *mind*, on which I commented at the beginning of chapter 2. "How are you feeling?" is a question used to inquire about a lot of things: sensations a person is having—nausea, backache, sleepiness; or emotional states: anxious, lonely, loving, sexy, angry; or the state of a personal relationship—as in "Are things OK with us?" A similar question, "What are your feelings on this?" takes the term in another direction. It could be asking for a person's hunches, intuition, speculation. It could be asking for a "gut reaction"—an emotional response—or a deliberate personal judgment, a reasoned conclusion.

Feeling can be used as a synonym for *empathy*, as in "She has a feeling for what's going on with me." It can mean savvy or having a knack, as in "She has a feeling for car engine problems." Or it can mean sensitivity of various kinds: sensations being picked up by fingertips or an alertness to nuances in things, such as music, seasoning foods, or speech patterns. Terms used so loosely get us into trouble when we are trying to get a clear picture of human functioning. Jung's work helps us sharpen the usage.

Its use in so many different ways gives *feeling* a fuzzy, indistinct quality. It becomes a vague and indirect way of talking about intangible experiencing. When we put *feeling* alongside *thinking*, the latter seems more substantial and definite. That impression leads to serious misperceptions, as Jung made clear in his work on types of mental processing.

In everyday language, *thinking* is used almost as loosely. "What are you thinking?" can mean a dozen different things depending on the circumstances of the question. Jung's special use of the terms *Thinking* and *Feeling* needs some elaboration. Most important are his distinguishing between feeling and emotions, and his identification of thinking and feeling as two equally valuable modes of *reasoning*.

People who read about Jung's work but miss the distinction he made between emotions and feeling can't tune into Jung's model of mental functioning. Interchanging "emotions" and "feelings," a common practice today, even among psychologists, is inconsistent with Jung's system. He reserved the term *Feeling* only for use in naming a judgment process in which personal priorities and values are used as the criteria for the decision. Feeling is a deliberate act of valuing. It is reasoning by weighing the relative importance of alternative actions, as they affect oneself and people and things held dear. For example, a person using Feeling judgment in arranging a business meeting would give priority to the participants' convenience, emotional agendas, personal needs, points of rapport and common ground, and potential interpersonal conflicts as elements of the meeting that will have an effect on accomplishing the tasks for which the meeting was called. Here's the main point: Jung defined Feeling judgment as a *rational* process, just a different kind of rationality than Thinking judgment.[14]

Emotions, on the other hand, are not rational. They happen to us without any reasoning being involved.[15] Jung used the example of loving versus being in love. Loving is active, an act of valuing. Being in love is a complex emotion that just happens. Emotions, of course, can be recognized in consciousness, taken as data, and used as information in a reasoning process, as criteria for either Thinking or Feeling judgment. For example, logical reasoning tells us the probability of being killed in a car accident is far greater than being killed in a plane crash. That is a widely accepted fact. But if someone decides not to fly because of fear of flying, is that being irrational? It may be, but it could also be a reasoned judgment, along these lines: "If I force myself to fly, I'll be so miserable with worry that I'll be tied up in knots for the whole flight and be a wreck at the meeting when I get there. I'll drive up the night before and be fresh for the meeting." People who favor Feeling judgment over Thinking judgment are better at recognizing emotions and taking them into account as data. Their unconscious emotional infrastructure is more available to them as a source of data. It also gives them access to the emotions of other people to a greater extent than for people who favor Thinking judgment. This ability makes them better able to anticipate emotional consequences of decisions and the impact of language choices in communication.

Using Thinking criteria in reasoning, in contrast to Feeling reasoning, is applying impersonal analysis to matters requiring a decision. Thinking judgment looks for logical, cause-and-effect relationships and consequences. Let's use again the example of planning a business meeting. The person using Thinking judgment in planning would be focused on the impersonal tasks—the resources and logical steps that are needed to advance the agenda—nonpersonal features that move the flow of the meeting toward a sound conclusion. Jung's clarification of rationality as having both Thinking components and Feeling components is a highly practical as well as a theoretical distinction, as suggested in the example of planning good meetings.

People who favor their Thinking function tend to be less in touch with their own emotions, and those of other people. My ENFJ wife, for example, with her well-developed emotional antennae, can often detect my emotions before I have any conscious awareness of them.

The Thinking and Feeling functions cannot be accessed in the same instant. We can move back and forth between Thinking criteria and Feeling criteria, but we cannot use both at once. And, of course, Jung's model is based on the assumption that each person prefers one over the other, uses it as the default reasoning process, and uses it more than the other.

The common use of the terms *thinking* and *feeling*—regarding thinking as rational, feeling as irrational, as well as the interchanging of the terms *feelings* and *emotions*—is a serious problem in psychology and in nontechnical use as well. It belittles the Feeling judgment process. All of us *are* irrational at times, but that is not a distinction between Thinking and Feeling; irrationality is the failure to use appropriate judgment, whether one favors reasoning by Feeling criteria or Thinking criteria. Thinking is commonly regarded as being more intellectual and more levelheaded. I see this conceptual sloppiness as doing a lot of harm. Those people who favor Feeling judgment—half of the general population by all estimates, including 40 percent of males—are misrepresented by this stereotype.

I have trained myself to use Jung's meanings for thinking and feeling in my work. In this book, I believe, the term *thinking* is not once used to mean general mental processing (as in "What are you thinking about?") or as a synonym for reasoning or rationality, or anything else but Jung's category as he defined it. This is a special circumstance, of course; but my intention is to show that Jung's way of characterizing reasoning—by Thinking criteria *and* by Feeling criteria—is one we can all adopt and would greatly benefit by if we did.

Similarly, I have not used the term *feeling* except to mean reasoning by Feeling criteria; and I avoid using the terms *feelings* and *emotions* interchangeably. What I have reasoned out for myself is limiting the term *feelings* to refer to the articulated outcomes of reasoning by way of Feeling criteria. So when I express my feelings, in this use of the term, I am not simply venting emotions, but stating reasoned conclusions and considered values—conclusions that may well represent emotional data that I have drawn into my reasoning by way of Feeling criteria. This is an important distinction to make when we consider the concept of emotional intelligence. Can there be any such thing as emotional intelligence if it is not an outcome of the process Jung called reasoning by way of Feeling criteria? The scholars who study and write about emotional intelligence and do not make the distinction between emotions and feelings have set up a roadblock in their work on understanding intelligence.

ONE OF THE FOUR FUNCTIONS IS DOMINANT

Through many thousands of hours with his patients, Jung observed that each person used all of the four mental functions—Sensation, Intuition, Thinking, and Feeling—but preferred one over the others. He referred to the favored one as the *dominant preference*, and saw the preference as distinctly shaping the way the person carried on his or her mental processing. By *dominant* he meant the function that automatically is in the lead in mental processing. It is the default mode, and the chairman of the board. The other three functions play their role in service to the dominant one. The order of preference of the four functions identifies the most comfortable and satisfying path of mental processing for a person. For example, my order of preference is Intuition, Thinking, Feeling, and Sensing. Intuition and Thinking processes predominate, with Feeling and Sensing being called upon occasionally. Jung came to the conclusion that the preference of one over the others was an inborn tendency. Today we would say the order of preference of the functions is hardwired. Below are the four dominant mental preferences he identified.

Jung saw that people who preferred *Sensing perception* over the other three functions relied fundamentally on what their senses presented to them. They attended mainly to what was immediately and literally in their present experiences. Direct, hands-on experience was what they wanted and trusted, and they tended to distrust Intuition and speculation about unproven possibilities. They sought out sensory richness in their lives. Their focus was on practical usefulness.

People who preferred *Intuitive perception* over the other three functions had a mind centered on finding intuitive impressions, possibilities, and abstract meanings that tie the bits and pieces of experience into insightful patterns and explanations. They sought the big picture first and the particulars later, using the particulars only as needed to reframe and improve the big-picture vision that guided their mental processing. They focused more on the future than the present and trusted imagination to give them a good view of the future; in doing that, they tended to neglect here-and-now sensory experiences.

People who preferred *Thinking judgment* over the other three functions had a mind centered on finding logical systems for sorting and organizing the sensory and intuitive perceptions they experienced. They used impersonal criteria to analyze and get clarity in perceptual data needed for sound conclusions. They sought reasoning detached from emotions, which they distrusted. Their conclusions were processed through such criteria as useful/not useful, true/not true, logically sound or not, and cause-and-effect connections. Their main focus was on having an ordered mind, built on a foundation of logical analysis.

People who preferred *Feeling judgment* over the other three functions had a mind centered on achieving objectives that were in harmony with inner values and harmonious with other people who are important to them. Their mode of reasoning was weighing the relative importance of things and events as they affect the welfare of people. New perceptions came into awareness as they found a niche among their own personal values and priorities. The people favoring Feeling judgment attended to the emotional content of experiences and used this information in decision making; they distrusted impersonal reasoning that neglected emotions. Their conclusions were processed through judgments such as better/worse, helpful/hurtful, high priority/low priority. Their main focus was on having an ordered mind grounded in caring and harmonious connections with people.

A SECOND FAVORITE AMONG THE FUNCTIONS

As he worked with his patients, Jung discovered that many of them had a one-sidedness; they were so wrapped up in their dominant function that the other functions were seriously neglected. For example, he saw patients with the Thinking function dominant who were preoccupied with Thinking to such an extent that they were seriously insensitive to emotions and to issues that required Feeling judgment. And they were so bent on having closure around their logical principles that they neglected letting their Sensing or Intuition give them needed new data. Jung saw that each person had to have not only a mature dominant function but also a well-developed second preference. He called it the *auxiliary*. The mental distress he encountered in his patients was often an outcome of having a poorly developed auxiliary. The auxiliary was needed to balance—that is, to supplement and complement—the dominant function.

And Jung recognized that if the dominant was a perception process (Sensing or Intuition), the auxiliary needed to be a judgment process (Thinking or Feeling) to counterbalance the dominant; likewise, if the dominant was a judgment process, the auxiliary needed to be perception process. A person could not manage in a healthy way having both the dominant and the auxiliary be judging functions, Thinking and Feeling, or having them both be perceiving functions, Sensing and Intuition. One's mental landscape is almost totally filled, most of the time, by the dominant and the auxiliary functions. If it was filled with Sensing and Intuition as dominant and auxiliary, there would be scant room for judgment processes—the weighing and sorting, keeping and discarding—that are so essential to good mental functioning. The opposite case, having Thinking and Feeling as dominant and auxiliary, would be equally dysfunctional: a landscape crowded with set decisions and rules, with too little space for new perception data to enlighten and enliven the judgments. Clear perception and sound judgment must both be present in good mental functioning. Perception without sound judgment is aimless, and judgment without good perception data is hollow. Thus, Jung saw that if the preferred judging function—Thinking or Feeling—were dominant, the preferred perception function—Sensing or Intuition—had to be auxiliary, and vice versa.

THE FUNCTIONS ARE EXTRAVERTED OR INTROVERTED

Jung also saw that each of the four mental functions could be used in one's inner life, the life of thought and ideas, or in one's outer life, the life of engagement in the world of people and things. Jung used the terms *introversion* and *extraversion* to represent the inward and the outward focus of the functions, and referred to these directionalities as the *attitudes*. Thus, a person with dominant Thinking judgment directed outwardly was referred to as an extraverted Thinking type. One with inwardly directed Thinking as the dominant was referred to as an introverted Thinking type. Similarly, an extraverted person with Intuition as dominant and extraverted was referred to as an extraverted Intuitive type. And so on for the other types.

Jung also saw that mental health depended on having one's auxiliary function in the attitude opposite that of the dominant. That is, if the dominant is extraverted, the auxiliary needed to be introverted so that both the inner and the outer worlds were adequately attended to. For example, if I extraverted *both* my dominant and auxiliary functions, my inner life would be relegated to my least used mental functions and, as a consequence, I could be quite a superficial person.

The directionality of each function in a person doesn't change, or switch back and forth, say, from extraverted Thinking to introverted Thinking. Extraverted Thinking is mental processing devoted to putting the events, ideas, and objects of one's *outer* life in logical order and keeping them working according to that order. In contrast, introverted Thinking is the process of operating the *inner* life of the mind according to logical criteria. People who introvert their Thinking function will not be running their outer lives with the Thinking function. They will certainly want to have both their inner and outer life working logically, but that is accomplished by having their preferred introverted function working in tandem with their preferred extraverted function.

Here's an example that highlights the effect of directionality of a mental function, in this case the distinction between extraverted and introverted Intuition. My wife and I share a preference for the Intuition mental function. In her case, ENFJ, Intuition is introverted and her auxiliary, while for me, ENTP, Intuition is extraverted and dominant. We both extravert our dominant function, but Intuition is her auxiliary. The example comes from our work on revising the design of a workshop we had conducted together. While we were sitting at the dining table with workshop materials spread out, trying to figure out how to change some components or sequences, I suggested that we consider brainstorming a new design from scratch then fit in the components we wanted to keep. "Brainstorming from scratch is a great idea," she said. "Let's do it. Wait a little and I'll be right back." While she was somewhere else, I glanced through the materials on the table and started making a few notes. After ten minutes or so of waiting I went to see where she was, to ask when we were going to start brainstorming. I found her in her study with her fingers flying on her keyboard. I said, "I thought we were going to brainstorm." She answered, "Of course. That's just what I'm doing. I'll be done in about five more minutes." My extraverted Intuition was primed to brainstorm in conversation, thrashing out ideas across the table. Her introverted Intuition took her to the privacy of her word processor for a brainstorming dialogue with herself. She wanted to have her ideas roughed out before we started talking about the new design. We quickly realized that our differences in psychological type were in play here, and we had a good laugh.

A Further Word about Extraversion and Introversion

I have already briefly described Jung's meanings for the terms *Extraversion* and *Introversion*: extraverting means turning outside oneself for energy, stimulation, and renewal; introverting means turning inward for energy, stimulation, and renewal. Life calls on all of us to extravert and introvert every day—turning out to engage the world of people and things, and turning inward to attend to our inner lives. But we prefer one over the other and try to seek out a life pattern that allows us to stay in our preferred mode more of the time.

While the terms *extraverted* and *introverted* identify the outward or the inward directionality of the dominant function, they also are the names of categories of mental preferences that have distinctive traits attached to them. For example, an extraverted Feeling person and an extraverted Thinking person are both Extraverts, and while they extravert opposite mental processes, they have in common some traits that define Extraversion: scanning the environment for values and stimulation; plunging in, using trial and error to learn; often speaking one's thoughts aloud to process them; being active and expressive; and focusing on people and things. Introverted types have in common contrasting traits: finding stimulation inwardly; considering things deeply before acting; keeping one's thoughts inside until they are polished and ready to be made public; taking plenty of time for reflecting before acting; and focusing on ideas and inner impressions. Individual Extraverts and Introverts may differ somewhat from these patterns, but these are the traits commonly associated with these two contrasting ways of being in the world. The literature on psychological typology offers considerably more-detailed descriptions. Jung devoted a large portion of his book *Psychological Types* to Extraversion and Introversion.

As you can see, Jung used the terms *extravert* and *introvert* in two ways: to indicate the outward or the inward directionality of the four functions, as in extraverted Sensing or introverted Sensing, and to give a name to the common tendencies of all the types who share the preference of turning outward or inward, as described in the previous paragraph.

Extraverting and introverting are essential for everyone. It is only through extraverting that we gain breadth in our development, and only through introverting that we gain depth. Extraverts who neglect their inner life run the risk of being shallow and Introverts who neglect their outer life may be ineffectual in translating their thoughts into outward action. But Jung's research showed him that everyone must have a dominant function, such as Sensing, and the dominant function must have a directionality, such as being extraverted. Likewise, everyone needs a well-developed auxiliary function that operates in the attitude opposite that of the dominant one. These are inborn predispositions that provide stability and continuity in one's life.

JUNG'S USE OF THE TYPE CONSTRUCTS

Jung kept careful logs on his patients and eventually wrote a fairly extensive description of each of the eight types. They appear in his book *Psychological Types*, first published in 1921. Because he worked daily with people in mental distress, their psychopathology showed up in his type descriptions. But it is important to mention that he saw the healthy use of the eight function attitudes as vital for society collectively. And as for his working with individuals, by having in mind an image of the *healthy* mental processes of the person's type, for example, an extraverted Thinking type, he had that image as a guide to essential clues to finding the therapeutic pathway for a patient of that type.

Jung was distressed when people used the type concepts to sort other people into the type categories and then treat the people *as categories* rather than as individuals. I wonder if he speculated that this kind of misuse of type could be happening now, so many years later. The misuse is evident in such commonly heard statements as, "She's a Thinking type, so don't expect her to be sensitive to feelings." Or, "He's an Intuitive type, so you'll have to feed him all the details if you want him to see them." Or, "He's a Sensing type. He'll be a good one for stuffing the envelopes." Such stereotypes and misuses of the concepts are discussed in chapter 5.

So far as I can detect, Jung did not address the issue of whether the types he identified were different kinds of mind or variations on a unitary model of mind. But it is clear that he saw the types as distinctly different patterns of mental processing. And in therapy he believed his patients needed to be approached according to the priorities and motivations embedded in their types.

PREFERENCES AMONG THE FUNCTIONS ARE INBORN

Jung and Briggs and Myers, who studied the type phenomenon more deeply than anyone, were convinced that a predisposition to a type is inborn. Emerging neuroscience and infant development research seem to be confirming this. Jung's view was that in very early life, once one of the four mental functions has emerged as the dominant, the psychic strain required to change the dominant cannot be endured. To use myself as an example, Intuition is my dominant function and Sensing is my least developed function. My Intuition manages my conscious processing. Sensing is my least conscious function, but I can bring it into awareness in a *helping* role. My staying focused on sensory data takes deliberate effort. Staying there a long time is very hard work. Reflecting on my own mental processing, I recognize the impossibility of Sensing taking the executive role, becoming the default mode. So far as I can tell, based on my earliest memories, I started life as the type that I am.

While my senses serve me very well, especially in my unconscious functioning, I cannot enter the world of Sensing types. Sensing people address their life experiences in ways not available to me, and my attempts at using my Sensing function will never equal the quality of sensory acuity the Sensing types find natural. Moreover, my Sensing function will always be in service to my dominant Intuition, my default mode. As I mature within my type framework, I learn to use my non-dominant mental functions more competently and get more enjoyment from then. But maturity never means achieving parity among the functions. The dominant one has to stay in charge to keep the mental system integrated. One's essential outlook remains directed via the dominant mental function. It is the dynamic core of the mental framework. The concept of an executive or dominant process being needed for managing mental activity has support outside Jung's system as well.[16]

TYPE TERMS ARE MENTAL CATEGORIES, NOT NAMES OF TRAITS

As you can see in the sixteen descriptions, the MBTI instrument identifies a person's preferences in four categories—four pairs of opposites: EI—Extraversion or Introversion, SN—Sensing or Intuition, TF—Thinking or Feeling, and JP—Judgment or Perception. The preference pairs—EI, SN, TF, and JP—are either/or kinds of categories; they are *not* continuous qualities, such as a continuum from "very extraverted" to "very introverted."

It is very easy to use the categories incorrectly. For example, although Jung introduced the terms *extraversion* and *introversion* into the language of psychology, they have been largely used not as he intended, as type categories, but as names of traits one can possess more or less of. When extraversion is treated as a trait, on a continuum from extremely extraverted to slightly extraverted, the usage implies that there is a middle ground that is better than either extreme. This usage is outside of Jung's system. In Jung's sense, Extravert refers to someone who uses the dominant mental preference *outwardly*. Introvert refers to someone who uses the dominant mental process *inwardly*. *Degree* of extraversion or introversion has no meaning in Jung's system. A person is either an Extravert or an Introvert. E or I is an aspect of a dynamic mental framework for processing experiences. To that framework individual people attach specific skills and traits. Using a personal example again, my wife is gregarious and I am not, but we are both Extraverts. When extravert is used as a name of a trait, it is often interchanged with gregarious. In Jung's system of mental types, my wife and I both extravert our dominant function. In terms of *traits*, she extraverts in an initiatory way, I in a responsive, less gregarious, way.

A THEORY OF MOTIVATION

We have come to the doorway of a broad theory of motivation that is radically different from nearly every other theory today in the field of psychology. In mainstream psychology motivation is seen as a three-way interaction of (a) an environment, (b) the basic inborn drives everyone has in common, and (c) the idiosyncratic collection of personality traits that each person acquires. Different theories in the field of psychology put different weights on the three components. Jung took a tack in another direction. His discovery was that traits are distributed in patterns, and the patterns point to the existence of different *types* of mental processing—categories that have boundaries and definitions.

If Jung's types are taken as different kinds of mind, different hardwiring, then the experiences people have with their environments are filtered and processed according to the kind of mind a person has. The experiences take on different meanings and trigger different emotions according to the type. The filtering/processing dynamic is different for each of the sixteen types. This discovery by Jung, were it acknowledged by scholars who study human nature, would make the findings of behavioral geneticists not nearly so shocking as they have been. The controversial findings can be summed up in one sentence: genes account for 50 percent of all human behavioral traits, with virtually all the rest of the variations being the results of the *unique* environment of each person. This conclusion virtually cuts out all influences of *shared* environments, such as family and other nurturing conditions.[17] The common assumption is that the research was saying parents don't count for much. From the perspective of psychological typology, the controversy is a tempest in a teapot. Of course parents count. But the shared or common environment of the family is modulated by the fact that people who live together usually are not of the same psychological type. They process their experiences through different types of mind, making the intrafamily experiences unique to each member rather than common among them all.

The filtering/processing dynamic of each type is suggested in the type descriptions. Take, for example, two contrasting types, ENFJ and ISTP. The descriptions are shown on the next page. Read through the two descriptions. Compare them line by line, giving attention to the filtering and processing contrasts: what comes into awareness, what is kept focally in mind, and what kinds of life experiences most engage their psychic energy. Each is an energy dynamic, each with its distinctive emotional infrastructure. Individual ENFJs will differ from each other in many ways, but they share the same underlying dynamic. They may differ dramatically in how adept or clumsy they are in pursuing the (bulleted) values they have in common. That's a matter of maturity. Likewise, of course, for ISTP and the other types.[18]

Reading the descriptions of opposite types side by side, such as ENFJ and ISTP, allows us to see that they will lead very different lives. Consider the first bulleted value in each description: "having a wide circle of friends" and "a reserved outer life." These polar-opposite motivations are built into the dynamic of each type. Each type of

ENFJ

Imaginative HARMONIZERS, workers with people; expressive, orderly, opinioned, conscientious; curious about new ideas and possibilities. Having extraverted FEELING as their strongest mental process, they are at their best when responsible for winning peoples' cooperation with caring insight into their needs. They value:

- Having a wide circle of relationships
- Having a positive, enthusiastic view of life
- Seeing subtleties in people and interactions
- Understanding others' needs and concerns
- An active, energizing social life
- Seeing possibilities in people
- Thorough follow-through on important projects
- Working on several projects at once
- Caring and imaginative problem solving
- Maintaining relationships to promote harmony
- Shaping organizations to better serve members
- Sociability and responsiveness
- Structured learning in a humane setting
- Caring, compassion, and tactfulness
- Appreciation as the natural means of encouraging improvements

ISTP

Practical ANALYZERS; value exactness; more interested in organizing data than situations or people; reflective, cool, and curious observers of life. Having introverted THINKING as their strongest mental process, they are at their best when analyzing experience to find the logical order and underlying properties of things. They value:

- A reserved outer life
- Having a concrete, present-day view of life
- Clear, exact facts; a large storehouse of them
- Looking for efficient, least effort solutions based on experience
- Knowing how mechanical things work
- Pursuing interests in depth, such as hobbies
- Collecting things of interest
- Working on problems that respond to detached, sequential analysis and adaptability
- Freedom from organizational constraints
- Independence and self-management
- Spontaneous hands-on learning experience
- Having useful technical expertise
- Critical analysis as a means to improving things

mental processing suggests a distinct pathway of development, and a distinct kind of mental distress if the pathway is blocked. For example, if life circumstances deny the ENFJ opportunities to maintain a wide circle of friends, the dynamic of that type is seriously disrupted. Energy is diverted from making progress along the development pathway and put into a struggle with whatever is deterring ENFJ from having the circle of harmonious relationships. Each type has its own set of stressors, and they can be seen in the descriptions above by considering whatever would block the type's pursuit of the values listed there.

In the context of the theme of this book, here is the practical side of Jung's types: the model of development they provide allows us *to predict the kinds of circumstances that will enhance or impede development—and that will open and close the door to the zone experience for each type of mental processing.* The values and priorities listed in each type description point to the circumstances and conditions that provide that type's motivation. Development *and* achievement for each type will follow naturally along the path suggested by the descriptors. Each feature of the type's description gives us a clue about how to tailor our coaching to someone of that type. The contrasting features of ENFJ and ISTP, for example, highlight the different potentials of each. An ENFJ person has to grow and develop on the ENFJ base, the ENFJ value system, the natural place of integration and strength. The idea of "motivating" the ENFJ to become more "well-rounded" by tackling her "deficiencies," such as the traits listed for ISTP, has no place in Jung's model of development. The ENFJ's motivation will flow naturally when the supervisor or teacher helps provide conditions and opportunities for the ENFJ to do what she does best. Working from her natural base, she can develop all sorts of needed skills, including some usually more associated with other types. By honoring the natural base of each type, we affirm each type, each person, as worthy. And the experience of feeling affirmed is by far the strongest motivator. By using type as our framework for promoting development, we can avoid the disaffirming, negative consequences that flow from seeking people's improvement by focusing on their deficiencies. We will play out this theme a little more in chapter 6.

TYPE VERSUS TRAIT

Finally, the sixteen descriptions reveal a key feature of Jung's view of human nature. They show that the approach to understanding behavior taken by the *type* model is distinctly different from the *trait* model. From the type point of view, behavior is seen as arising as a natural *expression* of one's type of mental processing in a given situation; the motivations are *observable* in behaviors, demonstrating the type dynamic in action. And mental distress is the disruption of the dynamic. Theories of motivation based in *trait* psychology, in contrast, treat behavior as being *caused* by *unobservable* drives that underlie one's traits, whether genetic or acquired, in interaction with the environment. And mental distress is caused by having too much or too little of important traits.

The trait view of behavior, the view that saturates the common perception of human nature, treats mind as a thing rather than as the minding behaviors of the whole person. In the trait view, Jung's mental functions (S, N, T, F) are seen as entities—components of the mind-thing—that trigger our behaviors. In Jung's typological view of behavior the mental functions are the organizing dynamic of the sixteen frameworks of mental processing—sixteen kinds of minding, each with its own distinct pattern of filters, values, priorities, and motivations. In the first two chapters we looked at evidence that babies are born with organized minds, or better said, born with organized ways of being mindful in the world. The contribution of Jung and Briggs and Myers is in showing us that the innate mental organization comes in sixteen types: sixteen dynamic patterns, each with its own distinctive kind of mental filter. The descriptions of the sixteen types embody not only the systems of mental organization and Jung's theory of motivation; they are also practical guides to making the theory useable in everyday life.

THE SIXTEEN TYPES

Jung's writings include descriptions of eight psychological types, not sixteen. While Jung emphasized the importance of having a well-developed auxiliary function, he did not include the role of the auxiliary in his descriptions of the types. If he had included the auxiliary in his descriptions, he would have had sixteen types instead of eight. The extension to sixteen type descriptions came about from Katharine Briggs and Isabel Myers, whose descriptions were published in 1962, in the manual for the Myers-Briggs Type Indicator instrument. One of their major contributions to Jung's work was writing the descriptions to show sixteen kinds of normal, well-functioning mental processing. They removed Jung's references to the kinds of mental illness he found associated with the types. The descriptions were then ready for general use in nonclinical settings—the family, the workplace, career planning, education, and so on.

Myers and Briggs identified the sixteen types as follows and gave them four-letter designations as shown.

The four Sensing dominant types:

Introverted Sensing dominant with extraverted Thinking as auxiliary	ISTJ
Introverted Sensing dominant with extraverted Feeling as auxiliary	ISFJ
Extraverted Sensing dominant with introverted Thinking as auxiliary	ESTP
Extraverted Sensing dominant with introverted Feeling as auxiliary	ESFP

The four Intuition dominant types:

Introverted Intuition dominant with extraverted Thinking as auxiliary	INTJ
Introverted Intuition dominant with extraverted Feeling as auxiliary	INFJ
Extraverted Intuition dominant with introverted Thinking as auxiliary	ENTP
Extraverted Intuition dominant with introverted Feeling as auxiliary	ENFP

The four Thinking dominant types:

Introverted Thinking dominant with extraverted Sensing as auxiliary	ISTP
Introverted Thinking dominant with extraverted Intuition as auxiliary	INTP
Extraverted Thinking dominant with introverted Sensing as auxiliary	ESTJ
Extraverted Thinking dominant with introverted Intuition as auxiliary	ENTJ

The four Feeling dominant types:

Introverted Feeling dominant with extraverted Sensing as auxiliary	ISFP
Introverted Feeling dominant with extraverted Intuition as auxiliary	INFP
Extraverted Feeling dominant with introverted Sensing as auxiliary	ESFJ
Extraverted Feeling dominant with introverted Intuition as auxiliary	ENFJ

One letter of each four-letter designation is larger than the others to indicate the dominant mental function in that type. In the case of ISTJ, for example, the S is larger because it is the dominant function. The T represents the second-most favored function, the auxiliary. Thus the four letters convey the dominant function, the auxiliary function, and the attitude of the dominant (E or I); and the last letter, J or P, shows whether one's *outer life* is run by the judgment preference—Thinking judgment or Feeling judgment—or the perception preference—Sensing perception or Intuition perception. In the case of ISTJ, the *auxiliary* Thinking judgment runs the outer life. In the case of ESTJ, the *dominant* Thinking judgment runs the outer life. (Because Extraverts use their dominant function in the outer world, the J/P indicates their dominant, as in ENFJ and ENFP. Introverts reserve their dominant for the inner world, so the J/P reports their *auxiliary* function, as in INFJ and INFP.) The J types have in common a strong tendency to run their outer lives planfully—having things decided, settled, and running according to a plan. They aim for closure. The P types have in common a strong desire to keep things open and flexible so they can spontaneously adjust their actions as new perceptions flow in.

WHY SIXTEEN?

Why sixteen and not eight or twenty-four or some other number? If we accept Jung's hypothesis, we arrive at sixteen. His rationale was that:

- *all* conscious *mental* activity can be sorted into four categories (S, N, T, and F),
- one of the four functions is the center of mental processing for each person—the dominant,
- the dominant function is used introvertedly *or* extravertedly (thus we are already at eight types, because the ET dynamic is different from the IT dynamic, and so on),
- and each type is defined by both dominant *and* auxiliary functions.

The last feature splits the eight into sixteen. Could there be more than sixteen? Myers gave years of study to the variations within each type.

Of course all ENFPs are not alike. But are there *systematic* variations within the type, as well as idiosyncratic differences between people of that type? Yes, and those variations are identified by an instrument, the MBTI Step II, published by CPP, Inc. It sorts responses into five subsets for each of the eight preferences: EI, SN, TF, and JP. But this sorting does not result in more types than the sixteen. It reports patterns within the type. The number of psychological types will not be more than sixteen because Jung's construct is based on four functions—S, N, T, F—used in four different ways—E, I, J, P—and $4 \times 4 = 16$.

VALIDITY OF THE SIXTEEN TYPES

As mentioned earlier in the chapter, the development of the Myers-Briggs Type Indicator instrument made possible empirical validation of Jung's typology. Because the instrument was designed to represent Jung's construct exactly, a validation study of the instrument is a validation check of the typology underlying it. Hundreds of studies have demonstrated the validity of it. One especially important set of studies I have described in an endnote.[19] Despite the massive evidence of validity, Jung's typology has been almost totally neglected by mainstream psychology and is barely mentioned in psychology textbooks, as noted in chapter 1. I have written this book, in part, with the intent of nudging this aspect of Jung's work more into the mainstream. The resources referenced in the endnote highlight some of the reasons that Jung's types have been neglected.

Beyond statistical validation there is the personal validating that happens when people find themselves reflected in a type description and discover the usefulness of the concepts. The type descriptions demonstrate a symmetry and comprehensiveness in Jung's construct. As one reads them I believe the symmetry becomes evident. And the implications for finding the zone door for different types are clearly suggested in the pattern of values in each description.

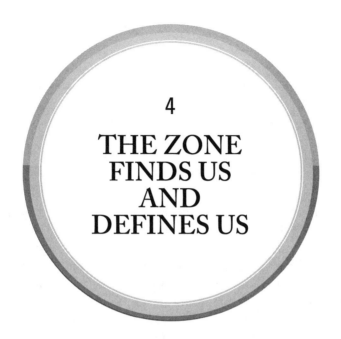

4

THE ZONE
FINDS US
AND
DEFINES US

Andre at twelve years of age is already a chess whiz. His fascination with the game started at age seven when an older cousin taught him how to play. From that day on anyone watching him play could see that he was totally in the zone when he had a challenging game going. His parents, neither of whom had played chess, support his interest and have been chauffeuring him to matches for several years. They're happy he has an absorbing interest and are especially pleased that it hasn't seemed to "mess up the rest of his life." They see him as "still well-rounded" in terms of school activities, friends, and family life. And they are still "amazed that chess took hold of him."

While chess is a game played virtually worldwide, what are the odds of any particular person finding chess to be a source of the zone? The odds must vary greatly from situation to situation: Is it a game supported by family, friends, and school, among other influences? Is there time and opportunity to play? Are there partners to play with who present the right level of challenge? Will the chess player be seen as a freak or a hero, or have some other status in between? All these cultural factors, and many more, are ingredients of the zone phenomenon. The zone experience that the chess player finds is not just his or her own *personal* experience. It belongs also to the culture from which it arises. From that viewpoint we can say that the chess zone has found the new player. Chess found Andre.

OPENING THE DOOR TO THE ZONE

The title of this chapter introduces a theme that is played out in chapter 5 as well as here. Essentially, the thesis is that the zone experience draws us like a magnet. We want the experience again and again. And there are forces in our environment and impulses in our genes, all beyond our conscious awareness, that draw us toward opening some zone doors and not others. Beyond each door is a different pathway for finding our individual flow. The forces and impulses are by no means deterministic, dictating our daily choices and behaviors. In any given setting we make our own choices that can turn out to be good, bad, or mediocre. But we are unconsciously drawn to open and enter some door(s) rather than others, and behind each door is a distinctive developmental path that influences the choices we make. Each path highlights some values and not others and suggests a set of priorities to follow among the options that life presents. And we are defined by the choices we make among the zone options.

What's in the previous paragraph applies to Andre, doesn't it? Factors in his environment and in his genes, such as a genetic disposition for "if . . . then" reasoning, steered him toward chess. We can easily suppose that the experiences he finds in the chess zone do influence, to some extent, many of the other aspects of his young life. And we can expect them to have a permanent effect on the rest of his life too, whether or not chess remains a major feature of his adulthood. Forces beyond his awareness attracted him to chess and hold him in that recurring zone.

Before we consider the factors that affect our choices among zone options—forces *beyond* the psychological aspects of the zone experience—let's review what psychologists have identified as the basic intrapersonal ingredients of any zone experience, summarized briefly in chapter 1 into five sets:

- When one is in the zone one's attention is concentrated and focused on a clear goal. The interest being pursued is so absorbing that it takes one out of ordinary experiencing and blocks out worry and distractions. And it is an interest freely chosen.
- The focus is on something other than the self. The self is out of consciousness, invested and absorbed in the action.
- A feedback loop that bypasses the self is in play. Data needed for making adjustments in one's actions to better reach the goal become immediately available without being routed through self-aware critical analysis.
- The tasks in pursuit of the goal are challenges that stretch one's skills, and typically they are well-practiced skills; they are a barely manageable difficulty that, when managed, brings the joy that sustains the zone experience.
- There is a sense of control over one's actions, a control that seems almost effortless.

These elements of the zone experience were derived from self-reports of thousands of study participants. Studies were done in North America, Asia, and Europe, all following the same protocol and research design devised by Mihaly Csikszentmihalyi. Over one hundred thousand participants were given a pager and a journal in which to make entries when they were paged at random times, about eight times a day for a week. They wrote in the journal what they were doing when beeped, what they were thinking about, and how they felt. On numerical scales they rated their state of consciousness and motivation, happiness, self-esteem, degree of concentration, and so on. Their entries supplied the raw material for the research. Out of these freeze-frames of people's experiences, the researchers extracted and summarized the conditions that were present when the people perceived themselves as being in flow—in the zone, as I am referring to it.[1]

It is important to note that the research was not designed to answer the question of how people *got to* the zone event; that is, what opened the door to the zone for them. The research doesn't show that the conditions summarized above *caused* the zone experience. Those reported experiences were present *along with* the flow event. But as statisticians say, correlation is not causation. What the research did do was shed light on universal features of experience that were present at the same time that the flow happened, *after* the door to the zone was opened. My interest is in what came before. That takes us into the realm of speculation and hypothesis making.

Looking again at the five conditions identified by Csikszentmihalyi and his colleagues, let's consider the clues they offer as to what opens the door to the zone—conditions that are, in effect, preconditions. One feature that jumps out clearly is having a strong interest in something, interest so engaging that the self is absorbed or submerged in the process. Common sense tells us that keen, active interest is a precondition for the zone. Without a compelling interest the zone experience does not begin. If interest wanes, the zone experience ends. In chapter 2 we considered the evidence that babies seem to get to the zone often and fairly easily. When something interests them and keeps them actively engrossed in work at the edge of their skills and understanding, they are in the zone. When an experience is new and challenging to them, it sustains the zone. But we saw evidence that babies drop out of the zone when the experience becomes familiar and no longer a challenging curiosity. For example, the experiment with the mobile above the crib attached by a ribbon to the baby's ankle: the baby's kicking to make the mobile move lasted only as long as the investigative curiosity did.

The first four zone conditions described above seem to all be part of babies' zone experience. They have the appearance of preconditions—zone opening and zone sustaining. I feel on solid ground in hypothesizing that these four are preconditions, door openers, to the zone. The fifth condition, a sense of almost effortless control over circumstances, seems a different sort of feature of the zone, a satisfying side effect that helps sustain it. A sense of control, by itself, would not be a precondition to the zone. In my view it would come after the preconditions were present.

Dropping a sense of control from the list reduces it to four preconditions. In chapter 2 I laid the groundwork for a different fifth element—that investigative minding is a condition needed for the zone, and it is the only kind of reasoning that participates in the zone.

Lower-level minding such as pat-answer reasoning, the natural outcome of blank-slate teaching, does not open the door to the zone. Higher-quality minding opens it. In the big picture, then, if we promote investigative minding, we promote the zone.

So far we have identified five door-openers to the zone. The list also helps us distinguish zoning out from being in the zone; the first three in the list are also present in zoning out, while the last two are conditions that shift one into the zone experience.

The zone phenomenon is a personal psychological experience, as the chess zone is for Andre. But it doesn't occur willy-nilly. It happens in a cultural context. *When* the zone happens and the *form* it takes depend on the forces in the culture and in our genes that support and shape it. For Andre, the conditions were right. The game found him, and it became his personal most important zone.

THE ZONE AS PLAY

ONE'S CULTURE CONTRIBUTES TO THE ZONE EXPERIENCE

There are other ways to study the zone experience besides using self-report data, as was done in the Csikszentmihalyi research and using the analytical work of John Dewey. In this chapter we look through other lenses to find additional insights into what opens the door to the zone. I will be drawing from the seminal work of the Dutch cultural historian Johan Huizinga and also Carl Jung's pioneering study of archetypes. While the zone experience is a personal psychological phenomenon, it only occurs because of a supporting set of cultural conditions, and we need to understand them. Huizinga and Jung gave us very useful ways of examining the contributions of one's culture to the zone experience.

Huizinga's book that bears on the zone phenomenon is *Homo Ludens: A Study of the Play Element in Culture*, first published in 1939.[2] *Homo ludens* means "man the player." He began the foreword to his book with the sentence "A happier age than ours once made bold to call our species by the name of *Homo Sapiens.*" Huizinga lived through the horrors of World War I and wrote this book while Hitler's Germany was obviously launching large-scale war and "ethnic cleansing." These events led Huizinga to believe that *sapiens*, meaning wise or thinking, needed to be reconsidered as the label for our species. He did not intend *Homo ludens*—man the player—to replace it but wanted to promote other ways of viewing the essential nature of humankind. His work highlighted the centrality of play in human nature.

As a cultural historian, Huizinga recognized that play is older than civilization. And play is not exclusively a human phenomenon. Animals play, just as humans do. "[All] the basic factors of play, both individual and communal, are always present in animal life—to wit, contests, performances, exhibitions, challenges, preenings, struttings and showings-off, pretenses, and binding rules." Now that Huizinga has called our attention to that fact, we can easily suppose that the human animal had play before human culture emerged. Studying play from his historian's perspective, Huizinga concluded that play is a fundamental and pervasive feature of human nature. He shows readers the elements of play in human activities ranging from silly games to sacred rituals. As I summarize here the cultural elements of play that Huizinga identified and described, consider how well they match the psychological conditions for the zone experience.

VOLUNTARY

"First and foremost," Huizinga wrote, "all play is a voluntary activity. Play to order is no longer play: it could at best be but a forcible imitation of it."[3] Play is an activity freely chosen. As we have examined the zone experience so far, it requires concentrated attention on something of absorbing interest. And an absorbing interest in something, by definition, is freely given. Forced interest cannot be play. When we teach/coach/nurture from the blank-slate assumption—teaching for pat-answer responses—we run a serious risk of blocking the play element, and blocking the door to the zone. Huizinga's comment about "forcible imitation" of play took me back to some gym classes I had in high school when we were required to "play" some game or other that seemed to me just a required chore we had to endure. For me there was no play in such a game.

OUTSIDE ORDINARY LIFE

Play activity stands apart from everyday life. When we play, we step "out of 'real' life into a temporary sphere of activity with a disposition all its own," a reality of its own.[4]

Group play gives members a feeling of being "apart together." There is a bonding that flows from the experience of "sharing something important, of mutually withdrawing from the rest of the world and rejecting the usual norms. . . . Even in early childhood, the charm of play is enhanced by making a 'secret' out of it. This is for *us*, not for the 'others.'"[5]

Solo play, it seems to me, has the same qualities, but the bonding occurs between the individual and the play activity, such activities as reading, writing, being a collector, a hobbyist or specialist in certain things, a jogger, and even doing the crossword puzzle in the morning newspaper. One is "apart together" with the solo activity, outside ordinary life.

BOUNDARIES

Play is "a temporary activity satisfying in itself and ending there. . . . It is 'played out' within certain limits of time and place. . . . It plays itself to an end. . . . It contains its own course and meaning."[6] There is a clear distinction between play and not-play. All people can sort their activities into the categories of play and not-play and recognize that they step across a boundary when they move from one to the other. And we can expect that some activity identified as play by one person may be labeled as not-play by another. While some people commonly make a sharp distinction between their play and their work, others tell of the importance of finding play *in* their work, with no boundary between them. But everyone can identify which of their experiences are play and not-play.

FORM AND FUNCTION

Huizinga's broad view of play is evident in the following passages concerned with form and function in play.

[As soon as play begins] it at once assumes fixed form as a cultural phenomenon. Once played it endures as a new-found creation of the mind, a treasure to be retained in memory. It is transmitted, it becomes tradition.

The arena, the card-table, the magic circle, the temple, the stage, the screen, the tennis court, the court of justice, etc., all are in form and function play-grounds, i.e., forbidden spots, isolated, hedged round, hallowed, within which special rules obtain.

The words we used to denote the elements of play belong for the most part to aesthetics, terms with which we try to describe the effects of beauty: tension, poise, balance, contrast, variation, solution, resolution, etc. Play casts a spell over us; it is "enchanting," "captivating." It is invested with the noblest qualities we are capable of perceiving in things: rhythm and harmony.[7]

ORDER

"Inside the play-ground an absolute and peculiar order reigns. [Play] creates order, *is* order. Into an imperfect world and into the confusion of life it brings a temporary, a limited perfection. Play demands order absolute and supreme."[8] Play also depends on the order that comes from limitation and mastery of the self. The self serves the play and is submerged in it.

RULES

All play has rules. When puppies play together they know that play bites are allowed, but not strong bites. In games, the rules are absolutely binding, and if they're not followed, the play dies and the game is broken. "The umpire's whistle breaks the spell and sets 'real' life going again."[9]

Huizinga's analysis led him to the thesis that civilization in its early phases arose as play. The order and rules required for the backbone of civilization were derived from the mind-set and habits formed in play. "[Civilization] does not come *from* play like a babe detaching itself from the womb: it arises *in* and *as* play, and never leaves it."[10]

But civilization in our time has a lesser place for play. "As a civilization becomes more complex, more variegated and overladen, and as the technique of production and social life itself becomes more finely organized, the old cultural soil is gradually smothered under a rank layer of ideas, systems of thought and knowledge, doctrines, rules and regulations, moralities and conventions which have all lost touch with play. Civilization . . . then . . . has grown more serious; it assigns only a secondary place to playing."[11]

TENSION, NOT ANXIETY

"Among the general characteristics of play we reckoned tension and uncertainty. There is always the question: 'will it come off?'" In play, the stretching of ourselves toward some outcome always involves tension. "Baby reaching for a toy . . . , a little girl playing ball—all want to achieve something difficult, to succeed to end a tension." Tension and the resolution/release of it are part of all play, whether group or solitary play. Tense attention accompanies having something at stake, doing something chancy. "To dare, to take risks, to bear uncertainty, to endure tension—these are the essence of the play spirit."[12]

But the tension in play is not the emotion of fear or anxiety. Play captivates us and carries us along in a flow of finding what is needed to keep the play going and to get us closer to the goal we want. Fear breaks the spell of the game, takes us outside of it.

PASSION AND JOY

Emotions in the play experience can range from mild to intense. But there is always an emotional engagement in the play activity. At the more intense end, play can proceed "with the utmost seriousness, with an absorption, a devotion that passes into rapture. . . . Any game can at any time wholly run away with the players."[13] The joy of taking the risks and getting through them seems to be unlike any other satisfactions that happen outside of play. The joy in play is vital in that it renews our energy for the essential daily activities that are not-play.[14] As I am writing this paragraph about the passion in play, the World Cup games are in progress. One television commentator said that in England, where it was invented, "Soccer isn't a matter of life and death—it's more important than that."

These elements of play just summarized need to be present for the zone to happen. But, of course, not all play is zone-play. Most play does not rise to the level of zone-play.

LOVE AND ART AS PLAY

In her book *Art and Intimacy*, Ellen Dissanayake makes the argument that love and art are "our closest encounters with perfection, experiences that may be likened to ideas of heaven and bliss."[15] While she does not characterize love and art as zone-play, her language clearly conveys all the play elements we have been discussing here. Dissanayake asks us to consider how our "own less-than-perfect selves and souls and those of our lovers . . . can sometimes transcend [our] imperfections and create together in the act of physical love something divine and transfiguring."[16] "How miraculous that our mortal bodies in these inelegant actions should become the instruments for a composition of sensations that, at their best, awaken us to—or immerse us in—a reality transformed beyond anything imaginable in ordinary life."[17] She applies this language to making music and other art forms as well as to making love.

> Both love and art have the power to grasp us utterly and transport us from ordinary sweating, flailing, imperfect "reality" to an indescribable realm where we know and seem known by the sensibility of another, united in a continuing present, our usual isolation momentarily effaced.[18]

Of course, sexual and art activities often do not rise to the exalted level described here. Some people seem handicapped in making that journey to zone-play. Dissanayake sees the capacity for love and art as being grounded in mother-infant bonds of mutuality. Without such a beginning in life a child may be emotionally limited for a lifetime. "The same rhythmic-modal capacities and sensitivities that evolved to make possible mother-infant mutuality also create and sustain these other ties of intimacy, including adult lovemaking—to be distinguished from copulation as dining is distinguished from feeding, or as expressing gratitude to a game animal after one has killed it is distinguished from throwing it in the back of one's pickup."[19]

CULTURE'S ARENAS FOR ZONE/PLAY

The parallels between the outcomes of Csikszentmihalyi's psychological research and Huizinga's historical analysis are striking. The former drew on the subjective experiences of individuals—an inside view of the zone phenomenon—and the latter on observations of cultural patterns—an external view. But they are describing the same feature of human experience. It seems very likely that participants in the research conducted by Csikszentmihalyi and his colleagues could easily recognize that their zone experiences had all the characteristics of play as described by Huizinga. The participants would confirm that their zone experiences were: freely chosen activities, interludes outside of ordinary life; bounded in time, space, and purpose; following their own form, function, rules, and order; energized with tension and release; and sustained by the joy of taking risks and getting through them.

The elements of zone-play need to be present for the zone to happen. But because play is an essential component of culture—it is built in—it *will happen* when the circumstances are right. When people can freely choose to play and opportunities are given for the play, it will happen. If any of the elements of play described above are removed, the play will end. The zone will end. Huizinga's work helps us see the role of the culture in sponsoring the zone experience. Those of us who want to extend zone opportunities to more people more of the time have Huizinga's help in seeing ways to shape environments to foster the zone. The essential elements of play he identified can serve us as a checklist to use in examining the quality of our efforts to teach or coach with zone-promoting play activities.

PRACTICE-PLAY

Huizinga devoted most of his book to characterizing play of the quality that we would call the zone. As I said earlier, he saw the term *play* as applying to a range of activities from trivial to sacred and profound. A large part of the range of play is encompassed by zoning out and just-play, with a much smaller part being in the zone. But there is also play of another quality as well, not highlighted by Huizinga. It could be called practice-play. We are all aware of it but don't generally distinguish it from other play. It has all the features of zone-play except one: in practice-play the self is not submerged in the activity, as it is when we are in the zone. Practice-play is self-aware play. For example, when Andre is practicing chess moves by himself and consciously analyzing the moves and their potential effects on opponents, he is playing, and it feels like play, but he is likely to be in practice-play rather than caught up in the zone. And when Andre is in practice-play, he is not zoning out. Because he is teaching himself and practicing skills with the intention of improving them, his playing does not fit the definition of zoning out—a play form that is essentially for comfort, pleasure, and relaxation. Viewing play in this way, we'd have to say that practice-play makes up a very large portion of the play that serious players engage in. The tennis player working on her backhand racket control, relay runners perfecting the baton handoff, and all sorts of players honing their reflexes for their particular game are examples of practice-play. This is skill building that lays the basis for potential zone-play, skills that become so automatic that they will need no *conscious* attention when put to use in The Game that carries the potential for the zone experience.

When The Game is in process, the self must be immersed in it, out of consciousness, or the zone can't be entered. Andrew Cooper, in his book *Playing in the Zone: Exploring the Spiritual Dimensions of Sport*, quotes the professional archer Tim Strickland in this regard: "Your conscious mind always wants to help you, but usually it messes you up. But you can't just set it aside. . . . The thing you have to do is anchor it in technique. Then your unconscious mind, working with your motor memory, will take over the shooting for you."[20]

Play, Zone-Play, Practice-Play, and Not-Play

The general use of the term *play* is looser than that described by Huizinga. He mainly focused on what I am referring to as zone-play. Playing that doesn't rise to the level of zone-play is just-play. When my wife and I take a break to play cribbage in an afternoon, what we mainly do is just-play. Athletes often allude to the shift in their game from just-play to zone-play. Billie Jean King is famously reported to have said, "When it happens I want to stop the match and grab the microphone and shout, 'That's what it's all about!'"

One more thought about the relationship of play and the zone. When people are involved in zone-play and something happens to break the play, by definition the activity becomes not-play and not-zone. We have all seen this happen to ourselves and others. If people are engaged in a *game* when the zone-play is broken and the game continues, their actions become just-play or just a performance that is not-play, if we stay with Huizinga's definition of what is essentially play. Similarly, a musician or a craftsman, for example, who loses the zone-play but must continue performing is *just* performing, not playing. Through the years I have been aware of this shift in the playing of jazz musicians: when their zone ends for some reason, the performance shifts from creative improvisation to uninspired imitation, a shift that other musicians and some jazz fans can hear.

When we are in the zone, our experiencing of it is something we want to continue. We neither *want* nor *choose* to end the zone. The end of it just happens when circumstances stop supporting the zone. When we lose play and go into not-play, we do not shift automatically into zoning out. As I see it, zoning out is different from not-play activity. Zoning out is voluntary, a choice. When the zone ends and we find ourselves in not-play, we can *choose* to continue the activity in a zoning-out mode, a nonstretching alternative to the zone. When the zone is gone, the musician, for example, has the choice of shifting into just-play or zoning out, or continuing the performance as not-play, or ending the performance. So zoning out is an order of play, but it is a quality of play that does not promote growth and development as does zone-play.

THE DARK SIDE OF PLAY

In his book, Huizinga offered no criteria for making the distinction between play of zone quality and what I am calling zoning out and practice-play. He did write about a dark side of play, using very harsh language to describe what he called *false play*:

> Modern social life is being dominated to an ever-increasing extent by a quality that has something in common with play and yields the illusion of a strongly developed play-factor. This quality [is a] blend of adolescence and barbarity which has been rampant all over the world for the last two or three decades. . . . [It presents itself as an] insatiable thirst for trivial recreation and crude sensationalism. . . .
>
> The club [as a vehicle for play] is a very ancient institution, but it is a disaster when whole nations turn into clubs, for these, besides promoting the precious qualities of friendship and loyalty, are also hotbeds of sectarianism, intolerance, suspicion, superciliousness and

quick to defend any illusion that flatters self-love or group-consciousness. We have seen great nations losing every shred of honour, all sense of humour, the very idea of decency and fair play. . . . True civilization will always demand fair play.[21]

As I see it, what Huizinga has described in these passages is play that has emerged or been co-opted in conditions of low morality. Just as Csikszentmihalyi sees flow as having no moral compass, Huizinga said play "lies outside morals. In itself it is neither good nor bad."[22] Let's consider the phenomenon of play "outside morals" with the example of warfare.

WAR AS DARK PLAY

War Is a Force That Gives Us Meaning is the title of a book by Chris Hedges, who served for years as a war correspondent in Central America, the West Bank and Gaza, the Sudan and Yemen, the Gulf War, Bosnia and Kosovo, and other conflicts.[23] He wrote the book, drawing on his experiences, to find sense in the enduring attraction of war despite the horrors that always accompany it. Hedges saw that "war forms its own culture. . . . [War] is a drug . . . peddled by myth-makers—historians, war correspondents, filmmakers, novelists, and the state—all of whom endow it with qualities it often does possess: excitement, exoticism, power, chances to rise above our small stations in life." Hedges concluded that "[war] can give us purpose and a reason for living. . . . , a resolve, a cause. It allows us to be noble."[24]

Let's consider Hedges's analysis in light of Huizinga's criteria for what constitutes play. Can we say that the attraction of war is the attraction of play? According to Huizinga, play consists of activities that are interludes outside of ordinary life, requiring undistracted concentration; bounded in time, space, and purpose; following their own form, function, rules, and order; energized with tension and release; and sustained by the joy of taking risks and getting through them. All these criteria for play fit the activities of war. Huizinga had one other criterion: play is an activity freely chosen. Does that one fit war? Hedges suggests how it is that people freely choose to participate in war: "The prospect of war is exciting. Many young men, schooled in the notion that war is the ultimate definition of manhood, that only at war will they be tested and proven, that they can discover their worth as human beings in battle, willingly join the great enterprise."[25]

America's entrance into World War II provides a striking example of the importance of free choice in participation in war. Before Pearl Harbor, even those Americans with friends and relatives in Europe caught up in war with the Nazis remained largely isolationist. It was "Europe's war." America was seen as blessed by being thousands of miles away. That sentiment changed overnight when the Japanese, Germany's ally, bombed Hawaii. With America attacked, its citizens freely committed themselves to the war against the Axis powers.

In our time, when suicide bombings are reported daily in our newspapers, we have continual evidence of the moral poverty that convinces people to "freely choose" to make horrendous war.

That the zone phenomenon is precipitated by war events and that humans are zone seekers by nature is borne out by people's reports of war experiences. We all know war veterans who tell stories that have the ring of zone experiences. I once had a neighbor, retired from a career in retail sales, who rode with me on a four-hour round-trip in my car. We didn't have many common interests that I knew of, and I wondered as I was picking him up what sorts of things we might talk about. He was a talker, and I wanted to steer the talk in a direction that would interest me. I knew that he had served in the army in Europe during World War II and that the memories of his service experiences were important to him. So I asked him to tell me about them, and he responded eagerly. In those four hours he was more animated and enthusiastic than I had ever seen him. The telling of his stories seemed to put him in the zone. It became evident that his war experience as a whole, despite the horrors that were part of it, was a time of zone experiences that made the rest of his life pale in comparison. From what he told me about his time in combat, I can now see that the conditions needed to make the zone possible, as identified by Huizinga and Csikszentmihalyi, were all there. And they were largely absent from the rest of his life.

The *quality* of play we engage in defines us. From the perspective that Huizinga offers us, intelligence and moral character have to do with the width or narrowness of our zone seeking—for example, socially responsible *versus* selfish goals and actions. Csikszentmihalyi makes a strong case that passive leisure, such as watching television, is far more common for many people than active leisure, to the detriment of the health of the culture.[26] Conscience and self-discipline are essential to steering play behavior constructively toward moral ends. Huizinga's view of the quality of play illuminates how morality, ethics, and esthetics are different facets of the same thing.

THE DARK SIDE OF SPORTS

The surge of excitement in war has its counterpart in sports. Andrew Cooper put it this way in his book *Playing in the Zone*:

> [Sport's] power to move us is as much a cause for concern as it is for celebration. Critics who rail against its pathologies are for the most part justified. It is a truism to say that the world of sport is a circus of greed, corruption, hypocrisy, and exploitation. Sports are indeed tools for the stimulation of frivolous appetites and base emotions. They provide a false sense of relief from the real problems of powerlessness, anonymity, and isolation that are imposed by our social institutions. They are in a playground of distraction and childish regression.[27]

We are zone seekers, whether we are looking for zone or zoning-out experiences. We take the initiative to find the experiences. But, as Huizinga reminds us, something *beyond* our conscious intentions calls us out to play. Play as a cultural phenomenon draws us into its activity forms. These play forms that call us are realities that exist apart from our specific experiencing of them. Church, casino, ballfield, movie house, MP3 player, shopping mall, theme park, or wilderness—all are arenas for different forms of play, from sacred to profane. They call and we respond, more attracted to some of them than others. Whatever arenas we choose, we are game players by nature. Zone/game playing keeps us in touch with our investigative side, and zoning out/game playing provides respite or comfort in an indifferent world.

ARCHETYPES SHAPE THE ZONE

Carl Jung gave us still another way of seeing how our culture shapes zone pathways, and why some of them attract us and others do not. This was his work with archetypes. Jung's formulation of the psychological types, explained in chapter 3, offers one set of lenses by which to view and make sense of human experience. It is a system concerned with *conscious* experience. Much more of Jung's work was about the unconscious side of human existence. One part of his work on unconscious mental activity, his study of archetypes, is particularly helpful in our understanding of the zone phenomenon. Jung's view was that each person's unconscious mind can be divided into a personal unconscious and a collective unconscious. The personal unconscious is a storehouse of memories and images from one's experiences that are out of awareness. The collective unconscious is the part that underlies and has no dependence on the person's unique subjective experiences. It is a deeper structure that is common to most or all people, passed down through the generations, from elder to younger, with their having little or no awareness of it being passed. It consists of cultural features, what Jung called *archetypes*, that provide continuity in human nature, forms that we accept unconsciously as givens and pay no attention to until we are prompted to notice them—and even then sometimes we can't see them. It is a major part of us, but it existed long before each of us came on the scene.[28]

Jung used the term *archetypes* to refer to the content of the collective unconscious. Archetypes are forms or patterns of experiencing, ways of being in the world. They are not the substance of our lives, but only the forms we inherit, within which we play out the substance in our individual ways. Archetypes are the structures of the stories we live, not the scripts of the stories. The stories show us ways of functioning in the culture. Through the study of the various religions, myths, legends, and fairy tales, dreams and historical accounts, Jung identified many archetypal themes and wrote descriptions of some of them. He said there are as many archetypes as there are common life situations. The commonalities we see across cultures, and through the centuries, are accounted for by archetypes.

Because archetypes are unconscious forms, we necessarily alter them when we bring them into consciousness to talk or write about them. That is, our descriptions of archetypes are colored by the personal experiences—conscious and unconscious—we must use in composing the descriptions. The characterizations of archetypes I offer in the paragraphs that follow certainly have been filtered through my own personal experiences.

For most of us, the first archetypes to come into our awareness are Mother and Father. Preschool children play "house": "You be Daddy and I'll be Mommy. Jan, you be the baby." And they play out the roles, and the behaviors, values, and attitudes they believe go with each role. No one had to "teach" them how to play house. The archetypes of Mother and Father were never articulated to them. How they shape the roles will depend a lot on the experiences they have in their own families. The young children playing house may correct each other according to their views of the roles: "That's not the way to be Mommy." But each of the children already had the archetypal forms of Mother and Father in their psychological makeup as structures within which they played out their version.

Mother and Father remain powerful archetypes in anyone's life. Many girls find their life's calling in the Mother archetype, and many boys find their identity in the Father archetype. But being a mother is different from being a Mother. One can be a biological mother without identifying with the Mother archetype. Someone who is a mother—and delights in being a mother—may find her essential identity and fulfillment in an archetypal theme quite different from Mother. Examining the major archetypal themes and their bearing on the zone experience is the subject of the rest of this chapter.

Jung and others who have taken up his work have identified and written about many archetypes in the context of explaining human behavior and development and in conducting therapy. Some of the archetypes most commonly referred to, besides Mother and Father, are Warrior and Amazon, Magician, Hero, Eternal Boy, Crusader, Trickster, Wise Man/Woman or Sage, the Innocent, and Wanderer or Seeker. Some who study human development in terms of archetypes hold the view that we all take on different archetypes at different stages of our development, in a linear or spiral way, as we work toward wholeness.[29] Others believe we each identify with one dominant archetype and that our development involves finding clarity in and mature use of the strengths in the one archetype, along with skills of working constructively with people of other archetypes. The latter represents my own view, which has been strongly influenced by the work of Tad and Noreen Guzie.[30] Their approach to the archetypes drew on the work of one of Jung's students, Toni Wolff.[31]

The Guzies' main thesis was that the archetypes provide powerful insights into where and how people find their *identity* and *fulfillment*. They identified four male and four female archetypes they called "the great stories." The male archetypes are Father, Seeker, Warrior, and Sage. The four female archetypes are Mother, Companion, Amazon, and Mediatrix. In their view, other archetypes influence people's lives, but they act as modifications or variations of these major ones. Following the lead of Wolff, the Guzies see each set of archetypes as polar opposites on two axes:

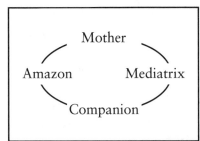 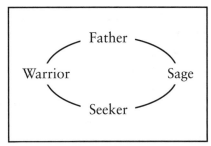

Mother and Companion, both fundamentally focused on *personal* relationships, are opposites in how they engage in relationships. The same is true for Father and Seeker. The other four archetypes essentially take a *nonpersonal* approach to events and relationships, but they are focused on opposite kinds of goals. So we have a personal axis and a nonpersonal axis with contrasting archetypes on each axis.

The female and male archetypes in the same positions in the boxes above, such as Amazon and Warrior, have much in common. In their descriptions of the archetypes, the Guzies identify both the commonalities and the gender differences in the male- and female-paired archetypes. For my purposes of highlighting the links between archetypal motivations and values and the zone phenomenon, I have chosen to combine the male and the female counterparts and work with just four archetypal themes that apply to either gender. Mother and Father combine into the Nurturer; I use the term Adventurer in combining Companion and Seeker; I have taken Warrior to cover both male and female; and I have used Sage to refer to both males and females of that archetype. In using Warrior and Sage to cover both sexes, I am not submerging the female attributes into the male. I just see Warrior and Sage as more unisex than Amazon and Mediatrix. I tried other terms for this axis, but they did not work as well to convey the archetypes. So I work with these four:

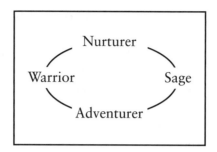

In the descriptions that follow on the next page, I have drawn liberally on the Guzies' phrasing, and I am very grateful to them for their thoughtful work. The bulleted descriptors are laid out in parallel fashion, to highlight the contrasts. Comparing the descriptions line by line shows the contrasts.

There is an assumption underlying the archetypes to keep in mind as you read the descriptions. In no respect is any of the four better than the others, that is, more valuable to the culture. If each were not essential to human culture, it would not have evolved and been sustained throughout the millennia. Affinity for one archetype or another says nothing about a person's intelligence or other gifts and talents. There is no reason to suppose that the Sage is wiser than, say, the Nurturer, or vice versa. The archetype patterns represent four different kinds of wisdom, four approaches to life in which to be wise or foolish, mature or ineffective.

I believe these descriptions catch the essence of the archetypes, but they are bare bones compared with those the Guzies wrote. Their descriptions also included personal development and relationship issues. Over a period of years, they introduced over two thousand people to the archetypes, along with Jung's psychological types, in two-day retreat seminars. They found that nearly all of their clients could solidly identify a best-fit psychological type for themselves (using Myers-Briggs Type Indicator reports, along with dialogue about the reports) and recognize the archetype that was the main influence in their lives. The Guzies also found that people's psychological type preferences did not predict the archetypes they identified with. That is, any type could be linked with any archetype; the two sets of Jungian categories were essentially independent.[32] Moreover, the Guzies' data showed that one's archetype orientation did not dictate choices of jobs or specific life roles. For example, people who

The Nurturer finds identity and fulfillment in:

- Relationships in which they can play out a protective-parental role
- Cherishing, aiding, rescuing, protecting those who need assistance
- Doing *for* others, bringing people along, promoting their development
- Directing things in traditional ways
- Protecting hearth and home, aiming for security and comfort
- Conserving group values; directing and managing people toward them
- Giving to others, irrespective of their own needs

The Nurturer's weak spots: over-nurturing, causing dependency, smothering; not trusting the other's strength; being authoritarian

The Warrior finds identity and fulfillment in:

- Accomplishing tangible things in the larger world, beyond close kin
- Competing successfully; excelling in all chosen tasks
- Setting doable goals and efficiently getting things done
- Winning and acquiring; bringing home the trophy
- Prodding, inspiring themselves and others to do and be the best
- Being tuned in to power structures and having their own positions of power

The Warrior's weak spots: ruthlessness, winning at any cost; acquiring to excess

The Adventurer finds identity and fulfillment in:

- Peer relationships in which they can play out a companion role, not a nurturing one
- Freedom in relationships; freedom of self-expression
- Doing *with* others, finding mutually interesting adventures
- Exploring, experiencing, taking risks
- Rejecting hearth and home, heading out over the next horizon; promoting change
- Finding new places, people, things; making one's distinctive mark
- Sharing with others— kindred individualists

The Adventurer's weak spots: fickleness, abandoning a relationship when the next horizon calls; being self-absorbed

The Sage finds identity and fulfillment in:

- Understanding the inner world of intangible experience
- Searching for meanings and explanations; bringing things to light
- Figuring out what is worth doing, what things and actions are worthy of support
- Having expertise; explaining and interpreting things to others
- Probing into complexities; trying to figure out how things work and why
- Influencing those who shape policy and who have power and control

The Sage's weak spots: being deluded about one's expertise, a buffoon; being unfocused identified with the Nurturer archetype were no more likely to have children than others. Virtually all roles in life can be played out in a Nurturing way, not just the management of a biological family. While the responsibility of being a parent requires nurturing, it can be approached in many ways. An example I know of is a single mother of a six-year-old daughter. The mother clearly identified with the Adventuring archetype. When she learned about the archetypes, she realized, in retrospect, that she had been rearing her daughter as a companion in her adventure in motherhood. It seemed to be working just fine for both mother and daughter.

While most of the Guzies' clients identified themselves clearly in one of the major archetypes, some felt that more than one was at work in them; one archetype was dominant, but another played a secondary role. For example, a Nurturer with Warrior as a secondary archetype. As I came to use the system with my own clients, I suggested they consider the four archetypes as placed on the face of a clock: Nurturer at twelve o'clock, Sage at three, Adventurer at six, and Warrior at nine. Then each person could find himself or herself at one of the twelve clock positions. Nurturer with Warrior as a secondary archetype would be at eleven o'clock. Warrior with Nurturer secondary would be at ten o'clock, and so on. I identify myself as a four o'clock Sage. My wife identifies herself as an eleven o'clock Nurturer. That puts us almost directly across the clockface, with nearly opposite archetype orientations. Our contrasting archetype values and motivations are something we experience every day. We feel very grateful to have the knowledge of the archetypes helping us in dealing with our differences.

Using the clock model, a person could not have an archetype combination of, say, Warrior and Sage. They are across the clock from each other, polar opposites with contrasting values. The person may feel the pull of both Warrior and Sage, but the most likely explanation is that the person is one or the other archetype and is living in a environment that contrasts with his or her archetype. For example, many business settings reward Warrior traits, irrespective of the archetypes of the people employed there. A Sage in that environment could easily identify with both archetypes. Knowing about archetype values could help the Sage find ways to make the job setting—with its Warrior values—more suited to Sage strengths. Or understanding the archetype differences could highlight the need for a job change. Policymakers in some organizations are now using the archetype concepts to study the organizational culture with the intent of making the workplace more congenial to all four archetypes and more supportive of the value patterns represented in them. All four are usually represented in any organization with a membership larger than about ten people. And the Guzies found that people from all walks of life distribute themselves around the clockface.

ARCHETYPES AS ZONE INDICATORS

Finally, we come to the relationship of archetype and zone. Look again at the lists containing the four archetype descriptions. If the phrase in each that reads "They find their identity and fulfillment in" were replaced with "They find their zone experiences in," we would have a good general guideline for using archetype concepts in helping people open the zone door. The phrases that describe the weak spots of each archetype—listed at the bottom of each box—give clues about the outcomes of what I would call zone deprivation. People's behaviors reflect their archetypal weak spots when they are not growing, not maturing. The zone experience fosters growth and development through the process of its inherent investigative minding. The zone experience provides confidence and, little by little, strengthens the constructive elements of our archetypal traits. Little by little it provides enough security to let us be open and sensitive to positive archetype values beyond our own. My view is that when we are deprived of zone opportunities, the less mature aspects of our archetype become more prominent in our behavior.

I began this chapter with the statement that *when* the zone happens and the *form* it takes depend on forces in the culture and in our genes that support and shape it. Our "great stories" are one of those forces that shape the zone. From the Jungian point of view, we don't choose our great stories, they choose us. We are born with a predisposition to take on one of the great stories. My wife's testimony is a case in point. From her earliest memories, and from what she was told about herself as a very young girl, she had a passionate interest in nurturing creatures—stray dogs and cats, birds and any other wild things that needed rescuing. She was the only one of her family of two parents and five girls who had this strong need to nurture. And she knew in first grade that she would become a teacher of first graders when she grew up. Which is what happened. Today, years after her retirement, she still gets in the zone tutoring (Nurturing) primary grade children who are behind in reading. And the zone she experiences in working with them is contagious; the children feel it and make amazing gains because they find their zone, too.

Getting a sense of one's natural great story early in life is a gift that doesn't happen to many of us. It could happen more often, I believe, if we were more alert to archetypal patterns and characteristics. When we see the zone happening to a young person, that event may be evidence of archetypal values finding expression. The kind of zone the person is experiencing, and the context of it, could be clues pointing to an archetypal path of development to explore. For example, does the zone event appear to be expressing Adventurer values or Sage values? What are some Adventurer or Sage resources we could supply that might help sustain the zone experience? The clear objective is to help the zone to continue because it is such a powerful vehicle for growth and development. The archetype way of viewing experience cautions us to observe, very closely observe, the budding interests of young people that are revealed in the zone events they experience and try to avoid pushing an agenda that comes out of our *own* archetype and may be a mismatch for their archetypes. For example, anyone who has ever attended a Little League baseball game has seen a Warrior parent in the bleachers loudly pushing his or her child into Warrior values, whether or not they are consistent with the child's own archetypal bent. At the same game one could see a Nurturing parent cautioning the Warrior coach to "tone down the tough stuff" or "give every kid a chance to play" because "skill development and character development are more the focus of Little League than winning or losing the game."

As parents, coaches, or mentors, we need to remember that zone-play is freely chosen, voluntary. If we prescribe for the other person an approach to life events that is not consistent with the person's psychological type or the archetypal values emerging in them, we block the zone rather than promote it. And when people of different archetype orientations find themselves at odds over policies or actions, the constructive way to tackle the problem is as fellow investigators looking for common ground.

5

ZONE DOORS, ZONE PATHWAYS

D oes knowing a person's kind of mental processing—her psychological type—give clues to the nature of what I am calling the zone pathway for that person? I believe it does, and I began drafting some answers to the question by reflecting on people whose zone experiencing I have observed and whose type I know. Then I shifted to people I know well who appear to share similar zone experiences but who are different in type. And I also thought of people who share the same type but seem to have quite different zone fields. All of this pondering helped me form some hypotheses to answer the question.

ZONE AND TYPE

Here are some examples of cases that occurred to me in the process. Two gifted visual artists I know, who are well respected by their peers, often find the zone in their work. They are opposites in their types of mental processing—ENFP and ISTJ—and their approaches to their work seem to reflect their type preferences. The ENFP, who works mainly in painting with acrylics and in mixed media, experiments continually and finds her zone through the novel effects she is able to create. Once she has achieved an effect she likes, she is drawn to find a new variation, something that feels fresh to her. Many of her creations sell well and many go back from the gallery to her storeroom for lack of buyer interest. The gallery director asks her to produce more of the sort that sell well, but she says she has to follow her muse, and her muse is not influenced by the economics, the sales response. The ISTJ works in sheet metal sculpting, mainly with copper and brass sheeting that he cuts with a torch then bends and mounts for wall hanging. In starting as a professional metal sculptor, he tried various forms and approaches, and when he found those that sold well, he stayed with that style. He finds the zone in improving and perfecting the techniques that are appreciated by customers. He has a steady demand for his creations from interior designers who mainly furnish office buildings and hotels.

Read the ENFP and ISTJ descriptions on the next page line by line to see the grounding of the two artistic pathways.

In some respects, the example of these two artists helps break the stereotype of what sort of person is drawn to and can be successful in fine arts, or any occupation. These two artists have the same occupation, at least on the surface, but they find a different niche in it. And the zone they find there is distinctly different, in line with their psychological type.

Another example of occupational niche in relation to type comes from a colleague of mine who is a consultant to organizations. Working with a large firm of certified public accountants, he had administered the MBTI instrument and explained the type concepts to a number of employees. He told them that their managers knew about type and were open to discussing any issues they individually might have about making their work setting a better fit to their type of mental processing. My friend told me about one CPA, Eric, who had a solid relationship with his manager and took the offer to talk with his boss. He told the manager about insights he got from learning his MBTI profile. Eric said it helped him get clarity on the nature of stresses he had been feeling in recent months. While he was proud of

ENFP

Warmly enthusiastic PLANNERS OF CHANGE; imaginative, individualistic; pursue inspiration with impulsive energy; seek to understand and inspire others. Having extraverted INTUITION as the strongest mental process, they are at their best when caught up in the enthusiasm of a project. They value:

- The surge of inspirations, the pull of emerging possibilities
- A life of variety, people, and warm relationships
- An exciting outer life fueled by imagination
- Following their insights wherever they lead
- Finding meanings behind the facts
- Creativity, originality, a fresh perspective
- An optimistic, positive, enthusiastic view of life
- Flexibility and openness
- Exploring, devising, and trying out new things
- Open-ended opportunities and options
- Freedom from the requirement of being practical
- Learning through action, variety, and discovery
- A belief that any obstacles can be overcome
- A focus on people's potentials
- Brainstorming to solve problems
- Work made light and playful by inspiration

ISTJ

Analytical MANAGER OF FACTS AND DETAILS; dependable, conservative, painstaking, systematic, decisive, stable. Having introverted SENSING as the strongest mental process, they are at their best when charged with organizing and maintaining data and material important to others and themselves. They value:

- Steady, systematic work yielding reliable results
- Practical systems and organization
- A controlled outer life grounded in the present
- Following a sensible path, based on experience
- Concrete, exact, immediately useful facts, skills
- Consistency, familiarity, the tried and true
- A concrete, present-day view of life
- Working to a plan and schedule
- Preserving and enjoying things of proven value
- Proven paths, commonsense options
- Freedom from emotionality in deciding things
- Learning through planned, sequential teaching
- Skepticism; wanting to read the fine print first
- A focus on hard work, perseverance
- Logical, detached problem solving
- Serious, focused work and play

his accounting skills and got satisfaction from helping people with their accounting issues, parts of his job were seriously dragging him down. The MBTI reported Eric's type as ENFP and he totally agreed with the profile. He and others in his group had shared their MBTI results, and he was the only one who wasn't an ST type. As his group talked about type in relation to their jobs, he realized the technical aspects of accounting were drawing on his Sensing and Thinking processes—definitely not his preferred processing skills. The manager was responsive and saw a constructive way to harness the ENFP energy. Within a few weeks a new role was created within the department that fit Eric very well: new account development. It was very much a customer relations job. His colleagues were glad to pass on to Eric some aspects of their work they didn't enjoy. A glance back to the ENFP and the ISTJ type descriptions, with this example in mind, gives an idea of why the solution was a good one. Eric later reported that he was much more energized and satisfied with his new assignment.

In my experience, even a rough estimate of a person's type can sometimes lead to identifying where his or her zone may lie. One instance came about when I was asked to work with a middle school faculty to coach them in using type as they planned their teaching lessons. It was a school for students identified as having emotional handicaps and other learning problems requiring special instruction. After I had helped the teachers figure out their own types, we turned to the topic of student motivation in relation to type. Students' motivation for schoolwork was a central concern for many of the teachers. Later, in small groups, we discussed individual students and how the teachers might estimate their types. I wanted to show them that motivation problems could be type related.

In one small faculty group, during first period, the teachers talked about a boy that three of them knew. I asked the three to guess with my help what the boy's type might be. They agreed on E, N, T, and J characteristics. The teacher who had the boy in class for three hours of each day described the problems he presented. She said his classroom behavior mostly alternated between bullying and sulking, and he did not do his assignments. I had them read a description of the ENTJ type. Then I explained that people of this type, with extraverted Thinking as the center post of their personality, would want, above all else, to put their own version of logical order into their environment.

I highlighted in the type description the phrase that ENTJs thrive on being in charge. When I asked the teacher what opportunities the boy had to be in charge of anything, she said, "None. He can't even manage his own behavior, so how could he be made responsible for anything else?" I suggested she try to find something he could be put in charge of and let me know the result.

At the close of the day that teacher found me and excitedly said, "You are not going to believe what happened with Duane! On the way back to my room this morning I thought of something for him to be in charge of. We have a classroom library that students check out books from, and I don't do a very good job of managing it. I asked Duane if he would manage it, and he almost instantly became a different child. No bullying, no pouting, just cooperation and doing his work all day. And he figured out how to run the library efficiently."

Of course this small change in Duane was just an opening into the complex task of helping him get onto his path. But I believe the results convinced the teacher that understanding type was a worthwhile investment of her time and energy. And I believe the teacher began to get a glimmer of a key principle of type development theory: to get a responsible behavior from someone acting irresponsibly, entice their dominant function, in this case extraverted Thinking, into something constructive. The type descriptions clearly suggest the kinds of responsibilities each type will *want* to undertake, will need to undertake, to find psychological nourishment. I never talked with or observed Duane. But my guess is he found the zone for a time that day.

ZONE, TYPE, AND ARCHETYPE

The interlacing of type and zone is evident in these stories. Estimating a person's potential zone by his type was a theme of chapter 3. Estimating potential zone conditions from one's archetype orientation was introduced in chapter 4. Here in chapter 5 I am combining type and archetype to suggest zone doorways and zone paths. I have chosen to do this by using brief descriptions of people I have become acquainted with who:

- are confident of their type, in MBTI terms;
- have told me which of the four major archetypes they identify with most strongly; and
- have told me where they find the zone in their work and in their leisure time.

Let me start with an illustration of four nurses who are all ISTJs but differ by archetype orientation. While, as you might suppose, about two-thirds of nurses in general are Feeling types, ISTJ is the most common type among nurses who are not Feeling types. The niche within nursing chosen by these four individuals reflects their type and archetype orientation.

Here's a review of the priorities of ISTJs in general. We can assume that nearly all are true of the four nurses described below.

- Steady, systematic work yielding reliable results
- Practical systems and organization
- A controlled outer life grounded in the present
- Following a sensible path, based on experience
- Concrete, exact, immediately useful facts, skills
- Consistency, familiarity, the tried and true
- A concrete, present-day view of life
- Working to a plan and schedule
- Preserving and enjoying things of proven value
- Proven paths, commonsense options
- Freedom from emotionality in deciding things
- Learning through planned, sequential teaching
- Skepticism; wanting to read the fine print first
- A focus on hard work, perseverance
- Quiet, logical, detached problem solving
- Serious and focused work and play

Let's also take another look at the four archetype orientations.

EXAMPLE: FOUR ISTJ NURSES DIFFERING BY ARCHETYPE

The example I have in mind of the *Nurturer* ISTJ is a home healthcare nurse. She visits patients who need daily attention with medications

The Nurturer finds identity and fulfillment in:

- Relationships in which they can play out a protective-parental role
- Cherishing, aiding, rescuing, protecting those who need assistance
- Doing *for* others, bringing people along, promoting their development
- Directing things in traditional ways
- Protecting hearth and home, aiming for security and comfort
- Conserving group values; directing and managing people toward them
- Giving to others, irrespective of their own needs

The Nurturer's weak spots: overnurturing, causing dependency, smothering; not trusting the other's strength; being authoritarian

The Warrior finds identity and fulfillment in:

- Accomplishing tangible things in the larger world, beyond close kin
- Competing successfully; excelling in all chosen tasks
- Setting doable goals and efficiently getting things done
- Winning and acquiring; bringing home the trophy
- Prodding, inspiring themselves and others to do and be the best
- Being tuned in to power structures and having their own positions of power

The Warrior's weak spots: ruthlessness, winning at any cost; acquiring to excess

The Adventurer finds identity and fulfillment in:

- Peer relationships in which they can play out a companion role, not a nurturing one
- Freedom in relationships. Freedom of self-expression
- Doing *with* others, finding mutually interesting adventures
- Exploring, experiencing, taking risks
- Rejecting hearth and home, heading out over the next horizon; promoting change
- Finding new places, people, things; making one's distinctive mark.
- Sharing with others–kindred individualists

The Adventurer's weak spots: fickleness, abandoning a relationship when the next horizon calls; being self-absorbed

The Sage finds identity and fulfillment in:

- Understanding the inner world of intangible experience
- Searching for meanings and explanations; bringing things to light
- Figuring out what is worth doing, what things and actions are worthy of support
- Having expertise; explaining and interpreting things to others
- Probing into complexities; trying to figure out how things work and why
- Influencing those who shape policy and who have power and control

The Sage's weak spots: being deluded about one's expertise, a buffoon; being unfocused and personal care but can live at home. Most are elderly. She reports getting special satisfaction in taking charge, planning out, and helping them organize and manage themselves so they can stay independent.

The *Sage* ISTJ nurse started out her career as a regular hospital floor nurse but realized the work was too emotionally draining. She found her niche in intensive/critical care nursing. Reflecting on why that role was so satisfying for her, she gave two reasons. First, she was drawn to the machinery, the life-support equipment that was expensive and needed regular, conscientious attention. She studied the equipment and became recognized as the resident authority on its functioning. Second, the fact that her patients were usually unconscious or heavily sedated meant she could concentrate on the equipment side of their care that gave her challenges that weren't stressful.

The *Adventurer* ISTJ nurse is a serious outdoorsman. To protect his opportunities to be out with fellow hikers and boaters, locally and in various parts of the country, he mainly works the night shift in twenty-four-hour walk-in clinics or hospital emergency rooms and prefers twelve-hour shifts, three days a week, which leaves him four days off each week to pursue his nonjob interests. In fifteen years as a nurse, he has worked in ten different facilities, with fairly long breaks in between jobs to allow for his trips. He is regarded as a highly competent nurse and never has any difficulty finding a new position. He prefers working in emergency medicine because he enjoys "being a problem solver more that a caregiver."

The *Warrior* ISTJ is the chief office nurse for a plastic surgeon. She assists him in surgical procedures that can be done in the office and she essentially runs the technical side of the doctor's practice—that is, seeing that all the necessary medical resources are well supplied and properly organized and cared for. Informally, she acknowledges, she runs the office, and, in many respects "protects the doctor from intrusions and diversions that often plague a doctor in private practice."

I did not ask these four specifically about the zone conditions they find in their work. But they all expressed satisfaction with their differing nursing roles. Clearly, both type and archetype are reflected in their chosen specialties. Each plays out ISTJ values and priorities in different ways, in line with his or her archetype orientation.

PROFILES OF ZONE CONDITIONS BY TYPE AND ARCHETYPE

Fortunately, I have a large file of people to draw from to provide examples of all the sixty-four type/archetype combinations. For each, I have information on what takes them to the zone in both their work and leisure activities. Where I have more than one example of each, such as *Nurturer* ISFJ, I chose to include here the one that seemed to me to offer the features most representative of the group.

Here are the sixty-four profiles. I have arranged the tables by type function preference combinations—ST, SF, NF, NT—because those preferences most relate to occupational choices.

The brief comments from sixty-four people presented in the tables are, of course, only suggestive of zone pathways. Reading all sixty-four straight through may not suit you. But I do suggest you read enough to catch the patterns. And watch for interesting contrasts; for example, consider side by side the descriptions of opposite types, such as ENTP and ISFJ, to note how archetype values are pursued differently, and how they affect the sources of zone experiences.

ISTJ
Analytical Manager of Facts and Details

They value:

- Steady, systematic work yielding reliable results
- Practical systems and organization
- A controlled outer life grounded in the present
- Following a sensible path, based on experience
- Concrete, exact, immediately useful facts and skills
- Consistency, familiarity, the tried and true
- A concrete, present-day view of life
- Working to a plan and schedule

- Preserving and enjoying things of proven value
- Proven paths, commonsense options
- Freedom from emotionality in deciding things
- Learning through planned, sequential teaching
- Skepticism; wanting to read the fine print first
- A focus on hard work, perseverance
- Quiet, logical, detached problem solving
- Serious and focused work and play

NURTURER ISTJ Andrea: Internet sales	SAGE ISTJ Ed: Consultant/Trainer	ADVENTURER ISTJ Al: War college teacher	WARRIOR ISTJ Ginny: Graphic designer
Work zone conditions: Quiet, well-organized space, no interruptions, working toward a firm deadline with familiar content.	**Work zone conditions:** Researching, preparing, then sharing training materials, following a clear plan, with no distractions and all needed materials at hand.	**Work zone conditions:** Time to concentrate in an orderly setting, without interruptions, honing lesson plans and exercises to make them more effective.	**Work zone conditions:** Uninterrupted time in a calm environment to organize my thoughts, plan, and follow my plan. Completing one project before starting another.
Leisure zone conditions: Hands-on activities—home improvements, gardening, cleaning—all such activities I can be absorbed in and that produce visible results in short order.	**Leisure zone conditions:** I devour information about all sorts of things, like researching what bike to buy, deciding what book to select, and what plants to put were in my garden, then planting them properly.	**Leisure zone conditions:** RV camping, being out in unspoiled nature, visiting as many of the wilderness sites, national parks, and war memorials as we can get to and hike through.	**Leisure zone conditions:** Anything that has to do with organizing and accomplishment, such as cleaning and yard work. Exercise does it—it is measurable and produces results.

ISTP
Practical ANALYZERS

They value:

- A reserved outer life
- Having a concrete, present-day view of life
- Clear, exact facts—a large storehouse of them
- Looking for efficient, least effort solutions
- Knowing how mechanical things work, based on experience
- Pursuing interests in depth, such as hobbies
- Collecting things of interest
- Working on problems that respond to detached, sequential analysis and adaptability
- Freedom from organizational constraints sequential analysis and adaptability
- Independence and self-management
- Spontaneous hands-on learning experiences
- Having useful technical expertise
- Critical analysis as a means to improving things

NURTURER ISTP	**SAGE** ISTP	**ADVENTURER** ISTP	**WARRIOR** ISTP
Zach: High school history teacher	Will: Clergyman, Salvation Army officer	John: Financial planning consultant	Georgia: Mechanical engineer
Work zone conditions: Digging out obscure curiosities of history to put in my lessons to get students interested. Being very well prepared with the facts and details so I can ad lib in dialogue with them. Getting them engrossed in my stories.	**Work zone conditions:** Focused study in areas of special interest to me, such as ill-defined problems that need considered solutions. The zone comes when I have confidence in my expertise in the issue at hand.	**Work zone conditions:** Quiet time when I can drop everything else and prepare for challenging work for a client—read, make notes by hand, and frame it out on the computer. Then, with the client, when totally tuned in to the moment.	**Work zone conditions:** Thorny problems that stump other engineers take me to the zone. I can't put into words the analytical process I use, except that it takes intense concentration, scanning over my prior experiences.
Leisure zone conditions: Planning my new house, clearing the lot by hand, being involved in its construction, making the yard classy. I also get in the zone as a serious shade-tree mechanic.	**Leisure zone conditions:** Solitude helps me get in the zone, and activities such as reading, especially biographies, computer games, walking, and photography with digital image manipulation.	**Leisure zone conditions:** Building something really challenging that requires hands-on design and construction (e.g., custom boats and cars). Risky outdoors activities that push my senses.	**Leisure zone conditions:** Playing poker seems to require the right mix of competitiveness, know-how, risk taking, and adaptability to put me in the zone—sometimes all night.

ESTP

REALISTIC ADAPTERS in the World of Material Things

They value:

- A life of outward, playful action, in the moment
- Being a troubleshooter
- Finding ways to use the existing system
- Clear, concrete, exact facts
- Knowing the way mechanical things work
- Being direct, to the point
- Learning through spontaneous, hands-on action

- Practical action, more than words
- Immediately useful skills
- Plunging into new adventures
- Responding to practical needs as they arise
- Seeing the expedient thing and acting on it
- Finding fun in their work and sparking others to have fun
- Looking for efficient, least effort solutions
- Being caught up in enthusiasms

NURTURER ESTP	SAGE ESTP	ADVENTURER ESTP	WARRIOR ESTP
Alan: College basketball coach	George: Cabinetmaker, part-time teacher	Ray: Golf pro	Rodney: Trial lawyer
Work zone conditions: Shaping the raw talent of each player is satisfying, but the zone doesn't come for me until the hard drills and practice pay off in real teamwork, everyone pulling together to play at a level that surprises us all. To get there I need elbow room to coach in my own style.	**Work zone conditions:** I learned cabinetmaking at my father's side and picked up his love of it, too. Turning top-grade hardwood into fine cabinets—precision cutting, shaping, sanding, finishing, and all the rich sensations that go with it—puts me in the zone.	**Work zone conditions:** I slipped into golf as a career because it was more fun than anything else in my teenage years. The fun of it every day keeps me here. There's no zone for me without fun at the center of it. Some "golfers" are a pain to work with, but this free life is great in general.	**Work zone conditions:** I get in the zone after I've done careful homework on witnesses and evidence. With the facts down pat, I have all the ammunition I need to throw myself into the courtroom action without second-guessing myself. I can read the judge and jury and make my case.
Leisure zone conditions: Each year some players come here from tough home situations and need extra personal guidance. Being a substitute father for them sometimes put me in the zone. Playing, watching, and talking sports does it, too.	**Leisure zone conditions:** Studying Civil War history and memorabilia often puts me in the zone. I also teach wood-working part-time to kids in juvenile detention. Mostly I teach them pride in workmanship, and when they get it, zone happens for me.	**Leisure zone conditions:** Golfing with good buddies can put me in the zone, easily. Softball and basketball can do it, too. We bought an old house on a river, so we often go canoeing, kayaking and fishing. There's zone out there, too.	**Leisure zone conditions:** I get in the zone when I am playing racquet ball or tennis against really stiff competition. Video games get me to the zone sometimes. Non-challenging competition doesn't do it for me, except with my daughter.

ESTJ
Fact-Minded Practical ORGANIZERS

They value:

- Results; doing, acting
- Planned, organized work and play
- Commonsense practicality
- Consistency; standard procedures
- Concrete, present-day usefulness
- Deciding quickly and logically
- Having things settled and closed
- Rules, objective standards, fairness by the rules

- Task-focused behavior
- Directness, tough-mindedness
- Orderliness; no loose ends
- Systematic structure; efficiency
- Categorizing aspects of their life
- Scheduling and monitoring
- Protecting what works
- Being in charge

NURTURER ESTJ Art: Team leader, auto assembly plant	SAGE ESTJ Jan: Consulting psychologist	ADVENTURER ESTJ George: Army medic	WARRIOR ESTJ Erma: University dean, commercial studies
Work zone conditions: Some days run so smoothly I barely notice time passing. I suppose that is the zone. It is when everyone is doing exactly what's needed, all pulling together and anticipating glitches to avoid them. I especially enjoy breaking in new people when they work hard and are responsive.	**Work zone conditions:** When I get to work with an organization's management that is very serious about the quality of employee worklife, I can get in the zone figuring our how to fit a plan of improvement to their unique situation. It challenges and stretches me.	**Work zone conditions:** Over the years I have worked in many field hospitals. My current assignment is a real zone maker: I am on a team working out really efficient clinic practices and making state-of-the-art equipment flexible and adaptable to field conditions in combat.	**Work zone conditions:** Working with the business community to devise instructional programs that meet their needs. Arranging student internship placements that are an especially good match to the workplace and often result in permanent employment, win-win all around.
Leisure zone conditions: My two sons and I are very involved in stock car racing—all aspects of it. I can stay in the zone a long time when I am working on one of our cars.	**Leisure zone conditions:** Reading takes me to the zone, especially when it is related to something I need for my work. Restoring our 150-year-old house to authentic, original condition is often zone work.	**Leisure zone conditions:** I joined the army "to see the world," as the expression goes. Travel has let me experience many different parts of the world and many cultures, and to make good friends everywhere.	**Leisure zone conditions:** Water sports are my play zone. Anything connected with the water. Especially sailing competitions, getting the very best performance out of my boat.

ISFJ

Sympathetic MANAGERS OF FACTS AND DETAILS

They value:

- Preserving, enjoying the things of proven value
- Steady, sequential work yielding reliable results
- A controlled, orderly outer life
- Patient attention to basic needs
- Following a sensible path, based on experience
- A rich memory for concrete facts

- Loyalty; strong relationships
- Consistency, familiarity, the tried and true
- Firsthand experience of what is important
- Compassion, kindness, caring
- Working to a plan and schedule
- Learning from planned, sequential teaching
- Set routines, commonsense options
- Rules, authority, set procedures
- Hard work, perseverance

NURTURER ISFJ Angie: College career counselor	SAGE ISFJ Gregory: Psychologist, writer	ADVENTURER ISFJ Lynne: Occupational therapist	WARRIOR ISFJ Grace: Real estate office manager
Work zone conditions: Planning events and schedules (career fairs, open houses); responding to e-mail (not voice mail—I hate that); organizing my office; editing/proofreading; researching interesting career fields.	**Work zone conditions:** Sitting in quiet in front of my computer trying to make some complex thing comprehendible, using parts and pieces I can assemble and tweak, but not having to develop something from scratch.	**Work zone conditions:** The zone can come when I am *very* well prepared to help a client with all the needed facts and resources at hand and have anticipated all their needs. Having things predictable is important.	**Work zone conditions:** Ours is a very busy office, but everyone there knows I need quiet time and space to do my best work. I find the zone when by myself doing research and working on sales brochures and such.
Leisure zone conditions: Uninterrupted quiet time for cleaning the house, bill-paying, making shopping lists, doing laundry, yoga class, reading.	**Leisure zone conditions:** Solitary activity, working in my backyard pond, planning travel in minute detail, and reading.	**Leisure zone conditions:** With a few close friends I volunteer in planning and managing a religious retreat center on a nearby mountain, a wonderful place to be in the zone.	**Leisure zone conditions:** I play competitive tennis, coach kids soccer, and work out seriously. All can take me to the zone. Intense focus seems to be the key.

ISFP
Observant, Loyal HELPERS

They value:

- Personal loyalty; a close, loyal friend
- Finding delight in the moment
- Seeing what needs doing to improve the moment
- Freedom from organizational constraints
- Working individually
- Peacemaking behind the scenes
- Attentiveness to feelings
- Harmonious, cooperative work settings

- Spontaneous, hands-on exploration
- Gentle, respectful interactions
- Deeply held personal beliefs
- Reserved, reflective behavior
- Practical, useful skills and know-how
- Having their work life be fully consistent with deeply held values
- Showing and receiving appreciation

NURTURER ISFP Jo: Pediatric critical care physician	**SAGE** ISFP Jack: College professor	**ADVENTURER** ISFP Kevin: Customer service	**WARRIOR** ISFP Darin: Carpenter
Work zone conditions: I find the zone in critical situations with patients' lives at stake, situations that get me totally focused and immersed in the details of the work, being highly sensitive to responses I get from the patient.	**Work zone conditions:** I teach statistics to students who are mostly not math oriented. I find the zone often when I devise concrete ways to convey statistics essentials and see the light dawn in their eyes. Their gratitude and relief do it for me.	**Work zone conditions:** I work in a very congenial, relaxed office and help customers one at a time. I think the zone comes because I am really relaxed here and accepted for who I am—which is a big contrast to my last job.	**Work zone conditions:** Working with a crew that gets along well, with everyone knowing their job and doing it—that's important to me. Pulling together and bringing a job in under schedule can put me in the zone.
Leisure zone conditions: Being caught up in my kids' play, helping them develop; exercising; getting absorbed in household jobs; cooking an especially nice meal.	**Leisure zone conditions:** Gardening, both at home and at our church, is a zone opportunity. It gives my wife and me quiet time to focus on bringing beauty into the world.	**Leisure zone conditions:** Exciting and risky activities take me to the zone—skiing, skydiving, climbing, underwater cave exploring with scuba equipment. They test and fine-tune my skills.	**Leisure zone conditions:** My kids are really into sports. Working out with them builds a bond between us, and I get to the zone by helping them perform at top level.

ESFP

REALISTIC ADAPTERS in Human Relationships.

They value:

- An energetic, sociable life, full of friends and fun
- Performing, entertaining, sharing
- Immediately useful skills; practical know-how
- Learning through spontaneous, hands-on action
- Trust and generosity; openness
- Patterning themselves after those they admire
- Concrete, practical knowledge; resourcefulness

- Caring, kindness, support, appreciation
- Freedom from irrelevant rules
- Handling immediate, practical problems and crises
- Seeing tangible realities; least effort solutions
- Showing and receiving appreciation
- Making the most of the moment; adaptability
- Being caught up in enthusiasms
- Looking for least effort solutions
- Easing and brightening work and play

NURTURER ESFP	SAGE ESFP	ADVENTURER ESFP	WARRIOR ESFP
Nora: Pediatrician	Luke: Car salesman	Jim: Owns/Runs kayak and canoe rental service	Angela: Department store clothing buyer/manager
Work zone conditions: I didn't find any zone in med school until I got to work in a clinic, treating several children over a period of time. Then I knew I was in the right job. Seeing my skills pay off in helping families be healthy is a real zone reward. Especially with families I get to know well.	**Work zone conditions:** When I started selling cars, I didn't know I was going to make a career of it, but I turned out to have the knack for it. And I'm now a walking car encyclopedia. Making real friends with customers and others puts me in the zone. I have a lot of repeat customers because of friendships.	**Work zone conditions:** This is my work because I love being outdoors, here on the river. The zone is always out there. We have lots of repeat business from regulars, over a nine-month season. I'm my own boss in a low-pressure situation, which is ideal for me—and probably a condition for getting to the zone.	**Work zone conditions:** I have always loved clothes, so this is an ideal job for me. While some of it is routine, I get a big surge from being among the first to see new fashions and deciding which ones to carry, staging local fashion shows, cultivating customers, and beating our sales projections.
Leisure zone conditions: I easily get into the world of my own two children and often find the zone there. I have also been a coach at a boys/girls club and that often does it for me, too, as I see their skills and character develop.	**Leisure zone conditions:** Learning about cars and being around them put me in the zone. That's why I'm often at car shows and rallies. I sing tenor in a barbershop quartet, and the church choir. And the music is often a zone trip for me.	**Leisure zone conditions:** Besides my river zone, I find the zone in my music. I play in a country/western band whose members are really good friends. We play gigs around the state and at folk festivals. Lots of zone there.	**Leisure zone conditions:** Getting to travel and hobnob with glamorous people in the fashion world feels more like zone-play than work. I teach aerobics classes for our department store staff, and that often puts me in the zone.

ESFJ
Practical HARMONIZERS, Workers-With-People.

They value:

- An active, sociable life, with many relationships
- A concrete, present-day view of life
- Making daily routines into gracious living
- Staying closely tuned to people they care about so as to keep relationships positive
- Talking through problems cooperatively, caringly
- Approaching problems through tried-and-true, familiar procedures
- Caring, compassion, and tactfulness
- Helping organizations serve their members well
- Responsiveness to others and to traditions
- Being prepared, reliable in tangible, daily work
- Loyalty and faithfulness
- Practical skillfulness grounded in experience
- Structured learning in a humane setting
- Appreciation as the natural means of encouraging improvements

NURTURER ESFJ	**SAGE** ESFJ	**ADVENTURER** ESFJ	**WARRIOR** ESFJ
Gwen: Real estate agent, homemaker	Art: Supervisor of intern teachers	Lise: Rental agent for a Florida condo group	Warren: Marketing for a cosmetics company
Work zone conditions: When my children were small, my zone was in the pleasure of caring for them. When they got older and needed me less, I took up real estate. I find the zone there in the relationships with great colleagues and in serving clients with TLC.	**Work zone conditions:** I get to know my interns well over a nine-month period. With some of them my coaching really connects and we get in the zone as they develop their skills. Getting closely tuned in to their situations seems to bring the zone experience.	**Work zone conditions:** I speak fluent German and French and work with European travel agents to get vacation renters for our condos. Building up relationships with clients overseas, often traveling to meet with them, is very exciting and satisfying.	**Work zone conditions:** Working very closely with our team to develop a marketing plan for a product. The blending of talents, under intense time pressure, in this highly competitive business is what helps bring the zone. Seeing the plan succeed.
Leisure zone conditions: My nonwork time is centered around our church. Mostly I network social events and coordinate outreach volunteers. I find a lot of joy in keeping people connected to one another, helping bonds to happen.	**Leisure zone conditions:** I coach in a community soccer league. The zone sometimes comes as I help players come along. I find the zone in doing local history and writing a column about it in our community newspaper.	**Leisure zone conditions:** During Florida's colder months I get to travel—for fun as well as to maintain relationships with my overseas clients in places I visit. Being with these far-flung friends puts me in the zone.	**Leisure zone conditions:** I am a sports nut, and I seriously collect sports memorabilia—eBay, swap meets, and so on. The high I get from doing my homework, working the details, and getting really good deals is what I suppose is the zone.

INFJ

People-Oriented INNOVATORS of Ideas

They value:

- A reserved outer life; spontaneous inner life
- Planning ways to help people improve
- Seeing complexities, hidden meanings
- Imaginative ways of saying things
- Understanding other people's needs and concerns
- Planful, independent academic learning
- Being inspired and inspiring others

- Reading, writing, and imagining; academic theory
- Being restrained in outward actions; planful
- Aligning their work with their ideals
- Pursuing and clarifying their ideals
- Taking the long view
- Encouraging others through appreciation
- Finding harmonious solutions to problems

NURTURER INFJ Gretta: Homemaker, retired teacher	**SAGE** INFJ Darlene: Writer, full-time parent and homemaker	**ADVENTURER** INFJ Kim: Potter, part-time adjunct art professor	**WARRIOR** INFJ Jim: Director, halfway house
Work zone conditions: Since retirement, I find my zone in cooking, especially baking and devising new recipes. I sell my baked goods at our farmer's market and have many regular customers who treat me as a second mother. That's a zone maker, too.	**Work zone conditions:** I write on religious and self-development themes. The researching and writing process, creating worthwhile ideas with words and imagination, often puts me in the zone. I homeschool my two kids, and we can get in the zone with their projects.	**Work zone conditions:** Potting captured me in a high school art class. It is so personal and challenging to my skills and creativity. I feel a spiritual connection between an ancient art form and new ideas and technology. Always something new to learn.	**Work zone conditions:** My job is hard, but it has its zone moments. I run a program for recovering substance abusers. Their day-at-a-time victories are often zone events for them and me. It takes total focus, eyes on the prize, and self-discipline to find the recovery zone.
Leisure zone conditions: I have played violin and cello since I was a girl. Music is a source of zone for me, playing or listening. I play in a string quartet. The warm discipline of blending with the other musicians to make something beautiful is pure joy.	**Leisure zone conditions:** Reading and bird watching are family affairs that sometimes take all four of us to the zone. They are absorbing activities that continually show us something new. I also find the zone in mentoring young writers.	**Leisure zone conditions:** Studying Native American history and art got me connected to my main zone activity: I volunteer at archeological dig projects for the university. Discovering the past through artifacts is very rewarding.	**Leisure zone conditions:** Reading is my zone place, not just escape but a source of renewal. Also I play serious bridge with some friends and enter tournaments whenever they come around. Bridge is always challenging and absorbing, every hand different.

INFP
Imaginative, Independent HELPERS

They value:

- Harmony in the inner life of ideas
- Harmonious work settings; working individually
- Seeing the big-picture possibilities
- Creativity; curiosity, exploring
- Helping people find their potential
- Giving ample time to reflect on decisions
- Compassion and caring; attention to emotional needs

- Adaptability and openness
- Work that lets them express their idealism
- Gentle, respectful interactions
- An inner compass; being unique
- Showing appreciation and being appreciated
- Ideas, language, and writing
- A close, loyal friend
- Perfecting what is important

NURTURER INFP Nick: School teacher	**SAGE** INFP Leanne: Organizational trainer	**ADVENTURER** INFP Ted: Jazz musician	**WARRIOR** INFP Rachael: Homemaker
Work zone conditions: I lead simulations in my teaching that require me to adapt quickly. I am prepared but with no script. The spontaneous energy I get from my students is what puts me in the zone—better energy than I can generate on my own.	**Work zone conditions:** The zone comes when I have created a space and invited people into it, a place of deep communion that is not cerebral but is a place of discovery. It comes when I know the subject by heart, I believe in it wholeheartedly, and become vulnerable.	**Work zone conditions:** Music takes me to the zone when it is close to my heart. The zone arises out of a place that is familiar but hasn't fully revealed itself before. I find new parts of myself there as I explore it. Performing there is work but it doesn't feel like it.	**Work zone conditions:** Caring for my family and managing home life are my full-time work. I homeschool my two children, ages nine and eleven. I work hard at it because I want them to excel. But that often takes me to the zone as I get caught up in their excitement in what they are learning.
Leisure zone conditions: Some situations cause me to stand outside myself, focus intently, and let my skills play themselves. One time, golfing with a friend who was seriously ill, I had the thought that this might be my last game with him, and I wanted it to be special. We both zoned.	**Leisure zone conditions:** When I can quiet the incessant chatter in my mind that is often critical and listen to the inner voice that wants to take me to unknown places. Music, dancing, and cycling can do that. Also creative writing, journaling, making greeting cards, and volunteering at church.	**Leisure zone conditions:** Music fills my "leisure" time as well. There are no real boundaries between working and playing. Some practicing is hard work but almost always has a "playtime" quality to it. Connecting with others through music, exploring new ideas, gives me most all the renewal I need.	**Leisure zone conditions:** Because our kids are way above grade level, we have more time for things besides books. We are big on sports and often find the zone there. Seeing them respond well to coaching and then play winning soccer and basketball is where my zone comes from. That, and my working out.

ENFP

Warmly Enthusiastic PLANNERS OF CHANGE

They value:

- The surge of inspirations; the pull of emerging possibilities
- A life of variety, people, and warm relationships
- Following their insights wherever they lead
- Finding meanings behind the facts
- Creativity, originality, a fresh perspective
- An optimistic, positive, enthusiastic view of life
- Flexibility and openness
- Exploring, devising and trying out new things

- Open-ended opportunities and options
- Freedom from the requirement of being practical
- Learning through action, variety, and discovery
- A belief that any obstacles can be overcome
- A focus on people's potentials
- Brainstorming to solve problems
- Work made light and playful by inspiration

NURTURER ENFP	SAGE ENFP	ADVENTURER ENFP	WARRIOR ENFP
Barbara: US physician in Kenyan village clinic	Greg: Assistant director, science museum	Lin: Stage designer for repertory theater	James: Motivational speaker, leadership coach
Work zone conditions: The inspiration I get in using my skills to help these people who are so grateful. Work aligned with my values. Creatively getting the max out of limited resources. Being a vital part of a large, extended family: this village.	**Work zone conditions:** I'm in charge of the children's galleries and lead the teams that create and make new hands-on exhibits. Imagining and designing them put me in the zone and it puts my science knowledge to the test. Seeing the kids' excitement is the payoff.	**Work zone conditions:** I found the zone in theater work when I was about fifteen. It's the rush of creating something fresh, the challenge of making ideas come alive, the association with kindred spirits. Acting isn't my medium; designing sets to frame the play is a joy.	**Work zone conditions:** Reactions from my audience and my clients set up the zone for me. I prepare carefully but often find myself going with the energy of the group, adapting to them and taking the work to a higher plane than I had expected. Synergy.
Leisure zone conditions: Leisure time is limited, but I find the zone in learning about and being involved in the culture of Kenya and the loving families who have adopted me. I also coach basketball and get caught up in the children's excitement.	**Leisure zone conditions:** We plan vacations so I can travel to other children's museums I have researched. Getting ideas for my work is my best playtime. My own kids are the best critics. When I see them in the zone in a museum, I know it's a winner.	**Leisure zone conditions:** My work is my play. It gives me all the variety I need. Theater people are a big part of my leisure time. The companionship is powerful—freewheeling, but close at the same time. There is always excitement in our group.	**Leisure zone conditions:** Competition sparks my zone. I love to win at any undertaking, including recreational activities. Golf is my special game. I get on a golf course whenever and wherever I can. Staying loose, with total concentration, gets me my wins.

ENFJ
Imaginative HARMONIZERS, Workers-With-People

They value:

- Having a wide circle of relationships
- Having a positive, enthusiastic view of life
- Seeing subtleties in people and interactions
- Understanding others' needs and concerns
- An active, energizing social life
- Seeing possibilities in people
- Thorough follow-through on important projects
- Working on several projects at once
- Caring and imaginative problem solving
- Maintaining relationships to avoid trouble
- Shaping organizations to better serve members
- Sociability and responsiveness
- Structured learning in a humane setting
- Caring, compassion, and tactfulness
- Appreciation as the natural means of encouraging improvements

NURTURER ENFJ Cleo: Homemaker, community volunteer	**SAGE** ENFJ Chris: College professor	**ADVENTURER** ENFJ Frank: Army chaplain	**WARRIOR** ENFJ Ed: Organizational development specialist
Work zone conditions: The zone comes for me in family life, in being an integral part of my children's development. When they find zest in life experiences it spills over to me, too. We are a family-centered family.	**Work zone conditions:** When I am very well prepared for my students and can take them to big insights, the zone comes for us. Also in my research, especially when my students are involved as co-researchers.	**Work zone conditions:** I had a stint in the army before I decided to be a clergyman. I liked army life but didn't find any zone there until I became a chaplain and started helping the young people get their lives sorted out. It's a counseling zone.	**Work zone conditions:** A close relationship with the CEO of our company gives me insights into the personnel issues that need my attention. My zone comes when I'm working with teams and we make breakthroughs to better functioning.
Leisure zone conditions: My husband says I get in the zone as a rescuer—of stray creatures and people in need. I am a longtime phone volunteer at a crisis intervention center. My wonderful colleagues there and I get deep satisfaction helping people through crises.	**Leisure zone conditions:** Family life has been a zone maker for me for years; for example, in our designing and hand constructing a lake cottage, detail by detail, nail by nail, over five years. Also I often find myself in the zone in reading serious stuff.	**Leisure zone conditions:** I love to travel, making new friends and experiencing new places. The zone comes in the broadening of myself I feel in different cultures. Army life let me travel, and I have a portable occupation within it.	**Leisure zone conditions:** Golf is my game. When I use it for play, the challenge often takes me to the zone. When I use it for work I have to reign in my competitive streak so as not to spoil the social tone, the rapport, that helps me accomplish my work.

INTJ

Logical, Critical, Decisive INNOVATORS of Ideas

They value:

- A restrained, organized outer life; spontaneous, intuitive inner life
- Conceptual skills, theorizing
- Planful, independent, academic learning
- Skepticism; critical analysis; objective principles
- Originality, independence of mind
- Intellectual quickness, ingenuity
- Nonemotional tough-mindedness

- Freedom from interference in projects
- Working to a plan and schedule
- Seeing complexities, hidden meanings
- Improving things by finding flaws
- Probing new possibilities; taking the long view
- Pursuing a vision; foresight; conceptualizing
- Getting insights to reframe problems

NURTURER INTJ Alan: Episcopal clergyman	**SAGE** INTJ Andrea: Clinical psychologist	**ADVENTURER** INTJ Roger: Newspaper reporter, writer	**WARRIOR** INTJ Neil: CEO, start-up bio-tech development lab
Work zone conditions: Intuiting the needs of my parishioners—my extended family—and crafting sermons and counseling sessions that help them find new perspectives on their problems and fresh ideas that improve their lives.	**Work zone conditions:** Exploring the complexities of human nature is what brought me to this career and keeps me here. Untying the knots of the problems my clients present often puts me in the zone. The issues are so engrossing.	**Work zone conditions:** Writing has been a source of zone for me since high school. I do investigative reporting. Tracking down the elements of a story, fitting together the pieces of the puzzle often gets me totally involved.	**Work zone conditions:** Our work is cutting-edge, and the discovery process puts us in the zone often. The drive to stay ahead in a highly competitive field keeps our juices flowing. Most of us are workaholics, oblivious of the clock.
Leisure zone conditions: Reading is a zone place for me for sure, with most of it being related to my work; chasing new ideas. My wife and I helped form and run a community organic garden and find a lot of joy there—with the earth and with our cofarmers.	**Leisure zone conditions:** Reading and writing have always been a trigger for the zone. I now write for professional journals, case studies, and book reviews. I am seriously involved in martial arts. The mental discipline of it is definitely zone inducing.	**Leisure zone conditions:** I like to get totally away from the pressures of my job at my lake cabin, where I can fish and explore the wild. My mind gets free to let ideas come for the books I write. It is a place and pace apart that lets the zone come.	**Leisure zone conditions:** When I do carve out leisure time, I can get in the zone playing handball; it takes total concentration, sharp instincts, and quick reflexes. Also do long-distance running and have been in seven marathons.

INTP
Inquisitive ANALYZERS

They value:

- A reserved outer life; an inner life of inquiry
- Pursuing interests in depth, with concentration
- Work and play that is intriguing, not routine
- Being free of emotional issues while working
- Working on problems that respond to detached intuitive analysis and theorizing

- Approaching problems by reframing the obvious
- Complex intellectual mysteries
- Being absorbed in abstract, mental work
- Freedom from organizational constraints
- Independence and nonconformance
- Intellectual quickness, ingenuity, invention
- Competence in the world of ideas
- Spontaneous learning by following curiosity and inspirations
- Using critical analysis to improve things

NURTURER INTP	SAGE INTP	ADVENTURER INTP	WARRIOR INTP
Darcy: RN, operational improvement advisor	B. J.: School counselor	Shana: Manager, grants program for university	Rick: Research and technical writing
Work zone conditions: Data analysis, devising new conceptual schemes. The zone comes when I'm free to follow and flesh out my insights of how to solve problems and when facilitating teams in generating ideas	**Work zone conditions:** When I can help students break through and get a new picture to guide them; when planning and writing a communication that makes dense stuff clear; when learning about complex systems.	**Work zone conditions:** Using my expertise in facilitating collaborative brainstorming regarding grants; working with bright, intellectually curious people who are excited about new possibilities and are seeking insights.	**Work zone conditions:** Brainstorming possible new products; doing data analyses; solving a mathematical problem; creating a new product; developing complex spreadsheets to track or store data.
Leisure zone conditions: Activities with family— yard games, volleyball, croquet, bocce ball, cooking, gardening.	**Leisure zone conditions:** Reading—especially nonfiction, such as history, political analysis, science, and biographies.	**Leisure zone conditions:** Exploring beautiful new terrain: cultural, natural, geographic, intellectual. The challenge of contra dancing.	**Leisure zone conditions:** Playing basketball and racquet ball; all kinds of reading; fly fishing.

ENTP

Inventive, Analytical PLANNERS OF CHANGE

They value:

- Conceiving of new things and initiating change
- The surge of inspirations; the pull of emerging possibilities
- Analyzing complexities
- Following their insights, wherever they lead
- Finding meanings behind the facts
- Autonomy, elbow room, openness
- Ingenuity, originality, a fresh perspective

- Mental models and concepts that explain life
- Fair treatment
- Flexibility, adaptability
- Learning through action, variety, and discovery
- Exploring theories and meanings behind events
- Improvising, looking for novel ways
- Work made light by inspiration

NURTURER ENTP Ralph: Judge, juvenile court	SAGE ENTP Anne: Public relations for a public utility company	ADVENTURER ENTP Rick: Graphic designer	WARRIOR ENTP Jack: IT specialist for a securities firm
Work zone conditions: Analyzing complex human issues in relation to the law. Finding ways the justice system can help in the reclaiming of lives of young offenders. Reframing families' problems so they can see how to manage them.	**Work zone conditions:** Working on plans for a company initiative I care about; for example, conceptualizing fresh ways to engage the community on serious energy conservation. Also, I have two co-workers whose lively minds can put me in the zone.	**Work zone conditions:** I run a small business, putting art on T-shirts. Creating new designs is far more likely to put me in the zone than is the business side. Artwork has fascinated me all my life. Working up new designs for clients is usually very satisfying.	**Work zone conditions:** Designing new, complex computer programs that make our company's work more effective. It is the challenge of doing what hasn't been done before that puts me in the zone. Hacking (legally!) to improve our security system does it, too.
Leisure zone conditions: My leisure time is mostly family time, and we got in the zone fairly often in the kids' sports when they were younger. Now we're involved in Habitat for Humanity projects. It is the passionate interest in the work that brings on the zone, I think.	**Leisure zone conditions:** Serious reading and sailing are my passions. They often take me to the zone, for different reasons. Reading feeds my restless mind, and in sailing, coping with the elements challenges me and calms me at the same time.	**Leisure zone conditions:** Skateboarding has been my zone since I was seven. Also basketball. Now I get in the zone with my young son. Exploring all kinds of things that are new to him make them fresh to me all over again.	**Leisure zone conditions:** Playing poker is my main zone producer. I can get totally absorbed in the process, lose track of time, yet stay sharp in the competition. I schedule casino high-stakes poker trips when I can. Playing the stock market does it, too.

ENTJ
Intuitive, Innovative ORGANIZERS

They value:

- Analyzing abstract problems, complex situations
- Foresight; pursuing a vision
- Changing, organizing things to fit their vision
- Putting theory into practice, ideas into action
- Working to a plan and schedule
- Initiating, then delegating
- Efficiency; removing obstacles and confusion

- Probing new possibilities
- Holding self and others to high standards
- Having things settled and closed
- Tough-mindedness, directness, task focus
- Objective principles; fairness, justice
- Assertive, direct action
- Intellectual resourcefulness
- Driving toward broad goals along a logical path
- Designing structures and strategies
- Seeking out logical flaws to improve things
- Being in charge

NURTURER ENTJ	**SAGE** ENTJ	**ADVENTURER** ENTJ	**WARRIOR** ENTJ
Jack: Agriculture management advisor	Christina: Grant writer for healthcare agencies	Richard: School district superintendent	Phil: Real estate broker, entrepreneur
Work zone conditions: I have specialized in helping government and NGO agencies in Central America improve agricultural practices. The zone comes for me when my clients and I get totally absorbed in analyzing the problems they face and trying out solutions.	**Work zone conditions:** Researching and getting clarity on complex social issues in healthcare services. Successfully fitting my analysis into the requirements of the grant funders. Captivating an audience when I present the details of my work.	**Work zone conditions:** Taking on a school system with knotty problems; figuring out the movers and shakers; working out the tricky politics of a school board; bringing talent forward, teachers and leaders, and seeing them make improvements.	**Work zone conditions:** Envisioning a new project, doing my homework to devise a persuasive proposal, successfully reading the players and anticipating snags, getting capital together, and riding the plan until it runs smoothly.
Leisure zone conditions: Being involved in my children's activities, especially their sports. I get caught up in their zone experiences. Getting insights into and becoming part of the culture and customs of the countries where I work.	**Leisure zone conditions:** Reading high-quality fiction and nonfiction. Conversation with really bright and gifted people. Engrossing projects having to do with fixing up our old house. Hiking and exploring. Swimming. Gardening and landscaping our property.	**Leisure zone conditions:** Hunting and fishing with friends, especially my old friends. Tracking down high-quality antique furniture, getting bargains, reselling, and swapping.	**Leisure zone conditions:** When I was young, the zone was in sports, mainly football in high school and boxing during my college years. I'm a competitor by nature, and the surge comes when I work out a winning strategy. Now it comes mostly in my work.

FINAL THOUGHTS

This is a good place to say again that type and archetype categories do not *determine* people's behavior. Rather, they point to a dynamic mental framework of values and priorities through which people process their life experiences. It is simply wrong to guess the type and the archetype of a person you are mentoring, coaching, nurturing, and so forth, and to then treat him or her *as the category* you selected for that person. It is just as wrong as assuming your child will or should be keenly interested in the same activities that produce zone experiences for you. If your child does share a zone field with you, that's a wonderful gift. But a young person's type and archetype affinities, or other factors, may steer him or her in another direction. Our role is to observe keenly their emerging interests and support budding zone experiences. Understanding type and archetype in this context helps us avoid using stereotypes and pressuring children against their nature, and this understanding provides us with ideas to use in dialogue with them, exploring possible zone doorways.

Although knowing about psychological types and the archetypes is valuable in guiding someone in finding zone opportunities, it certainly is not required. The parents of Andre, the young chess player, were not aware of type concepts. But they were able to support him in constructive ways as he pursued his zone. They did recognize that chess was a powerful force for his development.

How the zone and investigative minding are forces for development in an institutional setting is the subject of the last chapter.

6

BEYOND THE
BLANK SLATE

The previous chapters have suggested ways to read the motivations and priorities of individuals so as to help them move toward investigative minding and zone experiences. In this final chapter we look at the problem of breaking through the blank-slate assumption to make our *institutional* life more open to zone functioning. I am concentrating here on two institutions: the school and the workplace.

IN SCHOOLING

I begin with the problem of opening up the process of schooling. The false assumption that we are born with unformed minds—needing elders to provide organization as well as content—pervades the entire structure of schooling. It is so interwoven in the fabric of curriculum and instruction that it is all but invisible. When someone calls attention to the blank-slate assumption, as I do in this book, the existence of the assumption is dismissed as an unfortunate educational fact of life, an inevitable underpinning of the schooling process. The apologists for the blank-slate assumption can't imagine a formal education system without it. This mind-set is a huge barrier to introducing investigative minding and zone-sponsoring activities as central features of schooling.

In my view, getting through the barrier calls for a Trojan horse type of solution, one I am calling a "2 percent solution," as I explain later in the chapter. The background of my proposal is well illustrated in research highlighted in Annenberg Media presentations.[1] The Annenberg Foundation is dedicated to improving the quality of teaching and learning in K–12 schooling. The research I have drawn on from these projects bears directly on the thesis of this book, that children are born with organized minds, that they are natural investigators continually working to make sense of their world, and that they have formed mental modules, or intuitive theories, they use to guide their daily functioning. Children bring their theories with them when they start school. They are invested in them and don't change them easily. In effect, learning a new concept of how the world works means giving up—sometimes slowly and painfully—a conception they have already formed. In a general sense, learning is relearning. Schools have to be reformed to be based on this platform, connecting with already organized minds, rather than the blank-slate, pat-answer foundation.

The following pages draw from three videos produced by the Harvard-Smithsonian Center for Astrophysics. The first is an experiment in conceptions about electricity.[2]

Scene: A lawn on the campus of the Massachusetts Institute of Technology, following a commencement ceremony. A researcher-interviewer speaks individually with graduates still in their graduation gowns. With a C-size battery, a flashlight bulb, and some bare copper wire in her hand, she asks, "Do you think you could light a bulb with a battery and a wire?" Each student says yes and takes the material to demonstrate. One after another they try and fail to light the bulb. They act very puzzled as to why they fail, and mostly suggest that the bulb or battery must be faulty. One says, "I'm a mechanical engineer, not electrical." Just one student, after some false starts, makes the bulb light, saying, "I forgot. You have to make a complete circuit."

He makes the circuit by touching the wire to the battery, to the bottom of the bulb's base and to the side of the base at the same time, and the bulb lights.

The interviews were videotaped. Commenting on the video sequences, Harvard researcher Philip M. Sadler says, "It goes to the fundamental understanding of electricity. If one cannot light a lightbulb with a battery and a wire then everything built upon those ideas has problems. . . . Sometimes the simplest problems in science defy intuition, and the most basic technologies are difficult to grasp. Is it because of something we were not taught, or is it because of something deeper—something about the way we think?"

Sadler's research is concerned with the power of children's naive, intuitive theories—the mental modules—that they formed long before they were taught any science lessons. In effect he is saying that lessons taught without consideration of the already formed naive conceptions students bring to the classroom are cherry-picked by the students. That is, students attend to the aspects of the lesson that are consistent with and reinforcing to their prior theories and tune out the aspects that are contradictory. Not until the students' preconceptions are addressed *directly*, and the children are prompted to see that they can no longer make sense of events using their prior idea, are they then open to changing it. They themselves have to take the challenging data and *reconstruct for themselves* the new, more powerful concept. This viewpoint is the central feature of Dewey's theory described in chapter 2 and also reflected in the conclusions of Gopnik, Meltzoff, and Kuhl as they interpreted the studies of infants.[3]

The researchers conducted similar interviews with randomly chosen Harvard graduates and faculty, asking different science questions, basic questions in astronomy. One was, "Why do the seasons happen?" A typical response was that Earth's orbit around the sun is elliptical, so summer happens when we are closer to the sun and winter happens when we are farther away from it. Even one graduate who said he "took physics, planetary motion, and relativity" gave the same answer. Only two of twenty-three people interviewed correctly explained that Earth's orbit around the sun is circular, and it is the tilt of Earth on its axis in relation to the sun that accounts for the seasons.

Faulty, persistently held preconceptions of how the world works affect all aspects of science instruction. For example, other researchers turned up the fact that fewer than 40 percent of college chemistry graduates have a scientifically sound grasp of solids, liquids, and gasses in terms of the particles that make them up. Their science instruction apparently did not fully dispel their naive, private conceptions of the nature of matter.

Science educators in recent years have been systematically observing and recording the common naive ideas children bring to the classroom, ideas that teachers need to challenge and help students dismantle and replace with scientifically sound concepts.[4] Many of the naive conceptions that children have constructed for themselves are obviously grounded in the untutored experiences of their young lives. For example, the scientific explanation of gasses, liquids, and solids as consisting of particles viewed in terms of mass, density, volume, and so on, is not something children can intuit without instruction. It is completely natural for children to naively have such preconceptions as these: "Air is a gas but it has no weight and occupies no space." "Gasses aren't matter because they are invisible." "When gasses expand, more gas is present." "Gases make things lighter." "A deflated bike tire has less pressure inside it than out." But intuitive assumptions such as these need to be the starting point of science instruction.

Here are a few examples of children's self-constructed ideas about the nature of energy. "Things 'use up' energy." "An object at rest has no energy." "The terms *energy* and *force* are interchangeable." "If energy is conserved, why are we running out of it?" "Heat is not energy." And here are some examples of ideas about plants obtaining and using energy. "Plants get their energy directly from the sun." "Sunlight is a food." "Plants absorb water through their leaves." "Sunlight is 'consumed' in photosynthesis."

Lists of hundreds of naive conceptions have been made and sorted into two dozen categories of science, including: light, color, and vision; matter and its changes; living things and ecosystems; forces in fluids; and the life sciences. Seriously addressing each of them in the construction of science curricula and instruction is a massive task. But if the recent research on brain functioning is to be respected, and the blank-slate assumption is to be overcome and replaced with a commitment to connect with already organized minds, these conceptions children bring to the classroom are the starting point. Undoubtedly, some preconceptions are more important than others to address in the early grades because they are building blocks on which rest many more complex science concepts. Selecting the most seminal ones is part of the Trojan horse, 2 percent solution I offer in this chapter.

Besides a solid foundation of science concepts, young students need to start early in developing mathematical reasoning. Having computational skills and knowing math rules are not the same as mathematical reasoning. The blank-slate, pat-answer structure rests on the assumption that mathematical reasoning will follow naturally from a mastery of the skills and rules. But if children bring already organized minds, the prevailing structure needs to be stood upon its head. Rudimentary mathematical processing has been part of children's life experiences long before they start school, before the teacher begins teaching math skills. As with children's naive reasoning about the physical world being the starting point for science instruction, help with mathematical reasoning needs to precede math skills and rules. How that can be done is the subject of another Annenberg Media project depicting on videotape a long-term study by mathematics education specialists from Rutgers University in collaboration with the Kenilworth, New Jersey, school system, which serves a blue-collar community.[5]

Rutgers professor Carolyn Maher led the research team. They began their work with a randomly selected first grade class and followed the same children through the elementary years. When the students reached middle school, Maher and her team selected six of the children to follow as subjects through high school graduation. The children selected were representative of the range of ability in this classroom. Also, because data were collected by videotape, only relatively verbal students were selected. The sessions with these six children were videotaped as they were doing mathematics and being interviewed individually or in small groups. Maher described the research purpose as "following how particular mathematical ideas developed . . . to see what was possible, what students were capable of doing."[6] The work the students did with the researchers was totally separate from the regular classroom curriculum. The researchers met with the students typically five or six times a year. Here are some highlights.

Scene: Grade 2, students sitting around small tables in groups of two or three. The researcher presents a challenge: Stephen has three shirts—a white one, a blue one, and a yellow one—and a pair of blue jeans and a pair of white jeans. "How many different outfits can he make? Plan to show and convince me and your classmates that you got the highest possible number of outfits."

The students begin to work, mostly individually, talking easily, comparing their different ways of showing the combinations. The most common approach is to draw little pictures of three shirts and two pants and connect the drawings with lines to show the combinations. Five tables report that six outfits are possible and justify their conclusion by showing that no more lines can be drawn without duplicate lines running between any two items. One girl holds out for only five outfits being possible. When asked why, she answers, "*Everyone* knows you don't wear yellow with white!"

This brief exercise, representing the multiplication of 3 and 2, was conducted before the students were introduced to the multiplication process in grade 3. The exercise also oriented the students to the style of activity they would be doing with a Rutgers researcher in the future: being presented with a challenge, the "teacher" stepping back and observing, small groups working out and writing solutions for themselves, and then they justify their conclusions to each other without the teacher telling the right answer. The activity felt like play, and they were having fun. The structure of the exercise served to completely guide the work/play, without adult direction. In effect, the children were in charge of themselves during the whole exercise, except when the teacher probed with questions at the end to guide the discussion about solutions.

Here is a sample grade 3 session: The children are in small groups around tables, each with a pile of Unifix interlocking plastic cubes. The challenge: "Your job is to work together and build as many towers as possible of four cubes high using two colors, and then convince the other students that no two towers are alike and no more towers could be made that are different. Got the problem? Have fun!"

As the children start building towers, they reason aloud with each other how to know that no two towers were alike. At one table they hit on a system of being sure that each tower of two colors has an opposite, for example, a yellow-yellow-red-yellow tower has an opposite of red-red-yellow-red.

When all groups seem finished the researcher picks one table and says, "How many towers did you get?" "Sixteen." "How do you know that no two towers are alike?" One girl says, "We put all our towers in a row so we could compare each one with the others." She picks up one tower and holds it against each of the fifteen others. "We did this, checking each tower against every other tower to be sure no two are alike." Researcher: "How are you going to convince people, though, that maybe there aren't seventeen towers, or eighteen towers? Do you feel sure you have them all?" Student: "Yup, I am, 'cause I looked at all of them and I said that all of them had doubles ['opposites']." The discussion continues until all tables have shown and explained their work.

The following day the researcher selects one girl to interview about the towers activity. Included in the interview was this exchange.

> Researcher: What if we had two colors, red and yellow, and we made towers that were three cubes high instead of four cubes high. How many towers do you think there would be?
>
> Meredith: Well, maybe there would, there would still be sixteen.
>
> Researcher: Think so?
>
> Meredith: 'Cause if you just took one cube off of each one [tower four cubes tall] . . .
>
> Researcher: Now that's an interesting thought. If you took one off each of these. Want to try to, see what happens?
>
> Meredith: OK. [She takes the top block off each tower and detects eight duplicate towers. Meredith is then invited to consider why the number of towers decreased from sixteen to eight.]
>
> Researcher: Can you explain why you think that happened [the duplicate towers]?
>
> Meredith: Because this [tower] used to be four yellows . . . [and this tower used to be three yellows with a red on top of it] . . . and when you take the red off and the yellow off, the two towers are the same . . .
>
> Researcher: They become the same. Does that happen for all of those?
>
> Meredith: Yup. . . . We have to take eight [towers] away and eight would still be there.

The towers activity is visited again when the students are in fourth grade, with the challenge to find how many towers are possible when made five cubes high and using two colors. By the time they all solve the towers problem, the students are so excited about their proofs they can hardly sit still. Two children working together notice that with towers only two blocks tall, made with two colors of blocks, you can only build four towers. Comparing that finding with the fact that you can have eight different towers when they are three blocks tall, they hypothesize that each time you make the towers one block taller you double the number of towers that can be made. There will be eight different towers when the towers are three blocks tall, and sixteen different towers when they are four blocks tall, and so on. This kind of mathematical reasoning and proof-making is the main thrust of the project.

Each successive assignment stretches the reasoning with more complex tasks. In grade 5, the students are given this problem: A local pizza shop has asked us to help them design a form to keep track of certain pizza sales. Their standard "plain" pizza contains tomato sauce and cheese. A customer can then select one or more of the following toppings: peppers, sausage, mushrooms, and pepperoni. How many different choices for pizza does a customer have? List all the possible choices and find a way to convince each other that you have accounted for all the possible choices.

At their tables the groups begin to write out combinations. Then one group adopts a grid form with four columns, one for each topping, and starts adding rows as needed, putting checkmarks in the cells to show the presence or absence of the topping in each combination. Other groups see the idea and adopt it. Eventually, they have sixteen rows and realize that sixteen pizza combinations could be predicted because $4 \times 4 = 16$.

At this point in any of the activities, it was typical for the researcher to say, "Did anyone have the same answer, but a different approach?" "Is there anything about your solution that's the same as your classmates'?" "Can you explain what your classmate has done?" The goal is to extend student thinking.

One boy, Brandon, recognizes that the pizza problem is like the towers problem. His pizza chart has a 1 or a 0 in each cell of the chart to show the presence or absence of a topping. By sketching a four-cube tower lying horizontally, Brandon shows his classmates that with red blocks marked as a 1 and yellow blocks as a 0, he can create a towers chart that looks just like the pizza chart. Meredith observes that it is also like the shirts and jeans problem they had worked on in second grade. "It's patternlike. You couldn't have duplicates and you had to find as many as possible . . . and explain your answer."

Carolyn Maher observed:

> Some of the most dramatic data came when the students were coming up with justifications for their solutions and inventing the idea of mathematical proof. . . . You didn't wait for the authority, for the teacher to say if your thinking was right or wrong, or there is a way to think about this problem. And if you thought about it this way, you're a better thinker, a better student; you are a more successful mathematics student if your thinking followed a particular . . . expectation. I think that freed students. They were now able to trust themselves. Everyone's ideas were important. And they were able to pull from themselves and surprise themselves in what they could do.[7]

The narrator on the video: "When the Kenilworth kids were juniors, Maher pitched them a real brain twister. It's the World Series problem: how many different ways can a baseball team win a best-of-seven contest? . . . This is a classic combinations problem that might be taught in college. Even Carolyn Maher was often surprised by just how far the kids could take their own mathematical insights."

During all the middle and high school years the same smaller group of Kenilworth students met in informal afterschool sessions, also videotaped. In a discussion during their senior year, the students reflected back over their experiences with the researchers. Here are some comments from the students:

- "It made us different people."
- "We weren't scared of being wrong."
- "We were making our own theorems, our own formulas."
- "The kids ran the class during Rutgers time. You learn better when you own the process."
- "Rutgers never told us what the answers were."
- "We came to answers just by ourselves and could defend them."
- "Doing math like thought-steps . . . helps in every area of your life."

- "I thought I had no talents in math, but I can do it. Give me any problem and enough time."

There is hardly dispute about the depth of their understanding. What are noteworthy are their articulate expressions of how their personal understandings grew.

Nationally, most students stop taking math when the minimum requirements are met. All of the students who were in the Rutgers study through their high school years elected to take advanced placement calculus in their senior year.

Reflecting back over their analyses of the two-thousand-plus videotapes of the Kenilworth students, the Rutgers researchers came to a number of conclusions relevant to our interest in promoting investigative minding and precipitating the zone experience:

- The need for sense making, working together, negotiating reasonableness, and personal ownership of ideas characterizes the views of the students on how they learn mathematics.
- Analyses of the videotaped data indicate strong relationships between (1) a teacher's monitoring the process of a student's constructions of a problem solution and (2) the teacher's posing a timely question that invites or challenges students to revisit earlier thinking, revise it in the light of new experience, and, if appropriate, move forward to deeper, stronger understanding. The teacher is acting as a catalyst.
- Time for student reflection is also important. We have found that asking students to write about the way they are thinking about a problem during class and at home facilitates a prolonged interest in thinking about the questions posed by the teacher.[8]
- [Ownership] is an issue that is not often associated with problem solving, perhaps because it is not so much about actions taken in problem solving as it is about the students' attitude. However, the students' ownership of their mathematical activity was central in promoting their successful problem solving in the longitudinal study. Ownership of mathematical activity means that the students' mathematical ideas, representations, justifications, and decisions are emphasized over those

of the teachers, researchers, or other experts. Ownership was the issue most discussed by the students in their reflections.[9]

Let's consider the Rutgers math sessions in light of the themes of this book, beginning with Johan Huizinga's criteria for what constitutes play, as described in chapter 4. According to Huizinga, play consists of activities that are interludes outside of ordinary life, requiring undistracted concentration; are bounded in time, space, and purpose; follow their own form, function, rules, and order; are energized with tension and release; and are sustained by the joy of taking risks and getting through them. The comments of the participating students strongly suggest that they saw the Rutgers sessions as interludes outside of ordinary school, having a separate time and purpose. They spoke of being caught up in the form, function, rules, and order; being energized by the activities; and being stretched and feeling pleasure in working out the challenges. That's a good match. The children experienced the Rutgers sessions as play, in Huizinga's classic sense.

Were they involved in investigative minding? Clearly pat answers were not being evoked. The students were prompted into inquiry, reflective reasoning. And their group discussions and dialogues with the researchers kept them in inquiry. The children relied on their own proofs, validated their own work, and did not ask the teacher for the "right answer."

There is also some evidence that the sessions put them in the zone. The tasks kept them focused on an absorbing goal. Jeff spoke of typically losing track of time because he was so engrossed. The students collaborated and provided feedback for each other, apparently in ways that were not taken as criticism. Romina commented on her lack of fear of making mistakes. They felt their skills and understanding being stretched. Mike spoke of a sense of students owning the process. These features of the sessions all suggest zone experiences, and all are evident in the clips shown in the videotape.

When the Rutgers approach is used with science rather than math content, there is a slight shift in structure. Most aspects remain the same: a classroom group is divided into small teams of two or three students; the adult supplies materials and poses a challenge that involves the materials; the activity is set up as structured play, not a school assignment; the materials and the challenge guide the activity, while the adult becomes just an observer or assistant to the groups; the students have the responsibility to steer their own actions, in group dialogue; the adult asks groups to explain what they did in their work and convince others that their outcome is defensible; and, with the emphasis being on student reasoning, the adult does not supply a "right answer."

When science is the focus, the target for the activity is students' naive concepts of how the world works—the concepts not supported by science. The adult leader would be working from a plan that has children's typical naive conceptions identified and sequenced by topic in an order that lists the most basic ones first, the ones that are foundational for more complex concepts. A large variety of hands-on science experiments for children is available, from many sources. The ones I have examined have not been organized in order of foundational hierarchy. And they vary considerably in educational quality, with some seeming to be more focused on entertainment value— "Wow! Isn't science exciting!"—than on nurturing student reasoning. Obviously, the latter is what is needed here as the prime criterion for selecting experiments.

Another criterion is that the activity done by groups of two or three can be managed by them without adult assistance, after the adult has set up the conditions required for the experiment. In most cases, the first part of the setup is having students articulate their reasoning about some "fact" of how the world works. Here's an example of what I mean, addressing the misconception that summer is warmer than winter because Earth is closer to the sun in summer. After the opening explanations by the students, the adult sets up conditions for the experiment using, perhaps, a globe on a stand, tilted on its axis as Earth is in relation to the sun. Using a large flashlight as the sun, he or she shows that about half of Earth is illuminated by the sun at any one time in the earth's rotation, half experiencing day, half having night in a twenty-four-hour rotation. But some places on Earth get the sun's rays hitting it straight on, and other places on Earth's surface, at the same time, get the sun's rays at a glancing angle. The adult pastes spots on the globe along the same meridian and asks, "Would Earth pick up more heat from the sun: here, directly facing the sun, or at this angle, or here, or does the angle make any difference? Why? Can we test this?"

Each group of two or three gets materials for the experiment: two or three tin can lids, a lump of clay, some black tempera paint, and a brush. The experiment needs to be done in direct sunlight. Breaking into their small groups, they paint one side of each can lid, let it dry, and mount it with a small lump of clay, black side toward the sun. One lid is placed directly facing the sun, angled in the clay to be directly perpendicular to the sun. The other two lids face the sun at angles like those places where the spots were placed on the globe. While the lids stand in the sun to pick up heat from it, the whole group can talk about Earth's rotation using the globe and the flash-light. After ten minutes, the small groups check the warmth of each lid with their fingers or by putting the lids against their wrists.

The children in their groups discuss the meaning of the relative tem-perature variations of the lids and explain their findings and reasoning to the whole group. The adult says, "Is summer happening where the rays of the sun hit the earth most directly, straight on? And winter where the rays hit at a glancing angle?" The adult then calls attention to the location of the spots pasted on the globe in relation to the conti-nents and moves the discussion in the direction of showing why, for example, Christmas—of course, on December 25—is celebrated in the summer in Australia. Or why near the poles there are days when there is no daylight, or nights when the sun is always visible.

Now we need to consider what the insights of the Harvard-Smithsonian science education studies and the Rutgers math project suggest for making changes in the schooling process as a whole, a process that has not changed appreciably from the blank-slate assumption despite decades of reform efforts. Since the 1960s I have studied the diverse goals and strategies of groups that have champi-oned changes in instruction in math, science, social studies, and reading. On the whole, their good ideas and passionate efforts were unsuccessful, and they faded away. I have come to the firm conviction that these efforts underestimated the tenacity of the entrenched blank-slate assumption that permeates the institution of schooling. As with the Harvard-Smithsonian and Rutgers projects, the reform efforts were challenging the pat-answer approach to teaching. The reformers largely believed that the logical soundness and inherent attractiveness of the ideas they promoted would convince teachers to make the effort to incorporate the new ideas and techniques into their teaching agenda. The reformers did not adequately take into account the typically overloaded condition of teachers. The proposed changes further overloaded them, and the institutional bias toward pat-answer teaching pulled teachers back to a traditional mode that was more manageable.

It was this analysis and the successes of the Rutgers project that brought me to the proposal of a Trojan horse, 2 percent solution. The Rutgers project, by all indications, was highly successful in influencing its student participants in several ways: interest in math, reasoning ability, ownership of their own learning and development, self-confidence as learners, a constructive attitude toward problem solving, and others—all of which carried over into their regular school work. The carryover happened despite the fact that the Rutgers work with the students was totally separate from their regular classroom work. My rough estimate is that the Rutgers participants spent less than 2 percent of their 180 days of each school year engaged with the experimenters. Yet the effect on them was dramatic. What can we speculate about the effect on their schools and their teachers? The participants' enthusiasm and progress could not have gone unnoticed. Might not some of the Rutgers rationale and methods have been picked up by some of the teachers?

Now suppose that all the students in a school district, beginning in first grade, had the opportunity to participate in Rutgers-like sessions, activities that were set up outside the regular curriculum and not subject to any of the conventional accountability requirements, such as tests and grades, for these sessions. Suppose 2 percent of the students' schooltime would be given to carefully structured math and science play, conducted in Rutgers style by someone other than a regular teacher. Two percent would be about an hour a month per group of children. Might not this Trojan horse brought into the school yield more than a 2 percent gain in students' academic progress and character development?

The Trojan horse aspect of this proposal is not about science and mathematics. Teachers have known for decades that children's tangible experiments in science and mathematics have the power to help them gain clear and accurate concepts about how the world works. Many excellent hands-on materials and ideas for children's experiments are available. Teachers and curriculum planners are open to these teaching tools. The Trojan horse analogy applies to making an opening in the seemingly impregnable walls of the blank-slate assumption that dominates the institution of schooling. As the story goes, the Trojans didn't know that the intriguing giant wooden horse the Athenians had built ostensibly to honor Athena—and had apparently abandoned outside the walls of Troy—was a trick concocted by the Athenian army to get the Trojans to dismantle part of their city wall to bring the horse into their own temple to Athena. Once the wall was open, the Athenian army got in and prevailed. The analogy isn't perfect, but I believe the wall of the blank-slate assumption that dominates the schooling process has not yet yielded through the decades to any rational, direct confrontation, whereas it may open itself to the indirect approach of the 2 percent solution.

A word about the power of ownership. It was when the Trojans took ownership of the horse that they became vulnerable. When schools take ownership of the successes of the 2 percent plan, they tacitly acknowledge the concepts this book is about. The ownership means that the deeply ingrained blank-slate preconception held by educators and students alike becomes visible to them and open to inspection. The educators become primed to reconstruct or replace it.

The power of ownership is what the Rutgers participants spoke about: they owned the challenge put to them by the researcher. They owned the investigative process, as a group, and this put them into a state of play that carried them along until they came up with solutions, solutions they themselves owned and validated, without needing to ask the adult if they got the "right answer." These outcomes are totally consistent with the fact of human nature we have been discussing: from birth onward we are investigators trying to make sense of life experiences and forming our *own* private conceptions of how the world works. We have ownership of them because we made them. We are invested in them; our sense of who we are is tied up in them. If what we are "taught" in school is contradictory to them, we may "learn" the new concept in a superficial way but keep our *own* concept as a deeper underpinning. We give up ownership of our own version only when our own further investigating finds it inadequate and we invent a replacement that makes more sense.

This process of disowning something and embracing something new may sometimes be a very long one. The 2 percent solution proposed here is not a quick fix. When a process starts with first graders it is impossible to say how long it will take to influence the whole system. Schools with more resources could start it in more grades at the same time. There are, of course, schools that already have consciously rejected the blank-slate assumption. Most were founded for that purpose. Some, such as High Tech High, a magnet program in San Diego, are receiving a lot of attention for their innovations akin to those described in this chapter. Some of them can be identified by typing "constructivist schools" into your internet search engine. A related influence in schools can be found by searching under *constructionism*, a term coined by Seymour Papert. A 2008 book, *Blocks to Robots: Learning with Technology in the Early Childhood Classroom*, describes the Pappert-influenced programs.[10] The 2 percent solution is obviously intended for conventional schools steeped in pat-answer teaching, perhaps with budget constraints, rather than schools already committed to an experimental instructional program.

I have never been a teacher of mathematics or science, but I believe the structure of the Rutgers approach in this proposal of a 2 percent solution can be generalized to teaching most, if not all, aspects of these disciplines. The approach is characterized by Ellen Langer as *sideways learning*: neither top-down nor bottom-up, neither pat-answer nor student creative discovery.[11] The teacher sets the context for learning and the students investigate to make sense of their own experiences within the context. Her book includes reports of dozens of research studies related to sideways teaching.

I believe the Trojan horse aspect of the 2 percent solution could be characterized as a sideways intervention for bringing some reform into the schooling establishment. Top-down interventions have not worked to dislodge the blank-slate assumption. Nor have creative teachers managed to spread their innovations widely, bottom-up. My proposal for a 2 percent, Trojan horse approach to introduce change in schools addresses that problem. But in no way should my proposal be taken as a substitute for or replacement of other strategies for improving schooling. Eric Schmidt, CEO of Google, when interviewed on PBS in March 2009, spoke of communities of learning being made possible by the Internet. He commented on a spectacular rise in various kinds of Internet exchanges between teachers of science and mathematics in particular. It is easy to imagine Trojan horse teachers contacting each other this way extensively, sharing ideas, materials, and results of investigation lessons.

There are many ways to refocus schools toward the broad goals represented by this book. My own work toward that end, for over three decades, has been to introduce to school personnel the use of the concepts underlying the MBTI and the MMTIC (Murphy-Meisgeier Type Indicator for Children) instruments as a means to better match instruction to students' different kinds of motivations and ways of learning. As of 2007, the MMTIC resources have been substantially enhanced and made more available to teachers and parents. They can be found at www .capt.org. And they are fine tools for helping to break the blank slate.

IN THE WORKPLACE

As I said in chapter 1, identifying how we can promote the zone experience for others—in our coaching, supervising, parenting, mentoring, and teaching—has been my main focus in shaping this book. We recognize in our own zone experiences their power to be catalytic of our growth and development, and we want others to find the same level of motivating energy. When I started this book I did not know what I would find as evidence of the zone actually being promoted in systematic ways. As I began the writing I had no idea what would be in this last chapter, except that it should highlight practical uses of the ideas in the previous chapters. I decided to concentrate on two institutional applications, schooling and the workplace. The Rutgers and Harvard-Smithsonian investigations gave me the basis for the first half of the chapter. Research conducted by the Gallup Organization is what I found as the basis for workplace reform that promotes zone functioning and investigative minding.

The first part of the Gallup research with employees was for the purpose of devising a measuring stick, a set of questions to put to subsequent research subjects to identify the most high-performing workplaces. Hundreds of questions were drafted and asked, and all were dropped except for twelve. The most valued employees responded to these questions most positively. The Gallup researchers concluded that these twelve questions "capture the *most* information and the most *important* information" about the quality of a workplace.

In 1998 Gallup researchers used the questions in a study of twenty-four companies from a cross-section of twelve distinct industries. Within these companies they identified over 2,500 business units to compare with each other. They interviewed 105,000 employees. From those business units they had obtained measurements of four different kinds of business outcomes: productivity, profitability, employee retention, and customer satisfaction. "The Gallup research was the first cross-industry study to investigate the links between employee opinion and business unit performance, across many different companies."[12]

To explain the comparison of business units, they gave an example of an "extremely successful" retail company that employed thirty-seven thousand people spread across three hundred stores, with about a hundred employees per store. Although the stores were carefully designed to be alike in every detail, they differed dramatically in productivity, employee morale, employee turnover, and so on. Treating each store as a separate business unit, Gallup researchers compared employee responses to the twelve questions between stores to try to pinpoint the reasons for the differences. With organization-wide policies being consistent across stores, and with demographic and other such variables being taken into account, the researchers had to conclude that the differences between stores could only be accounted for by the main shaper of each store's culture: the immediate manager of the employees.

Employee responses to the twelve questions pointed directly to the quality of relationship between supervisor and employee; for example, responses to a question concerning employee opinion as to how well they were supplied with resources needed to do their work right. The store that rated highest on the twelve questions had 45 percent of its employees strongly agreeing with this question, while the lowest-ranking store had only 5 percent agreeing strongly with it. In fact, the two stores had the same materials and equipment, "yet the employees' perception of them was utterly different. Everything, even the physical environment, was colored by the supervisory behavior of the store manager. . . . The manager was the key."[13]

This is what they found in comparing the 2,500 business units. "First, we saw that those employees who responded more positively to the twelve questions also worked in business units with higher levels of productivity, profit, retention, and customer satisfaction. . . . Second,

the meta-analysis revealed that employees rated the questions differently depending upon which business unit they worked for rather than
which company."[14] For companies with multiple business units the
results meant "there was a limit to what they could control from the
center. . . . On the brighter side, however, these results revealed that
this company was blessed with some truly exemplary managers. These
managers had built productive businesses by engaging the talents and
passions of their people. . . . The talented employee may join a company because of its charismatic leaders, its generous benefits, and its
world-class training programs, but *how long that employee stays and
how productive he is while he is there is determined by his relationship
with his immediate supervisor*" [emphasis added].[15]

The power of the employee-supervisor relationship is reflected in
another outcome. Of the twelve questions, the most powerful ones are
those with a combination of the *strongest* links to the *most* business
outcomes (productivity, profitability, employee retention, and customer satisfaction). And the six most powerful questions are most
linked to the actions of the immediate supervisor. They are the first six
on the list. We will examine, a little later in the chapter, the implications of these six questions for our central theme: promoting the zone
phenomenon, investigative minding, and working with people of different types of mental processing.

The other major Gallup study addressed the question of what
great managers do to bring out the best in their employees. Eighty
thousand managers were interviewed. Gallup compared the answers
of great managers to those of "average" managers to look for patterns, to learn what, if anything, the great ones had in common that
distinguished them from their less successful colleagues. The exemplary ones, those who managed the most productive business units,
had an approach to supervision quite distinct from the others. Here is
a summary of the findings.

In dealing with employee strengths and weaknesses, the exemplary managers concentrated on identifying and enhancing
employees' natural strengths and working around their weak spots.

Rather than comparing each employee to a set of ideal competencies and coaching each one in the skills they lack, great managers
focus on finding *strengths* in individual differences, strengths that represent the motivational core of the employee—her distinctive way of

thinking. They draw on the strengths to help her become a better version of who she already is. Then the manager adjusts work roles to fit the individuals.[16]

The exemplary managers characterized their role as that of *catalyst*. The first six of the twelve questions that identified strong workplaces contain the guidelines for the catalyst role:

- negotiate clear expectations
- provide needed resources
- provide opportunity "to do what I do best every day"
- give recognition and praise
- connect in a caring relationship
- encourage personal development[17]

The great managers resisted the trend of their organizations to assign the catalyst role to special departments, such as human resources or training. What they wanted to manage themselves was selecting employees, helping them find the best fit within the work of the team, setting expectations, motivating and developing each one, one on one.

Marcus Buckingham and Curt Coffman, the authors of the Gallup report, distinguished the catalyst role from the conventional role of manager as follows.[18]

Key Roles	Conventional View	Catalyst View
Select a person:	based on her experience, intelligence, and determination	for talent (disposition, temperament)
Set expectations:	by defining the right steps	by defining the right outcomes
Motivate the person:	by helping him identify and overcome his weaknesses	by focusing on strengths, not on weaknesses
Develop the person:	by helping her learn and get promoted	by helping her find the right fit, not simply the next rung on the ladder

The authors of the report gave extended descriptions of the catalyst role as it was characterized by the exemplary managers identified in the research work, summarized in the table. It is a role fully consistent with the thrust of this book: helping people find zone functioning and investigative minding by engaging them through their own type of mental processing, their motivations and priorities. We will briefly look at the four features of catalytic management.

1. Great managers select a person for talent. The report's authors define *talent* in a special way. What great managers try to identify in their employees are *recurring patterns of thought, feeling, or behavior* that can be productively applied to the work at hand. They look for an employee's "mental filter" that is constantly, unconsciously "sorting, sifting, creating a world in real time." The filter is the source of the recurring patterns of behavior. To this the authors have given the shorthand name *talent*. It could just as well have been called predisposition or temperament. In my view, of course, the best system for identifying the recurring mental patterns and filters was given to us by Carl Jung—the psychological types. Buckingham and Coffman offer an example of accountants' talents:

> Through Gallup's studies of great accountants, we have discovered that one of their most important talents is an innate love of precision. Ask a great accountant—not any accountant, but a great accountant—when he smiles and he will tell you, "When the books balance." When the books balance, his world is perfect. He may not show it, but inside he is aglow. All he can think about is, Oh, when can I do that again!
>
> A love of precision is not a skill. Nor is it knowledge. It is a talent. If you don't possess it, you will never excel as an accountant. If someone does not have this talent as part of his filter, there is very little a manager can do to inject it.[19]

"Great managers are not troubled by the fact that there is a limit to how much they can rewire someone's brain. Instead they view it as a happy confirmation that people are different. There is no point wishing away this individuality. It's better to nurture it. It's better to help someone understand this filter and then channel it toward productive behavior."[20] "There is nothing very special about talent. . . . Talent is only potential."[21] No one should be taking credit for talent because it is commonplace. "However, each person can and should take credit for cultivating his unique set of talents."[22] The best way a manager can help an employee cultivate her distinctive talents and move toward excellence is by helping her find roles that match and tap into those talents.[23]

2. Great managers set expectations by defining the right outcomes rather than by defining the right steps. Then they let each employee find his own route toward the agreed-upon outcomes.

> [This approach] resolves the great manager's dilemma. All of a sudden her two guiding beliefs—that people are enduringly different and that managers must focus people on the same performance—are no longer in conflict. They are now in harmony. In fact, they are intertwined. The latter frees her up to capitalize on the former. . . . [She] can go with each person's flow, smoothing a unique path toward the desired result.[24]

This approach also frees the manager to be more straight with the employee who is consistently not meeting expectations. Rather than being stuck in issues shaped by categories such as poor work ethic, weaknesses, disobedience, or disrespect, the manager and employee can approach the problem as one of miscasting—a mismatch of talents and role. The matter of finding the right fit takes us to the next aspect of catalytic management.

3. Great managers motivate a person by focusing on strengths, not on weaknesses. When working with an employee whose performance shows him to be miscast, the great managers hold up a mirror, prompting a reflection process in which the employee examines missteps to learn more about his unique set of talents and nontalents. This is the beginning of finding a better fit. "They use language like 'This isn't a fit for you, let's talk about why' or 'You need to find a role that plays more to your natural strengths. What do you think that role might be?' They use this language not because it is polite, not because it softens the bad news, but because it is true."[25] The manager's job is to set the person up for success.

When looking for a good fit of employee talents to the roles to be filled, there are often times when managers cannot select for talent from a large pool. But one can always scan for it in the existing personnel, scanning to find the best fit of person to role. Out of the vast array of personal qualities that can be scanned for, two can be especially important indicators of talent, according to the authors: what roles the people have been able to learn rapidly in the past, and their sources of satisfaction. "Everyone breathes different psychological oxygen. What is fulfilling for one person is asphyxiating for another. . . . A person's sources of satisfaction are clues to his talent. So ask him what his greatest personal satisfaction is. Ask him what kinds of situations give him strength. Ask him what he finds fulfilling. His answers will help you know what he will be able to keep doing week after week after week."[26]

Great managers don't try to fix the weaknesses; they work around them. They work to help each person become more of who he already is. Why is it so tempting to try to fix people, including oneself? Because we've been taught to take stock, find the gaps, and try to build up our skill set, to be come more "well-rounded." The most effective managers reject this. "Why? Because if the focus of your life is to turn your nontalents, such as empathy or strategic thinking or persuasiveness, into talents, then it will be a crushingly frustrating life."[27] Taking stock of one's weaknesses is not what promotes development. Great managers don't manage with weaknesses in mind. They know that "no matter how well intended, relationships preoccupied with weakness never end well."[28] This finding is echoed in research cited by Daniel Goleman.[29] He reminds us that a leader's emotional tone can have surprising power, for better or worse. In exchanges based on weaknesses the subordinate feels isolated and threatened. In exchanges based on strengths, the impact is positive, and the subordinate feels empathy and support.

4. Great managers develop the person by helping her find the right fit, not simply the next rung on the ladder. The best managers know that "*self-discovery is the driving, guiding force for a healthy career,* . . . not just filling oneself up with marketable experiences. Self-discovery is a long process, never fully achieved. [Great managers] give self-discovery a central role, making it an explicit expectation for each employee."[30]

However far along on a career path the person is, the manager's role is to help her take the responsibility "to look in the mirror and ask, 'Do I thrill to this role? Did I seem to learn this role quickly? Am I good in this role? Does this role bring me strength and satisfaction?'" The manager helps her find clues that this role plays to her talents.

> As she looks in the mirror, she learns. Each step is the chance to discover a little more about her talents and her nontalents. These discoveries guide her next step and her next and her next. Her career is no longer a blind hunt for marketable experiences and a breathless climb upward. It has become an increasingly refined series of choices, as she narrows her focus toward that role, or roles, where her strengths—her skills, her knowledge, and her talents—converge and resound.[31]

Readers interested in more detailed suggestions and examples of catalytic managers in action can find them in a follow-up book, published by Gallup Press: *12: The Elements of Great Managing*, by Rodd Wagner and James. K. Harter. It draws on the same research base as *First, Break All the Rules: What the World's Greatest Managers Do Differently*, by Marcus Buckingham and Curt Cuffman, plus data from thousands of additional interviews. Gallup has also published a book applying the same principles to schools: *Building Engaged Schools*, by Gary Gordon.[32]

The Gallup focus of managing people with an emphasis on their natural strengths rather than their deficiencies led to research on how to describe the strength patterns. Donald Clifton, with the help of Tom Rath and other researchers, derived from the huge pool of Gallup data thirty-four "themes" of natural strengths, such as Adaptability, Connectedness, Developer, and Self-Assurance. In 2001 they introduced an online self-report instrument, the StrengthsFinder, to help people identify preferences and patterns in themselves that could give clues to a better match between personal inclinations and career roles. In 2007, Gallup released a revised version of the online instrument, StrengthsFinder 2.0, to accompany the publication of the 2007 book by Tom Rath.

Clifton's thirty-four themes emerged from a kind of factor analysis of Gallup's data. In contrast to Jung's sixteen psychological types, the thirty-four themes are not derived from or linked to a comprehensive *theory* of human mental functioning. These are two different ways of identifying patterns of natural mental inclinations. As readers might suppose, I prefer the Jung/Myers work as I have described it in chapter 3. The type descriptions offer a means for people to identify and explore a match of their priorities and motivations in relation to many life choices and roles, including career choices and work roles. And Jung's symmetrical theory shows the interconnectedness and dynamic interplay of personality variables in ways that go beyond trait-based descriptions.

Let's review the content of this chapter and consider how the main themes of this book run through the Rutgers, Harvard-Smithsonian, and Gallup research processes and outcomes. First of all, those studies highlight the blockage to human development caused by the blank-slate assumption and show the energy for growth that is released when the blank-slate/pat-answer barrier is bypassed. The Rutgers study showed the gains in mathematics children could make when their natural investigative side is engaged—gains especially impressive because the intervention took up less than 2 percent of the children's time in school. Their small group investigations—totally bypassing pat-answer instruction—seemed to spark the zone for them.

The Harvard-Smithsonian project demonstrated that many graduates of prestigious colleges, with years of science instruction, had only a veneer of science pat answers to show for the hundreds of hours of their time invested. Underneath the veneer, and largely unfazed by science instruction, were the naive theories they had formed in childhood by their own untutored investigations to make sense of their world. "Scientific" explanations they had worked out for themselves had an emotional hold on them that could not be broken unless their teacher and curriculum abandoned the blank-slate assumption and "held up the mirror." Teachers holding up the mirror are acknowledging the reality and power of the students' preconceptions, prompting students to see inconsistencies and reflect on ways to reconcile conflicting data. Acknowledging that children come to the classroom with already organized minds, and that deep learning comes only when the children reorganize their ideas of how the world works, is a big step.

The Gallup studies give strong evidence that great managers treat their employees in the ways identified in the main themes of this book. They treat people fairly by carefully identifying and respecting their differences, rather than treating them alike. They focus on using people's strengths, matching people to roles that give them both satisfaction and manageable challenges. And the managers work around people's weak spots. These practices are fully consistent with the objectives of Jung and Myers of bringing out the best in people by honoring their differences in types of mental processing. The great managers break the blank-slate barrier. They avoid pat-answer supervision and give employees latitude in how they use their different talents to reach the common objectives. The great managers engage people as fellow investigators who share ownership with them in the process of finding good solutions. In doing so they set up conditions for the zone experience, conditions that release in people highly productive energy.

THE SCHOOL AND WORKPLACE LINKAGE

There is a serious disconnect between school and workplace, between what schools are currently preparing students to do and what the twenty-first-century workplace requires. Several foundations concerned about the disconnect funded the National Center on Education and the Economy (NCEE) to study the problem and prepare a comprehensive report and recommendations for public policy. The funding foundations were the Annie E. Casey Foundation, the Bill and Melinda Gates Foundation, the William and Flora Hewlett Foundation, and the Lumina Foundation for Education. The carefully prepared and critiqued report, *Tough Choices or Tough Times*, was published in 2007.[33]

The report argues convincingly that the ability of the United States to hold its own in the changing global economy will require a change in education to put a much heavier emphasis on fostering in students higher qualities of mind: "a deep vein of creativity . . . comfort with ideas and abstractions . . . innovation . . . investigative thinking . . . ingenuity . . . quick   learning . . . flexibility . . . self-discipline . . . cross-cultural empathy . . . capacity to work on ever-changing teams, . . . and mathematical reasoning" in addition to the familiar goals of "a very high level of preparation in reading, writing, speaking, mathematics, science, literature, history, and the arts." Few people would argue with the goals. The report makes many policy recommendations for well-thought-out process reforms, but at the heart of the NCEE proposal are two key strategies: recruitment of highly talented, "world-class" teachers, through considerably higher pay, and a much-improved student testing process. "The kinds of examinations and assessments that will capture these and other qualities at the level of accomplishment required will entail a major overhaul of the American testing industry. If that is not done, then nothing else will matter, because the old saw that what gets measured is what gets taught is essentially true."[34] Given its emphasis on higher qualities of mind, I was deeply disappointed to find the report totally captive to the blank-slate assumption. Here are the problems:

- There are no existing paper-and-pencil tests that can measure the qualities of mind mentioned above. They are measurable but not by this means. These qualities are deep dispositions that competent teachers can recognize in students' interactions. Teachers can identify them and chart their development over time. Teachers—not tests—are the yardstick that can measure progress on these objectives. Perhaps these qualities can be measured to a modest extent by psychological inventories, but they are in a different ballpark from the competencies that are measured by educational exams. I seriously doubt that paper-and-pencil exams can ever be designed to measure them.
- These qualities of mind can indeed be fostered in schools, provided that the teachers themselves already have the qualities and are eager to help students develop them. They are qualities that the Rutgers and Harvard-Smithsonian projects were able to stimulate. But accountability exams do not help the process. They tend to hinder it by steering attention and effort away from creative and investigative learning processes.
- Yearly administered statewide accountability exams have taken over American education, and they drive the curriculum and teaching practices. They are also driving out of education the very teachers who have the qualities the NCEE report is looking for, because they feel stifled by the exam-driven curriculum. This outcome is not surprising. Statewide accountability exams came into existence because legislators were disappointed with the quality of work being done by teachers. So they instituted high-

stakes testing to micromanage classrooms. They wanted to see yearly progress of all students on basic minimum skills—all students measured against common standards. Some teachers I have interviewed don't mind the test-focused worksheets and practice exams that have come to dominate the system. But the inventive, ingenious teachers largely see the change as a slap in the face, and they hate it for cramping their autonomy and demeaning their professional judgment. And they leave teaching. My wife—a retired elementary school principal—and I have seen this firsthand, many times.

- The problem is not with the existence of exams, but with the fact that they are competency post-tests. They are the tools of a carrot-or-stick view of motivation, a view that will not under any circumstances foster the qualities of mind we are talking about. They are grounded squarely in the blank-slate assumption. The teachers we want to attract and retain are not afraid of exams; they don't want passing tests to be what is most focused on in the classroom. Legislators, representing the public, want accountability exams. There is a solution that has a chance of satisfying both interests, as well as improving schools in the ways proposed in this book.

Here are my suggestions for policymakers. First, alter the statewide accountability testing in two ways. Existing statewide exams measure student year-to-year gains in the aggregate, school by school, not child by child. They take a snapshot of each classroom group toward the end of each school year. They are not designed to help teachers and parents track an individual child's progress from year to year or give guidance on how to match instruction to each student to enhance her progress. That is a critical flaw that can be fixed by moving the exam to the beginning of the school year and converting it to a *diagnostic-developmental* inventory. When the test is given early, the results can be returned to teachers soon enough in the school year to be used in pinpointing each child's level of learning and identifying the gaps that need attention. Teachers and principals can move beyond a test-driven curriculum and teaching process that moves lockstep for all children irrespective of their level of prior achievement or individual differences in base strengths and motivation. With the new testing, parents can get a more accurate measurement of their child's status and progress. Data from this kind of diagnostic-developmental inventory will identify a child's gains against her previous year's status and show the baseline skills and concepts to which the teacher can match instruction. Data from this new test can also be aggregated to show school-by-school progress—the classroom snapshot. From the point of view of the legislators and the public they represent, the statewide annual tests will remain a year-to-year accountability tool. The measurement will simply change from September to September.

When the test is removed as an end-of-the-year test, the pressure to learn for the sake of the test is reduced. This is a good thing. Anxiety about doing well on high-stakes tests is detrimental to learning for many children. High-stakes tests provoke emotional reactions quite different from diagnostic tests or the regular, frequent tests that teachers prepare to accompany lessons. The latter are not a drag on the learning process. And, most important, so long as the lessons continue to be aimed toward the common statewide basic goals, the accountability system continues. The statewide testing retains its constructive features and loses unwanted baggage.

If they are to have diagnostic value, the yearly statewide test results need to be returned to schools quickly in the fall, and they also have to be packaged in a way that teachers can easily identify from the data where each child stands on the various threads of skills and concepts—information they can use in mapping out their lessons. That will mean a change of reporting format for most states, to provide the kind of data teachers expect from a *diagnostic* test. The emphasis will be on identifying the prerequisite concepts and skills that each student has or doesn't have in entering the curriculum typical for that year's studies. Without such data on each child, the teacher will have a much, much harder time matching instruction to the individual child's level of reading, math knowledge, and so on. Research has shown again and again that children's confidence in themselves as learners and their competence in school tasks are seriously set back when they do not encounter materials that match their instructional level. We know, of course, that the range of levels is very wide, even in first grade. And in our present mode of undifferentiated instruction—one lesson plan fits all—the gap between skill levels never closes; it only gets wider.

From a student's point of view, the proposed annual test administered in the fall is a pre-test, not a post-test. For example, the fall-administered math test given to students just starting geometry will show how well the students grasp the foundation skills needed for starting geometry, not specifically how well they mastered algebra in the previous year. This concept of diagnostic testing is fully consistent with the NCEE's intent of getting students more engaged and energized in their studies. Moving the testing to September administrations and adapting its reports to provide diagnostic, developmental data should help release a lot of constructive energy among teachers and students that should boost achievement scores and have many other positive consequences. The research on effective instruction is very clear: lessons that are active, varied, and hands-on are far more effective than those organized around test-focused worksheets, which have come to dominate the curriculum. The effect of the change should be welcomed by teachers, especially teachers who have the qualities we are trying to keep in, and attract to, our schools. They would welcome diagnostic data they can take into account in lesson plans. For teachers to stimulate curiosity, ingenuity, investigation, initiative—and the other qualities we are looking for—they need to know the fund of understandings the individual students bring to the learning situation.

The present system of annual statewide tests has another serious flaw. It is a validity issue. A little reflection raises the strong impression that the statewide competency test results are padded with unreliable right answers, in other words, trained responses with little to no understanding of meaning. All of us who have taken a competency test right after studying specifically for that test know that some of our answers were something we held in memory just long enough to put on the test. This is especially true when we used aids such as worksheets and practice tests containing items that mirror those on the final test, a practice now taken up in schools in many states. Many of the facts and skills implied by our test scores never entered our long-term memory—they were "just test learning."

If the purpose of statewide testing is to measure how well the public money for schools is being spent, this kind of testing—one that encourages teaching to the test and inflates test scores—is a flawed notion of accountability. True accountability comes from accurate data. Having the measurement points be in September is a straight-forward way to remove the padding and get better evidence of student gains. September-to-September measurement will give more accurate evidence: children's unreliable, not-understood, right answers will largely disappear from their memories over the summer break. From this cleaned-up evidence of gains, teachers will be better able to tell what was taught well enough to survive into permanent memory and what needs to be taught again in more effective ways.

Beyond testing is the issue of improving the school as a work-place, for teachers and students alike. Getting and keeping a higher caliber of teachers in schools will only be effectively done if they work under school leaders who give them the support and latitude they need to do their best work. Suppose some of the great managers Gallup identified were brought in to consult on school management. No doubt they would emphasize the four key catalytic roles any man-ager should play, including the school principal: select teachers for talent, that is, deep dispositions that fit the roles; set expectations by defining the right outcomes and allowing teachers latitude on how to reach them; motivate teachers by focusing on their strengths, not their weaknesses; and allow them to develop their skills by helping them find the right fit in the teaching program.

Finally, I want to emphasize the need for a new focus in instruc-tion. If schools are to develop in students the mental and emotional qualities that take our next-generation workforce to a higher level, then the school experience must be mainly about giving children daily opportunities to *do* the kinds of tangible and practical investigations, creations, initiatives, and self-managed work we expect of them after they leave school. There is no other way to develop these traits than by being immersed in situations that foster them daily. I would call the new focus investigative learning. When students engage in investiga-tions that draw on their base of strengths—their own type of mental processing—they then can get beyond the blank-slate barrier we have perpetuated and get to a place where the zone experience is more freely available to take them to higher-level functioning.

AFTERWORD

Chapter 6 addressed the issue of developing a zone culture in our institutional life, specifically in schools and the workplace. For some readers, that is not their main reason for reading the book. Their focus is on finding useful ideas for their own personal development. In closing the book, let's loop back to that topic. Readers puzzling with such questions as, Why don't I find the zone more often? or How can I tinker with my job to get more zone in it? or How can I find the zone more often with my children? are looking for clues as to what precipitates the zone experience and sustains it.

My suggestion for a starting point is to decide, at least tentatively, which archetype description (see p. 143) and which psychological type description (starting on p. 78) best fit you. The archetype descriptions give four distinct ways that people find identity and fulfillment. The psychological type descriptions show sixteen kinds of mental processing, each with different sets of values and priorities. Your preferences among them point to zone doorways for you.

As I am writing this, my wife, Carolyn, suggests herself as an example. When you read the Nurturer archetype description and the ENFJ type description, you are getting a mental picture of what energizes Carolyn. Is it surprising that she finds the zone these days by tutoring children who have trouble in reading? Tutoring is a natural fit for her archetype and type. In contrast, I know other ENFJs who have no interest in bringing along young children. One of them, a Warrior/Adventurer and a state legislator, finds her zone in the hurly-burly of politics. Same type, different archetype, different zone field.

The phrases in the type and archetype descriptions suggest general areas of priority interests that may spark the zone. The phrases also remind us that the *absence* of these conditions will block the zone—and the growth and development that arise from the zone experience. For example, in the case of an ENFJ type, the lack of opportunity to have a wide circle of relationships would be serious blockage.

How does an interest beget a zone experience? When it takes us to investigative minding. Someone looking to find more zone in her work can start by reflecting back on work activities that prompted her to go beyond pat answers to investigation that had a life of its own, that caused work to feel like play. Those sorts of activities point to others that have the same energizing qualities.

How do we recognize investigative minding when it is happening? We are alert, highly attentive to events and people, focused on an absorbing interest, and wholly engaged and probing. Whatever the activity at hand, these experiences indicate the zone is not far behind them. We can't will the zone to happen, but we can intentionally engage in investigative minding, in work and in leisure. Watch for these cues, keep them going, and follow them.

What does it take to sustain the zone? The biggest self-inflicted zone breaker is self-conscious self-criticism. Look for ways to get feedback on your actions that don't engage self-analysis—feedback that gives you data for adjusting your actions without the baggage of *shoulda, woulda, coulda*. The zone sustains itself when the self remains embedded in the task and the flow isn't broken by distractions.

How can we find the zone more often with our children and our partners? By inviting them to be fellow investigators, as Carolyn does with the children she tutors. They join forces in tackling the peculiarities of language, finding rules for how it works. Carolyn has a knack for seeing the world through a child's eyes, seeing what investigations might grab them, and that leads to mutual zone experiences. Jung's characterizations of the psychological types help us see the world through the eyes of types other than our own, and those insights help us find common ground—the basis for mutual zone—with our partners, children, and adults alike. Studying the psychological types is an investment that keeps paying rich dividends.

I wish you well as you build these ideas into your life.

ACKNOWLEDGMENTS

This book has benefitted from the ideas and critiques of many people I consider wise and talented. I am especially grateful to those who read portions or all of the manuscript as it evolved and offered their thoughtful suggestions: Jane Kise, Judy Provost, Nancy McKenzie, Paul Lawrence, Charles Martin, Andrew Meltzoff, and Sue Scanlon. At Prometheus Books, Steven L. Mitchell, editor-in-chief, and editors Joe Gramlich and Jade Zora Ballard were very helpful in getting the book launched.

John Dewey's ideas have been part of me since Clyde Curran introduced me to them fifty years ago. Ten years later Mary McCaulley introduced me to Carl Jung's psychological typology. These two gifted people and the ideas they shared have enriched my life and work ever since. I hope they would see this book as a valuable extension of the ideas they exemplified and planted in me.

Most of all, I am grateful to my wife, Carolyn, whose love, support and wisdom is woven into every page of the book.

NOTES

CHAPTER 1: IN THE ZONE

1. Steven Pinker, *How the Mind Works* (New York: Norton, 1999), p. 44.

2. Steven Pinker, *The Blank Slate: The Modern Denial of Human Nature* (New York: Viking Putnam, 2002).

3. Alison Gopnik, Andrew Meltzoff, and Patricia Kuhl, *The Scientist in the Crib: Minds, Brains and How Children Learn* (New York: William Morrow, 1999), p. 30.

4. Ibid., p. 69.

5. Lise Eliot, *What's Going On in There? How the Brain and Mind Develop in the First Five Years of Life* (New York: Bantam Books, 1999), p. 29; Matt Ridley, *The Red Queen: Sex and the Evolution of Human Nature* (New York: Macmillan, 1993).

6. Howard Gardner, *Frames of Mind: The Theory of Multiple Intelligences* (New York: Basic Books, 1983).

7. Clyde Kluckhohn and Henry A. Murray, *Personality in Nature, Society, and Culture* (New York: Alfred A. Knopf, 1953), p. 53.

8. Mihaly Csikszentmihalyi, *Flow: The Psychology of Optimal Experience* (New York: Harper and Row, 1990); Mihaly Csikszentmihalyi, *Finding Flow: The Psychology of Engagement with Everyday Life* (New York: Basic Books, 1997).

9. W. Timothy Gallwey, *The Inner Game of Tennis*, rev. ed. (New York: Random House, 1997).

10. Csikszentmihalyi, *Flow*.

11. Andrew Cooper, *Playing in the Zone: Exploring the Spiritual Dimensions of Sport* (Boston: Shambhala Press, 1998), p. 41.

12. Joseph LeDoux, *Synaptic Self: How Our Brains Become Who We Are* (New York: Viking Penguin, 2002).

CHAPTER 2: THE INVESTIGATIVE MIND

1. Lise Eliot, *What's Going On in There? How the Brain and Mind Develop in the First Five Years of Life* (New York: Bantam Books, 1999), p. 334.

2. John Dewey, *Art as Experience* (New York: G. P. Putnam's Sons, 1958), p. 163; John Dewey and Arthur Bentley, *Knowing and the Known* (Boston: Beacon Press, 1960), p. 56.

3. Dewey, *Art as Experience*, p. 263.

4. The contributions of Piaget and Vygotsky have been well documented. McGraw's work is well summarized in Thomas Dalton and Victor Bergenn, eds., *Beyond Heredity and Environment: Myrtle McGraw and the Maturation Controversy* (Boulder: Westview Press, 1995).

5. Alison Gopnik, Andrew Meltzoff, and Patricia Kuhl, *The Scientist in the Crib: Minds, Brains, and How Children Learn* (New York: William Morrow, 1999), pp. 26–27.

6. Ibid., p. 29.

7. Ibid., p. 27.

8. These studies are all reported in ibid.

9. Daniel Goleman, *Social Intelligence* (New York: Bantam Dell, 2006), p. 163.

10. Ellen Dissanayake, *Art and Intimacy: How the Arts Began* (Seattle: University of Washington Press, 2000), p. 10.

11. Gopnik, Meltzoff, and Kuhl, *The Scientist in the Crib*, p. 69.

12. Ibid.

13. Ibid., p. 74.

14. Dissanayake, *Art and Intimacy*, p. 104.

15. Gopnik, Meltzoff, and Kuhl, *The Scientist in the Crib*, p. 33.

16. Ibid., p. 32.

17. Ibid., p. 25.

18. Elizabeth Spelke, "Initial Knowledge: Six Suggestions," *Cognition* 50 (2006): 433–47.

19. Martin Brune et al., eds., *The Social Brain: Evolution and Pathology* (Sussex, UK: John Wiley, 2003).

20. Gopnik, Meltzoff, and Kuhl, *The Scientist in the Crib*, p. 36.

21. Dissanayake, *Art and Intimacy*, p. 29.

22. Gopnik, Meltzoff, and Kuhl, *The Scientist in the Crib*, p. 104.

23. Ibid., p. 94.

24. Steven Pinker, *How the Mind Works* (New York: Norton, 1999), p. 14; Steven Pinker, *The Blank Slate: The Modern Denial of Human Nature* (New York: Viking Putnam, 2002).

25. Eliot, *What's Going On in There?* p. 372.

26. Gopnik, Meltzoff, and Kuhl, *The Scientist in the Crib*, p. 117.

27. Matt Ridley, *Nature via Nurture* (New York: HarperCollins, 2003).

28. Goleman, *Social Intelligence*, p. 151.

29. On the relationship of the "inner" and "outer," John Dewey said: "Whatever else organic life is or is not, it is a process of activity that involves an environment. It is a transaction extending beyond the spatial limits of the organism. An organism does not live *in* an environment; it lives by means of an environment. . . . The processes of living are enacted by the environment as truly as by the organism; for they *are* an integration." John Dewey, *Logic: The Theory of Inquiry* (New York: Holt, Rinehart and Winston, 1938), p. 25.

30. Eliot, *What's Going On in There?* p. 41.

31. Donald Symons, *The Evolution of Human Sexuality* (New York: Oxford University Press, 1979).

32. John Dewey, *Essays in Experimental Logic* (Chicago: University of Chicago Press, 1917), pp. 183–219.

33. Joseph LeDoux, *The Emotional Brain: The Mysterious Underpinnings of Emotional Life* (New York: Touchstone, 1998), p. 12.

34. Dissanayake, *Art and Intimacy*, p. 14.

35. Ibid., p. 39.

36. Joseph LeDoux, *Synaptic Self: How Our Brains Become Who We Are* (New York: Viking Penguin, 2002), p. 236.

37. LeDoux, *The Emotional Brain*, p. 280.

CHAPTER 3: FRAMEWORKS OF MENTAL PROCESSING

1. Steven Pinker, *How the Mind Works* (New York: Norton, 1999), pp. 33, 58, 88, 142; Joseph LeDoux, *The Emotional Brain* (New York: Touchstone, 1998), p. 210.

2. Gordon D. Lawrence, *Descriptions of the Sixteen Types* (Gainesville, FL: Center for Applications of Psychological Type, 1998).

3. Isabel Myers in Gordon D. Lawrence, *People Types and Tiger Stripes*, 4th ed. (Gainesville, FL: Center for Applications of Psychological Type, 2009), p. 86.

4. Humphry Osmond, Miriam Siegler, and Richard Smoke, "Typology Revisited: A New Perspective," *Psychological Perspectives* 8:2 (1977): 206–19.

5. Nancy Schaubhut and Richard Thompson, *MBTI Type Tables for Occupations* (Mountain View, CA: CPP, 2008); Isabel Myers, Mary McCaulley, Naomi Quenk, and Allen Hammer, *MBTI Manual: A Guide to the Development and Use of the Myers-Briggs Type Indicator*, 3rd ed. (Mountain View, CA: CPP, 1998).

6. Carl Jung, *Psychological Types* (Princeton, NJ: Princeton University Press, 1971), sec. 512.

7. Pinker, *How the Mind Works*, pp. 21, 89, 95; LeDoux, *The Emotional Brain*, pp. 35, 105; Alison Gopnik, Andrew Meltzoff, and Patricia Kuhl, *The Scientist in the Crib: Minds, Brains, and How Children Learn* (New York: William Morrow, 1999), pp. 49, 99, 108, 122.

8. Pinker, *How the Mind Works*, pp. 33, 58, 88, 142, 144.

9. Carl Jung, *Memories, Dreams, Reflections* (New York: Pantheon, 1963), sec. 512.

10. Pinker, *How the Mind Works*, pp. 448–49.

11. Ibid., p. 33; Robert Ornstein, *MultiMinds: A New Way to Look at Human Behavior* (Boston: Houghton Mifflin, 1996); Marvin Minski, *The Society of Mind* (New York: Simon and Schuster, 1988).

12. Jung, *Memories, Dreams, Reflections*.

13. Jung, *Psychological Types*, preface to the 7th ed.

14. Ibid., secs. 729, 787.

15. LeDoux, *The Emotional Brain*, pp. 63, 161.

16. Pinker, *How the Mind Works*, p. 143.

17. Judith Harris, *The Nurture Assumption: Why Children Turn Out the Way They Do* (New York: Free Press, 1998).

18. Isabel Myers, *Gifts Differing* (Mountain View, CA: CPP, 1980).

19. The validity studies of the MBTI instrument, reviewed in the *MBTI Manual* (3rd ed. 1998), a selection of studies that span fifty years, demonstrate clearly the validity of the indicator, and of Jung's typology that undergirds it. While there is no need to revisit those reviews here, I do want to highlight a review article and a set of studies that didn't get into the *MBTI Manual*. They strike me as very important in two ways: in demonstrating the existence of types and in clarifying that the types are something other than

traits or composites of traits. Both are reported in James Newman, ed., *Measures of the Five Factor Model and Psychological Type: A Major Convergence of Research and Theory* (Gainesville, FL: Center for Applications of Psychological Type, 1996).

In the chapter "A Brief History of the Science of Personality," Newman observed that in recent years the research on personality has shifted dramatically toward a "search for a scientifically compelling taxonomy of personality traits." The taxonomy that has emerged is referred to as the "five factor model" (FFM) of personality. Numerous studies involving factor analysis of many thousands of responses to various personality instruments have produced five remarkably robust factors of personality. Different researchers have given different labels to the factors, but the five factors are considered to represent the major personality traits that account for a very substantial portion of personality variations among people.

Newman reviewed the work of two personality researchers at the National Institutes of Mental Health, R. R. McCrae and P. T. Costa Jr., who developed an instrument called the NEO-PI, designed specifically to measure the five factors. "They have looked at the NEO-PI in relation to just about every major personality test available. In virtually every comparison, they have found significant correlations between major scales of other instruments and those of the NEO. But nowhere did they find more strikingly convergent results than when they compared the NEO-PI with the MBTI." The NEO-PI scales are termed Extraversion, Openness, Agreeableness, Conscientiousness, and Neuroticism. Results on the first four of these NEO-PI scales correlate with the four MBTI scales at a remarkable level: Extraversion/EI, .70; Openness/SN, .70; Agreeableness/TF, .45; and Conscientiousness/JP, .47. It is *very* unusual to find correlations this high of outcomes on different psychological instruments. The sample size of the NEO-PI and MBTI study was 468, and the level of significance was $p < .001$ for all four correlations. The NEO-PI fifth scale is Neuroticism, a factor concerned with mental health. The MBTI has no dimension addressing mental health.

Quoting Newman, "McCrae and Costa (1989) agree that their comparison of the two instruments revealed 'impressive convergence,' but . . . they urge MBTI users to 'seriously consider abandoning Jungian theory [and] . . . adopt the perspective of the five-factor model of personality.' Their advice strikes me as rather odd, given their own admission that the FFM 'is purely descriptive; it does not explain the origins of personality nor the mechanisms that account for individual differences.'"

McCrae and Costa's advice to MBTI users seems upside down to me. Jung has provided an elegant construct to account for individual differences. Science always is concerned with a search for the most clean, parsimonious, comprehensive, and seminal explanations of phenomena—in this case, human personality phenomena. An impartial observer, one with no stake in any particular instrument or preconception, it seems to me, would marvel that an instrument, such as the NEO-PI—derived from factor analysis, and representing no underlying theory of personality—would map behavior so closely with an instrument, such as the MBTI, that was developed expressly to represent a *theory*, Jung's theory of conscious mental processing. The two instruments were constructed in total independence of each other. I believe the impartial observer would regard this convergence of the two instruments as a remarkable validation of Jung's construct.

The convergence of the five-factor model and the MBTI needed examination from another angle. The NEO-PI was designed to measure *traits*. The MBTI was designed to identify *types*. The high correlations of results on the two instruments do not help to demonstrate whether types are distinct from traits. When high correlations were found between the NEO-PI and the MBTI, the correlations were accomplished by treating scores on the MBTI dimensions *as if* they were points on continuous scales rather that distinct categories (e.g., a continuum of sweetness to sourness rather than grapes vs. lemons). For example, the MBTI Extraversion/Introversion dimension was treated as a continuum from high Extraversion to lower Extraversion to low Introversion to high Introversion. In Jung's construct there are no *degrees* of Extraversion; one is an Extravert (outward turner) or not. A study that treats type preference scores as continua does not distinguish between type and trait. Traits are continuous, types are discrete categories. Other research was needed to demonstrated the distinction. Wayne Mitchell's studies addressed that issue directly.

In his report "Empirical Verification of the Jungian Typology," in Newman 1996, Mitchell described a set of type versus trait studies involving the Expanded Analysis Report (EAR) subscales of the EAR version of the MBTI instrument. Each of the four dimensions of the MBTI—EI, SN, TF, and JP—has five subscales. For example, the subscales of TF are: Critical/Accepting, Tough/Tender, Questioning/Accommodating, Logical/Affective, and Reasonable/Compassionate. He used 1,568 people's MBTI results, taken randomly from a large data base. Essentially he tested their subscale results to see if they were more explainable as *traits*, that is, as if no *type* influence was exerted on the scores. A description of the research is beyond the scope of this book, but I am including a quotation from his summary:

> The analyses presented here yield clear evidence in support of Jung's theory, his typology, and the MBTI as a typological instrument. . . . There were clear differences between the trait and typological predictions, sufficiently clear, in fact, that there is no middle ground

between them. There are few times in the behavioral sciences, and especially personality research, when one encounters such dramatic, clear-cut differences between two opposing viewpoints in as many different empirical tests as were presented here. The results, in every case, support the MBTI version of the Jungian typology and refute a trait interpretation of its dimensions. . . . It is normally inappropriate to make such strong claims for one's findings. However, in this case the trait and typological predictions were so starkly opposed, and the results so clearly supported the typology, that to draw weak conclusions would be misleading.

The conclusions that these analyses warrant seem clear to me: the Jungian type preferences have been documented as fundamental psychological elements; and these phenomena are explained distinctly better by Jung's model of personality dynamics than they are by any theory that treats them as bundles of traits.

CHAPTER 4: THE ZONE FINDS US AND DEFINES US

1. Mihaly Csikszentmihalyi, *Flow: The Psychology of Optimal Experience* (New York: Harper and Row, 1991).
2. Johan Huizinga, *Homo Ludens: A Study of the Play Element in Culture* (Boston: Beacon Press, 1955).
3. Ibid., p. 7.
4. Ibid., p. 8.
5. Ibid., pp. 9, 12.
6. Ibid., p. 9.
7. Ibid., p. 10.
8. Ibid.
9. Ibid., p. 11.
10. Ibid., p. 173.
11. Ibid., p. 75.
12. Ibid., p. 10.
13. Ibid., p. 8.
14. The neurological link between play and joy are well documented in Jaak Panksepp's 1988 book, *Affective Neuroscience* (New York: Oxford University Press). He also demonstrates that play promotes neuronal and synaptic growth, particularly in the circuitry in the amygdala and frontal cortex.
15. Ellen Dissanayake, *Art and Intimacy: How the Arts Began* (Seattle: University of Washington Press, 2000), p. 4.
16. Ibid.

17. Ibid.

18. Ibid.

19. Ibid., p. 20.

20. Andrew Cooper, *Playing in the Zone: Exploring the Spiritual Dimensions of Sport* (Boston: Shambhala Press, 1998).

21. Huizinga, *Homo Ludens*, pp. 205, 211.

22. Ibid., p. 213.

23. Chris Hedges, *War Is a Force That Gives Us Meaning* (New York: Public Affairs/Perseus Book Group, 2002).

24. Ibid., p. 3.

25. Ibid., pp. 62, 84.

26. Mihaly Csikszentmihalyi, *Finding Flow: The Psychology of Engagement with Everyday Life* (New York: Basic Books, 1997).

27. Cooper, *Playing in the Zone*, pp. 17, 18.

28. Carl Jung, *The Archetypes and the Collective Unconscious* from *Collected Works of C. G. Jung*, vol. 9, pt. 10 (Princeton, NJ: Princeton University Press, 1963).

29. For example, Carol Pearson, *The Hero Within: Six Archetypes We Live By* (New York: HarperCollins, 1998).

30. Tad and Noreen Guzie, *About Men and Women* (Mahwah, NJ: Paulist Press, 1986).

31. Toni Wolff, *Structural Forms of the Feminine Psyche* (Zurich: Jung Institute, 1956).

32. Tad and Noreen Guzie, "Masculine and Feminine Archetypes: A Complement to the Psychological Types," *Journal of Psychological Type* 7 (1984): 3–11.

CHAPTER 6: BEYOND THE BLANK SLATE

1. See Annenberg Media, Teacher Professional Development and Teacher Resources across the Curriculum, www.learner.org.

2. The video, *Surprises in Mind*, is also viewable from Annenberg Media at www.learner.org/ resources/series130.html (accessed January 25, 2010).

3. Alison Gopnik, Andrew Meltzoff, and Patricia Kuhl, *The Scientist in the Crib: Minds, Brains, and How Children Learn* (New York: William Morrow, 1999), esp. pp. 13, 49, 56–57, 101, 155–56, 161–62, 164.

4. One educator, Valerie L. Talsma, maintains a Web site that includes lists of children's naive conceptions, organized by topics in science, with citations to those who have collected the data: http://homepage.mac.com/ vtalsma/misconcept.html (accessed January 25, 2010).

5. See note 2.

6. Ibid.

7. Private Universe Project in Mathematics, see www.learner.org/channel/workshops/pupmath/workshops/surprises.html (pp. 4, 5).

8. The research design and detailed reporting of the processes and outcomes of the long-term Rutgers study were reported in a series of journal articles, including: C. A. Maher and A. M. Martino, "The Development of the Idea of Mathematical Proof: A Five-Year Case Study," *Journal of Research in Mathematics Education* 27 (1996): 194–214; A. M. Martino and C. A. Maher, "Teacher Questioning to Promote Justification and Generalization in Mathematics: What Research Practice Has Taught Us," *Journal of Mathematical Behavior* 18, no. 1 (1999): 53–78; C. A. Maher, "How Students Structure Their Investigations and Learn Mathematics: Insights from a Long-Term Study," *Journal of Mathematical Behavior* 24 (2005): 1–14; J. M. Francisco and C. A. Maher, "Conditions for Promoting Reasoning in Problem Solving: Insights from a Longitudinal Study," *Journal of Mathematical Behavior* 24 (2005): 361–72; and in a transcript: Robert B. Davis Institute for Learning, Rutgers University, Private Universe Project in Mathematics, transcript of Annenberg Foundation video *Surprises in Mind*, 2001, viewable at www.learner.org.

9. Francisco and Maher, "Conditions for Promoting Reasoning in Problem Solving," p.369.

10. Marina Bers, *Blocks to Robots: Learning with Technology in the Early Child Classroom* (New York: Teachers College Press, 2008).

11. Ellen Langer, *The Power of Meaningful Learning* (Cambridge, MA: Da Capo Press, 1997).

12. Marcus Buckingham and Curt Coffman, *First, Break All the Rules: What the World's Greatest Managers Do Differently* (New York: Simon and Schuster, 1999), p. 28.

13. Ibid., p. 30.

14. Ibid., p. 32.

15. Ibid., pp. 31, 32, 39.

16. Ibid., pp. 56–59.

17. Ibid., pp. 33, 38.

18. Ibid., pp. 66.

19. Ibid., pp. 84, 85.

20. Ibid., p. 32.

21. Ibid., pp. 83, 93.

22. Ibid., p. 93.

23. Ibid., pp. 83, 93.

24. Ibid., p. 110.

25. Ibid., p. 209.

26. Ibid., p. 219.

27. Ibid., p. 145.

28. Ibid., pp. 145, 146.

29. Daniel Goleman, *Social Intelligence: The New Science of Human Relationships* (New York: Bantam Books), p. 194.

30. Buckingham and Coffman, *First, Break All the Rules*, p. 194.

31. Ibid, p. 197.

32. Ibid.; Rodd Wagner and James K. Harter, *12: The Elements of Great Managing* (New York: Gallup Press, 2006); Gary Gordon with Steve Crabtree, *Building Engaged Schools: Getting the Most Out of America's Classrooms* (New York: Gallup Press, 2006).

33. NCEE, *Tough Choices or Tough Times: The Report of the New Commission on the Skills of the American Workforce*, rev. and expanded ed. (San Francisco, Jossey-Bass, 2008).

34. Ibid., p. xxv.

INDEX